VISUAL & PERFORMING ARTS
CHICAGO PUBLIC LIBRARY

W9-AVG-173

SARAH CALDWELL

The First Woman of Opera

DANIEL KESSLER

VISUAL & PERFORMING ARTS
CHICAGO PUBLIC LIBRARY

THE SCARECROW PRESS, INC.
Lanham, Maryland • Toronto • Plymouth, UK
2008

SCARECROW PRESS, INC.

Published in the United States of America
by Scarecrow Press, Inc.
A wholly owned subsidary of
The Rowman & Littlefield Publishing Group, Inc.
4501 Forbes Boulevard, Suite 200, Lanham, Maryland 20706
www.scarecrowpress.com

Estover Road
Plymouth PL6 7PY
United Kingdom

Copyright © 2008 by Daniel Kessler

All rights reserved. No part of this publication may be reproduced,
stored in a retrieval system, or transmitted in any form or by any
means, electronic, mechanical, photocopying, recording, or otherwise,
without the prior permission of the publisher.

British Library Cataloguing in Publication Information Available

Library of Congress Cataloging-in-Publication Data

Kessler, Daniel, 1934–
   Sarah Caldwell : the first woman of opera / Daniel Kessler.
      p. cm.
   Includes bibliographical references (p.   ) and index.
   ISBN-13: 978-0-8108-5947-0 (cloth : alk. paper)
   ISBN-10: 0-8108-5947-5 (cloth : alk. paper)
   ISBN-13: 978-0-8108-6110-7 (pbk. : alk. paper)
   ISBN-10: 0-8108-6110-0 (pbk. : alk. paper)
   eISBN-13: 978-0-8108-6368-2
   eISBN-10: 0-8108-6368-5
   1. Caldwell, Sarah, 1924–2006. 2. Conductors (Music)—United States—Biog-
raphy. 3. Opera producers and directors—United States—Biography. I. Title.

ML422.C225K47 2008
782.1092—dc22
[B]   2007045884

∞™ The paper used in this publication meets the minimum requirements of
American National Standard for Information Sciences—Permanence of Paper
for Printed Library Materials, ANSI/NISO Z39.48-1992.
Manufactured in the United States of America.

R0414742993

VISUAL & PERFORMING ARTS
CHICAGO PUBLIC LIBRARY

CONTENTS

PREFACE

My original aim in recounting the life of Sarah Caldwell was one of scholarship, but I soon felt defeated at every turn by none other than Ms. Caldwell herself. In her prime, she skillfully manipulated the levers of publicity in a way that no agent could ever have accomplished in her behalf. While sustaining her twenty-hour days in getting her show on the stage, she never denied sleeping in her theater and moreover relished the retelling of it. In other words, she wanted nothing written about her that she could not control, and she would not cooperate in telling her story, which is unfortunate since I feel her personal story is more interesting than her accomplishments alone might indicate.

If Sarah Caldwell left behind production manuals, books, or articles that would inform such a project as this, none could be accessed or found. Considerable time was spent chasing down rumors. A rumor that she had dropped off all of her materials relating to opera production at the Library of Congress proved false. Another fool's errand was spent searching for her memorabilia, reportedly sent to a library in San Antonio funded by a onetime backer. While it is true that Ms. Caldwell spoke cogently at several annual conferences, such as the Central Opera Service (later morphed into Opera America in 1990), no minutes were taken of those meetings, and the files from that time show only a brief list of daily topics.

In the end, I was obliged to draw Ms. Caldwell's portrait from interviews and press accounts. Many of her close associates were helpful in offering their shared impressions. Fortunately, I experienced a fair number of her productions on the various stages in Boston from 1964 onward. A meeting with Ms. Caldwell six months before her death, when she was gravely ill, offered only a fleeting glimpse of her larger-than-life persona.

Those who worked with Ms. Caldwell claimed her methods were "free-form." Might I add "seat of the pants"? Still, many of her inspirations, coups-de-thèâtre, were sheer "moments of magic," as she defined them, and came together in a way that astonished her colleagues (and perhaps even Ms. Caldwell). If she deemed an opera's plot to lack contemporary relevance, she was more than happy to provide the Botox injection to iron out any sagging, outdated references.

Sarah seldom spoke of her creative muse, although there was no question that it was in play as exhibited in her best work. Early on, she learned for herself how to assume the various tasks related to opera production and did not delegate well, partly out of financial constraints and partly out of the need to control all aspects of opera production. Still, the end product could often be quite startling in its vision and execution, causing music critic Andrew Porter, writing in the *New Yorker*, to proclaim, "Sarah Caldwell was the best thing about American opera."

ACKNOWLEDGMENTS

The author gratefully acknowledges the following people who were so very helpful in preparing this biography: Helen Pond and Herbert Senn, Edgar Vincent, Jon Vickers, James Billings, Eunice Alberts, Osbourne McConathy, William Fred Scott, Lisi Oliver, Richard Leacock, Schuyler Chapin, Blanche Thebom, Linda Cabot Black, Jean Haffenreffer, Betty Hale, John Cunningham, Joseph Evans, Robert O'Hearn, Geraldine Baretto, Nalora Steele, Michael Kaye, Mike Richter, Norman Kelley, David Lloyd, Adelaide Bishop, Beverly Bower, Mac Morgan, Charles Kondek, Carole Bogard, Christopher Mahan, James Curran, Thomas Jamison, Jo Ann Manda, Betty Barnes, Vadim Ladygin, Olga Voskoboinikova, Thomas Smilie, Louis Scalmagi, Angelo Mammano, Henry Wieman, and David Jefferson.

SARAH CALDWELL:
BOSTON FINALE

Summoned by Sarah Caldwell, a band of wealthy (and dedicated) music fans gathered at the remains of a former vaudeville house on the edge of Boston's shabby Combat Zone. Caldwell, for decades the face of opera in Boston, called on those hardy enough to brave the intense summer heat to revive her Opera Company of Boston.

Caldwell was attempting to jump-start her now-defunct company, which had not performed since 1991. Boston Edison, despite substantial arrears, consented to turn on the electricity for a few more hours to accommodate her last pitch. Friday, August 26, 1994, was not the most suitable time for this meeting. Many of Boston's power brokers were likely down on the Cape, up on the North Shore, or possibly still in Nantucket.

Outside, there was the oppressive inner-city heat and humidity. Inside, crews from a Workfare program were concluding the last touches of a cleanup that had gone on for several weeks. The strong smell of mildew and mold still lingered in the air. The Opera House, formerly the Savoy movie palace and B. F. Keith Memorial Theater, had been closed for health and safety reasons in 1991.

Before appearing onstage with two soloists and a pianist, Caldwell stopped to have a few words with the supervisor of the cleanup crew: "As soon as you get the signal from me, you'll bring the boys out on stage. Don't worry, they won't have to say anything; I'll do the talking."

Sarah shuffled slowly to the lip of the stage to address the audience, her wiry gray hair coiffed for the occasion. At one time, her focus on musical studies was so intense that she neglected her appearance. Then, at the height of her notoriety, her picture gracing the cover of *Time* magazine, she had learned to be more conscious of how she looked. On this occasion, a subdued summer-print dress and a jacket slung over her shoulder exuded an air of casual earnestness. The usual bags under her eyes were not so evident. Now things were different.

As she introduced her soloists, soprano Karol Bennett and baritone David Arnold, Sarah surveyed her audience with her shrewd, wary eyes. Her voice, still resonant with its dulcet tone, rang with the self-assurance and matter-of-fact confidence she always showed under trying circumstances. The recital was not standard operatic fare; the singers performed mostly upbeat show tunes. "Blue Skies" and "Over the Rainbow" were to set the tone of renewed possibilities. Bennett and Arnold were not the celebrated artists who once graced the stage of the Savoy Theater in the heyday of Sarah's opera company, stars like Eva Marton, Dame Gwyneth Jones, or Tatiana Troyanos, all still active performers. Also notably missing was Beverly Sills, who could have flown up to Boston from Martha's Vineyard, where she was vacationing, to help with the pitch. The singers were the best Caldwell could manage. After the short recital, Caldwell renewed her plea to the invited guests. She read a statement by tenor Plácido Domingo, who sang with her company in its early years. In an optimistic message, the tenor stated he was "looking forward to performing with the opera company again, in the not-too-distant future."

Sarah made no effort to wipe away the beads of sweat gathered on her brow. Instead she spoke enthusiastically of a spring 1995 "April in Paris" season that would showcase three operas Sarah identified with that city, Puccini's *La Bohème*, Charpentier's *Louise*, and Debussy's *Pelléas et Melisande*. The latter opera's setting was not Paris, but it was premiered there, Sarah added. The problem, as it always had been, was money.

Years earlier in the century, Boston's last homegrown opera company to mount a full season had closed its doors in 1919, with Sarah's company making its debut after a thirty-eight-year gap. With the conclusion of her last Boston season in 1990, Sarah's mood had been more stoic. She merely commented, "The money didn't show," as she sat in her small office and pondered the uncertainties ahead. The company's debt was already $8.3 million. There was not enough money to pay the contributions to the musicians' pension fund as mandated in their contract.

Musicians were advised by their union that the default precluded further performances with the Opera Company of Boston.

Despite ominous signs, Caldwell had gone ahead with the planning of her thirty-third season and sent out an announcement to subscribers. Her lineup for the 1991 season promised a reprise of Leonard Bernstein's *Mass*, Tchaikovsky's *Eugene Onegin*, and a double bill of Mascagni's *Cavalleria Rusticana*, with Shirley Verrett as Santuzza, and Leoncavallo's *I Pagliacci*. Urged to buy tickets, many responded by sending in checks to prepay their renewals. However, one by one, each of the announced operas was canceled in notices sent before the scheduled dates. The company did not offer alternate dates, nor did it tell subscribers how to obtain refunds.

Many of the problems plaguing her company had already come to a head in a previous season when Sarah organized one of her most ambitious ventures, the Soviet-American "Making Music Together" festival. She was hailed as a latter-day Diaghilev for having the vision to bring together such a formidable array of talent ranging from the Bolshoi Ballet to the American premiere of *Dead Souls*, an opera by Soviet composer Rodion Shchedrin. That season ended with a huge deficit. Sarah claimed she had delegated the fund-raising to someone who failed to raise the needed sums. A very substantial shortfall loomed menacingly from both public and private contributors.

The mayor of Boston and the governor of Massachusetts pressed individuals and corporations to contribute the needed funds. Even the U.S. secretary of state, George Shultz, indulged in some arm-twisting with members of the Boston corporate group known as "the Vault." Exacting of corporate money under duress eventually led to sour feelings toward Sarah and any future enterprise in which she was involved. Sarah's hopes that she and her company would continue to be treated as a carefully nurtured asset by the Boston corporate community were dashed when word got back to her regarding comments such as "How dare she ask us for money?" or "Why should we be obliged to do anything for her?"

Sarah's local support dwindled sharply. By the early 1990s, Boston demographics began to change, with immigrants from all over the world pouring in and the city no longer a white ethnic bastion. In 1993, Thomas M. Menino was elected as mayor of Boston, the first Italian-American to hold that post and the first non-Irish-American since 1925. Some of Sarah's backers began to sponsor private musicales and receptions to keep her profile elevated in the changing Boston community. When introduced to new people, Sarah would sometimes say ". . . and don't believe what you read about me in the papers." Sarah's old-time backers were conspicuous by their absence. Often she found herself wandering alone among a gathering of faces strange to her, causing her to utter, "Nobody knows me here."

With her theater closed and boarded, Sarah had every reason to drop into a deep depression. However, her spirits were elevated when she was paid a visit by a search committee representing the Yekaterinburg Philharmonic Society. They had traveled from the industrial city in Russia, next to the Ural Mountains—the same city where Czar Nicholas and his family spent their final days, detained and later assassinated by Bolsheviks during the Russian Revolution.

When the Soviet Union broke up, several orchestras in Eastern European satellite countries feared lost state subsidies and began to cast about for conductors in the West. They believed such connections would raise their orchestras' profile and provide additional income through tours and recording contracts. An association with Sarah Caldwell might have brought such a result, despite her single complete opera recording. Still, memories of Sarah's prowess lingered with former contacts of the USSR Ministry of Culture. These may have raised the hopes and expectations of the Yekaterinburg delegation. After all, Sarah had single-handedly put together the prodigious Soviet-American "Making Music Together" festival in Boston and a reprise in Moscow. This early contact eventually led to Sarah becoming an associate conductor with the ensemble in the spring of 1994.

Now Sarah's August concert was drawing to a conclusion with Sarah speaking about her connection with the Yekaterinburg Philharmonic. She promised to conduct the Russian orchestra in a series of concerts at the opera house as a part of the "April in Paris" salute in programs featuring Stravinsky's *Le Sacre du Printemps*, first heard in that city, Sarah reminded her audience.

An awards ceremony followed, and, on cue, the inner-city youths who cleaned up the theater were brought onto the Savoy stage and thanked for their services. They received plaques, which Caldwell stated would hang in the lobby when the theater reopened. Sarah had always been successful in getting groups like the Workfare inner-city youth corps to expend their time and efforts free or for little or virtually no cost.

As the crowd began to file out of the theater, some stopped to speak to Sarah. Some offered weak excuses in place of firm commitments to contribute. Others walked out without comment, leaving Caldwell as empty-handed as when the concert began. Two longtime financial backers stayed on and corralled Sarah. They explained to her the difficulties they perceived in future fund-raising in the Boston area. During the short conversation, they demanded a level of fiscal responsibility and control in return for their help in raising money. Sarah turned and walked away.

Sarah was overtaken by a glow of nostalgia as she sat alone in the darkened theater, before the hired attack dogs were set loose to guard against vandals. In former times she would often remain in the theater long after rehearsals had ended and crews left the house. On those occasions, Sarah would wrap herself in her overcoat, ease her three hundred pounds into a seat, and stare mesmerized at the stage, as if plotting the blocking for the next rehearsal or conjuring up a bit of "stage magic" to wow her audiences. Focusing her thoughts on her predicament, she pondered what else she could do to reenergize the Boston community that had often come to her aid in the past, that same Boston community that considered itself the hub of the universe, that same Boston community, as Irving Kolodin, music critic of the *Saturday Review of Literature*, expressed it, "that forced Sarah to settle for shabby vaudeville houses which they imposed on her as a liability for daring to enlighten them."[1]

NOTES

1. Irving Kolodin, Review of *Montezuma*, Music to My Ears, *Saturday Review of Literature*, May 15, 1976, 42.

2

THE EARLY YEARS

The performing arts community in Boston was suffering from a general malaise when Sarah Caldwell first burst onto the operatic scene, fully formed, like a latter-day Minerva. The demolition of the city's acoustically fine opera house, one that had seen Enrico Caruso, Leo Slezak, Emma Eames, Mary Garden, Frances Alda, and Lillian Nordica on its stage, cast a pall of sadness over Bostonian music lovers. Opened in 1909, the house had served as the home for two local companies, however briefly (five and two years), and showcased nine yearly Chicago Opera visits (1917–1932), then from 1934 had hosted annual visits by New York City's Metropolitan Opera and served as the occasional venue for prizefights. By 1957, the venerated old house, which had remained dark most of the time, but was still thought to be structurally sound, was to be demolished to make way for a parking lot for Northeastern University.

But Sarah was undeterred by the fact that, as the bricks of the opera house were falling, her own fledgling opera company would never play there. She was in an upbeat mood, buoyed by the unanimous praise from local critics for her role in developing her Boston University Opera Workshop, by the clutch of enthusiastic supporters she had attracted, and by the fact that she had been tapped for the upcoming 1958 outdoor summer arts festival, an event to be held on the Boston Common. Other local groups had performed under this umbrella in prior years; now it was Sarah's turn. Unfortunately, none of the previous participating summer arts festival groups, such as Boris Goldovsky's New England Opera Theater, had had a sufficiently well-funded base to launch and maintain a full season in Boston. Neither, at the time, had Sarah's. That her company, known as the Boston Opera Group, and later the Opera Company of Boston, would grow to become a vital force in American opera in the coming decades might well have been beyond her wildest dreams.

Few who were then dazzled by this Minerva's theatrical invention and innovation would have imagined her prosaic origins among the gentle rolling hills of Nodaway County, located in the quaint and more or less forgotten northwestern panhandle of Missouri, 110 miles north and slightly west of Kansas City. Sarah was born on March 6, 1924, in Maryville (the county seat), the only child of a brief union (less than two years) between Carrie Margaret Baker of Maryville and Edwin Fletcher Caldwell of Burlington Junction, some twelve miles distant. As a mere infant, Sarah resided for a time at the Caldwell family farm outside Burlington Junction. Locals in Burlington Junction recall her parents as an attractive couple, but the marriage was doomed from the outset by Edwin Caldwell's bouts with alcohol. While a bitter divorce ensued, mother and daughter removed themselves to Maryville, setting up permanent housekeeping in the childless home of Sarah's great-aunt and great-uncle, where they remained until Sarah was twelve years old.

The Caldwell family of Burlington Junction were people of substantial means, whose wealth stemmed from raising herds of Black Angus cattle. No known records show child support forthcoming from the Caldwell clan. Instead, Sarah's maternal grandfather, a prominent banker in Maryville (population 10,500), sent his daughter Carrie Margaret to Northwestern University in Chicago, where she graduated with a doctoral degree in music. Carrie Margaret would soon join the faculty of Maryville's Missouri State Teacher's College and become a working mother,[1] while Sarah's doting aunt Emily—"Auntie Em"—would attend to Sarah's needs. To supplement her income, Carrie Margaret gave piano lessons. Since the union with Caldwell ended when Sarah was still a toddler, it is doubtful that Sarah retained any recollections of that sad time. Still, divorce carried a stigma then, difficult to imagine in our own day. Children can be cruel, although those who knew Sarah do not recall any taunts that came her way. She was known as a serious-minded child among her somewhat giddy classmates. Still, the problem of how to deal with the question, "Where's your daddy?" was probably the beginning of a protective shell Sarah cultivated, the Buddha-like mask so much a part of the adult Sarah's responses.

Records of Sarah's early years suggest she suffered from respiratory ailments. To ward off further complications, a mentholated handkerchief redolent of Vicks VapoRub was appended to the collar of her dress while at elementary school. Sarah's bouts with these ailments would return to plague her health through her declining years.

In later interviews, Sarah would imply that her mother at this point had gone back to Juilliard to finish her musical studies. Given the family economics, this is unlikely, and the reality gives us insight into the origin of Sarah's resilience, inventiveness, and determination to overcome obstacles. Teaching at the college, giving piano lessons, and training choruses brought only a modest income, but it was enough to ensure independence for Carrie Margaret and her daughter.

For all of the cosseting from her mother and great-aunt (perhaps because of it), Sarah was growing up a protected but talented child who did not suffer the obesity that was later her characteristic when she became the driving force behind opera in Boston. Even at an early age, she was playing the violin, practicing up to seven hours a day and astounding locals with her skill with the instrument. Sarah also stunned them as a would-be impresario of Fourth of July fireworks. She recalled her happiest days in Maryville fiddling with elaborately planned pyrotechnical displays from the vantage point of her backyard. She later told *Time* magazine, "I was not allowed to bring [any fireworks] home until the night before, but I had them put aside for me in stores all over town. I would set them all out on a table and look them over, sparklers, snakes, cherry bombs, Roman candles, firecrackers. Then I'd make my plans." Her displays were a hit with neighbors every Independence Day. Sarah remembered, "I was a specialist in nighttime fireworks."[2] Locals were so impressed with her fireworks displays that they saw a prodigy in their midst.

In the early 1930s, a festival called the Jubelesta was held in Kansas City each fall, headlined by a lesser star of vaudeville and early low-budget Western films, a comedy hack by the name of Bob Burns. An annual competition to name the most talented newcomer drew Sarah as an entrant. Votes in the form of mailed postcards were tallied by the contest judges. In an act of ballot stuffing, over five hundred postcards were sent from Maryville by "friends" of Sarah, leading to the final competition, which she won. Her contest entry was a jury-rigged musical instrument, an improvised violin she had fashioned from a cigar box and some stretched catgut that could be struck with a bow to make musical sounds. As the contest winner, Sarah thrilled an enthusiastic Kansas City audience, whose numbers were swelled by many well-wishers from Maryville for the occasion of her concert.

When the Ringling Bros. and Barnum & Bailey circus played Kansas City, Sarah's mother introduced her to Mrs. Ringling, a former classmate at Northwestern. Sarah and a school chum were special guests. They were allowed to eat in the circus commissary with acrobats, clowns, jugglers, and trapeze artists, who later showered them with attention at the subsequent performance as if they were VIPs.

Sarah's first brush with professional performing artists left an indelible mark. The incident became a catalyst for Sarah, who devised circus acts and "musical happenings" with her playmates as participants in the privacy of her backyard. On these occasions, Sarah played the violin while Carrie Margaret provided accompaniment on an upright piano pushed up against an open window.

Sarah's mother was determined to keep her daughter from feeling any maternal abandonment when Carrie Margaret was away training high school choruses in the summer months. To this end, she arranged with Auntie Em to distribute small notes, often with gifts, daily as if by regular post, to Sarah so that Sarah would feel as much the center of her mother's world as if her mother were present. When she returned to Maryville, she regaled Sarah with her tales of her college days at Northwestern University, the musical life there, the occasional performances at the Symphony, and the old Chicago Opera Company of that era. Carrie Margaret also told Sarah of something mostly reserved for adults, an excursion to Kansas City for concerts and theater on a Saturday afternoon, "a special treat," which her mother explained to her as "the most important ritual in the world." With this early seed planted in Sarah's mind, it would only be a matter of time before she would seek to make some connection or fusion with both music and drama.

It is easy to understand how these stories gave Carrie Margaret authority and glamour in Sarah's view, prompting her to remark later in an interview, "Because my mother was gone, I was raised with pictures of her and stories of how bright and smart she was. Her report cards seemed inhumanly good."[3] In this context Sarah's lifelong devotion to Carrie Margaret was a foregone conclusion, even as Sarah's growing success spurred a proportionate belittlement from her mother, whose and age rendered her increasingly difficult. Sarah would later present her mother as "Margaret," rather than "Carrie Margaret," sensing that her mother's name would have a decidedly Southern ring to Boston women.

By the time Carrie Margaret took her adolescent daughter to Kansas City to accept another position, she had already formed a special bond with Dr. Henry McMillan Alexander, a bachelor approaching his forties. He had earned a doctoral degree and was an associate professor at the teachers college. Alexander was one of five sons of a prominent jurist, Charlton Henry Alexander of Jackson, Mississippi, once nominated for the U.S. Supreme Court by President Woodrow Wilson.[4]

When Sarah was seventeen, Alexander proposed marriage to Carrie Margaret, and she immediately accepted. The newlyweds next moved to Fayetteville, Arkansas, the seat of the state university, where Dr. Alexander took a teaching position. Eventually, a child was born of this union, George Baker Alexander. Sarah was pleased and established a lasting bond with her stepfather.

With her schooling in Maryville and later Kansas City, Sarah showed a formidable grasp of mathematics that enabled her to finish school well ahead of her class. It was said that she demonstrated an uncanny ability to figure all of the odds in any given situation of probabilities, a talent that could have taken her all the way to the gaming tables of Las Vegas.

Sarah's desire for knowledge, however, was omnivorous and didn't stop at mathematics. She was encouraged in this endeavor by her step-father. He understood her and cared about her. As she recalled, "He kept a dictionary on the dinner table to familiarize me with new words. He told me I could study all the music I wanted but that he hoped I would choose to study something different in college."[5] For a time, she followed Dr. Alexander's advice, enrolling in the University of Arkansas as a psychology major, but transferred to Hendrix College, a small liberal arts college in Conway, Arkansas, where she continued her studies with the violin from the spring of 1940 to 1942. Afterward, she attended a summer semester at the University of Iowa while auditioning for scholarships. But everyone other than Dr. Alexander, including Sarah herself, believed she would follow in her mother's footsteps and take a doctorate in music, possibly with an eye for teaching.

Sarah had taken violin lessons from the age of five. Years later, she recalled that her early prowess with the instrument drew invitations to play with local chamber music groups in the Midwest, even while she was still a child. Sarah had hoped to study under David Ritchie

Robinson, director of the Conservatory at Oberlin College in Ohio and applied for a scholarship. But even if locals in Fayetteville had no doubts, her level of accomplishment failed to impress Robinson during her audition.[6] On that occasion, feeling uncharacteristically insecure and nervous, Sarah hid her shoes in her handbag, then presented herself barefoot—as a mendicant—before the auditioner. Robinson was not fooled; in any case, her gambit failed to win the desired scholarship, but Robinson did accompany her to buy a new pair of shoes. Her demanding mother was not pleased with the outcome, even though Sarah subsequently won a scholarship to pursue her violin studies at the New England Conservatory of Music (NEC).

Sarah's violin teacher at the NEC was Richard Burgin, then concertmaster of the Boston Symphony Orchestra (BSO). He later recalled, "Sarah wasn't particularly talented on the violin."[7] He had suggested she study some other line of music. Her viola studies with professor Georges Flourel fared better. He had a higher opinion of her talent.

At the NEC, Sarah's scholarship paid her tuition, but she was otherwise financially strapped, obliged to supplement her income by odd jobs, including such chores as babysitting. In a twist that seemed designed by the gods, watching over children landed her at the Brookline, Massachusetts, home of a man who would become one of her most important mentors. Boris Goldovosky was the founder of the New England Opera Theater. His passion for work as a conductor, producer, author, onetime head of the NEC opera department, and director of the opera program at the Berkshire Music Center in Tanglewood made him a well-known and respected figure in musical circles. He was a frequent presence on the intermission commentary for the Metropolitan Opera's Saturday-afternoon broadcasts. Sarah's studies with the violin had faltered, and she seemed uninspired with her subsequent switch to the viola. Under Goldovsky's tutelage, Sarah caught the opera bug. She became his assistant, doing everything from translating libretti into English (Goldovsky preferred his products to be in the vernacular) to writing his scripts for the broadcast intermission features to running errands or acting as "prop girl" (her own definition) for his staged productions. Again, that omnivorous desire to learn. Sarah eagerly took on any related task or semi-related chore with a zeal that astonished those around her.

There were those who maintained Boris invented Sarah, while others insisted that she carried his ideas forward to a wider currency. But moving into the Goldovsky household in Brookline for a time was ill advised. Her lack of personal hygiene irritated Boris's wife, the soprano Margaret Goldovsky, who was also a devotee of psychoanalysis as were many suburban matrons of that era. After considerable prodding by her hostess, Sarah agreed to seek help, but her stab at therapy was doomed to end after one visit. Though she had felt pressure to please Margaret, Sarah was not of a mind to having her psyche plumbed and probed. Those familiar with the situation claimed that it was Margaret, with her intense fixation on psychology, who drove a wedge between Sarah and Boris. But the break did not come until Sarah had lured away his backers a considerable time later. Besides, Sarah realized that more than any other American city, Boston had a tradition since the nineteenth century of tolerating, even revering, homegrown writers and thinkers, many of whom were quite eccentric. Why really, should she try to change? Her quirks appeared to be no more troubling than those of other locals and hardly seemed to disturb even the most staid Bostonians, whose dress code was often that of shabby gentility. Boston women, in particular, gravitated toward Sarah, believing she was an example of what Yankee ingenuity could be in a woman.

When the BSO resumed summer concerts at Tanglewood in 1946 after World War II, Sarah won a new scholarship as a violinist to play in a student orchestra with the Berkshire Music Festival. Although distantly located at the western edge of Massachusetts, Tanglewood was functionally a part of the Boston musical scene. Sarah would later recall her time at the summer festival as her happiest years, attending all the concerts. She wore T-shirts and heavy shoes that clunked, with hair straight to the nape of her neck. Sarah's appearance was more Junoesque than grossly overweight—she was even reported to have worn a size fourteen dress. But that all changed. By the time of her graduation in conducting, Sarah is shown in a class photograph as having gained considerable girth, seated among those standing. One fellow student recalled the time Sarah got stuck in the tub where she was billeted and was rescued by colleagues: "It was not a pretty sight!"

The winter of 1947 saw a double bill of Giacomo Puccini's *Il Tabarro* and Gian Carlo Menotti's *The Old Maid and the Thief* as produced by Boris Goldovsky's New England Opera Theater at Boston's Jordan Hall, with Sarah listed as "musical assistant on stage."

By 1948, Tanglewood witnessed Sarah's first fledging endeavor, what she called "my first lucky piece," the one-act opera *Riders to the Sea* by

Ralph Vaughan Williams, which she staged and conducted. In this work the atmospherics are crucial, and Sarah excelled at getting the audience to feel its moodiness and the introspective brooding of its characters. Her unusual student workshop production drew the attention of Serge Koussevitzky. He invited her to join the Berkshire Music Center faculty and return the following summer.

Koussevitzky's involvement with the BSO stemmed from 1924, when he took over from Pierre Monteux, and he continued to hold the post of music director until 1949. His tenure was marked by ninety-nine world premieres of works by Ravel, Stravinsky, Britten, Martinu, Copland, and a host of others. His second-greatest legacy was Tanglewood. Although the BSO was not the first orchestra to perform there, he did much to raise its profile from 1936 onward. He also founded the Berkshire Music Center in 1940 and became its first director. Koussevitzky's stewardship of the Boston Symphony became emblematic of a phenomenon that Sarah was to inherit. According to music critic Alan Rich, writing for *Boston* magazine, "The tendency of the city to build a widespread culture around one monolithic figure or institution [was] a situation far different from the abundant, varied, but helter-skelter musical life in New York. To some degree, the phenomenal success of Sarah's operatic career in Boston can be traced to the city's musical monotheism."[8]

Sarah's Tanglewood connection introduced her into a circle of young musicians, opera administrators, and composers such as the young Leonard Bernstein, Roger Sessions, Robert Shaw, Lukas Foss, and Boris Blacher—all then active in the Berkshires. For an aspiring artist, Tanglewood of the post–World War II decade (1946–1955) was a wonderful place for music making and spiritual growth, a place where one could forge useful contacts, bonds, and introductions. Sarah later told an associate, "At the time, I felt as if treading among giants."[9]

After performances in the Tanglewood Shed, it was the custom of the apprentices to adjourn to the Log Cabin, a nearby pub in Lenox, to discuss the performance. Not so with Sarah, who never appeared there. She was always back at the opera center workshop, busy putting additional touches on improvised sets for scenes that she would rehearse with students. She continued to astound colleagues and critics with her Tanglewood 1950 student production of Puccini's *Gianni Schicchi*, which *Opera* hailed as a "sheer delight, a performance worthy of any first-rate opera house. . . . The production by Sarah Caldwell was a mas-

terpiece of wit, grace, and humor, and the young singers became sea-
soned veterans."[10]

Still with Goldovsky at this time, Sarah continued her development,
graduating to other duties that burgeoned into general factotum, capable of any task. Her ability to grasp all the basics of the backstage and
production business was as sweeping as it was relentless, allowing her
increasingly to exert control over every aspect of opera production.
That same Tanglewood summer, on July 25, Sarah was deputized to
conduct Mozart's *La Finta Giardiniera* when Goldovsky suddenly fell ill
and was hospitalized. Word of her abilities got around. By 1951, when
Boston University was looking for someone to head its modest music
department, Sarah was hired.[11]

Setting aside her occasional work with Goldovsky and his New England Opera Theater, Sarah lost no time coming up with ways to put
what was to be her opera workshop on the map. Her first effort occurred on January 15, 1952, when she mounted Alessandro Scarlatti's *Il
Trionfo dell'Onore* (The Triumph of Honor.) Sarah gave the opera the
English title *The Rake's Reform*, as if to foreshadow her next bold effort
later that inaugural season. Harold Rogers of the *Christian Science Monitor* deemed it a "conspicuous and hilarious success."[12] For this piece,
Sarah reconstructed a streamlined version of the Scarlatti opus and
wrote the English lyrics herself. Sarah was not sufficiently fluent in foreign languages to create a nuanced translation and felt obliged to engage Eugene Haun, a friend and onetime fellow student from her days
at Hendrix College. Haun's superior command of languages helped
Sarah overcome the rough spots and turn out the spoken dialogue.

Later that spring, she was audacious enough to approach Igor Stravinsky and convince him to come to Boston to conduct his opera *The Rake's
Progress* at her workshop, a scant three months after the work's Met
premiere under the baton of Fritz Reiner. Stravinsky would conduct the
piece in the United States for the first time. Sarah staged it in its eighteenth-century setting with her student group, including Loren Driscoll
as Tom and Robert Mesrobian as Nick Shadow. In reality, it was only a
student production, but its impact went far beyond the implication of
that term. Cyrus Durgin, music critic of the *Boston Globe*, hailed the student *Rake* as "the most important event of the 1952 musical season . . .
with the orchestra, the sets, costumes, and other details of the production all . . . of superior quality."[13] Sarah obviously treasured the special
bond she felt she had forged with the composer. Among her prized

possessions were several autographed photos of Stravinsky adorning the walls of her BU studio, which she was quick to point out to any visitor.

In the early fifties, Sarah shared an apartment with two members of the BU drama department faculty. The three prided themselves on being a part of an intellectual wave that was thriving in Boston at that time, centering on the Brattle Theater in nearby Cambridge. This regional theater was thought of as an island of excellence, offering dramas by Shaw and Chekhov and Restoration comedies. Its productions became a crucible in Sarah's life, a place where she tested her own keen powers of observation, discussing with her roommates bits of stage business or deportment that would not normally register with the average theatergoer. What she saw at the Brattle inspired her and intensified her own theatrical creativity. Goldovsky had awakened her to the idea that opera and drama need not be mutually exclusive, but she was now realizing she could go further. As her mission evolved, she vowed to bring Promethean fire (as decreed by the gods), challenging opera's dramatic trappings and vastly expanding on what she'd learned from Goldovsky. Years later she told the *Boston Herald* that "it was her aim to make opera-going as much a habit as theater-going."[14]

In August 1952 Sarah was again at the Berkshire Festival opera department at Tanglewood. There she directed Leonard Bernstein's one-act opera *Trouble in Tahiti*, a thirty-eight-minute opus that has more to do with "trouble" than "Tahiti," in that we see a newly married couple rapidly growing apart in their suffocating suburban milieu. The composer had not been pleased with the premiere at Brandeis University two months earlier, in June, and understandably was hoping for a better production this time around.

Sarah found herself surrounded by Bernstein and his high-powered New York entourage, pressing her with their suggestions and their advice. Finally she had had enough, telling them, "Either you let me do it, or I step aside." The rebuke quelled the New Yorkers, and she was given full rein.

Her directorial touches turned heads, with minimal but striking black-and-white sets that had the look of architectural plans (black line drawings on white paper) but also served as a splendid backdrop for props and other devices cleverly used to effect quick scene changes. In a stroke of Sarah's magic, which was becoming known more and more as her signature, the very first scene appeared to dissolve from a silhouette of two male members of the Greek-styled chorus.

To the degree that the piece could be judged as ironic, Sarah injected moments of humor and occasional levity. During a brief scene in a milliner's shop, totally invented by Sarah, the faces of audience members were wreathed in smiles when odd-looking hats were struck as if they were musical instruments. With these and other devices, she kept the focus away from the banalities uttered by a trio of choristers and the diffident couple (Sam and Dinah), all of whom might strike the spectator as grating and irritating. Sarah's presentation is still recalled by those who felt they had witnessed a landmark production of the short work, one that has never been equaled.

With her summers free, Sarah used them to continue her quest for ideas in Europe, sampling everything from the Comédie Française to operas in great and lesser European houses. But opera in Paris was at an all-time low, so Sarah moved on to Hamburg, Germany, where she had friends, and then to East Berlin, where she became an admirer of the productions of the Komische Oper under Walter Felsenstein. With the absence of stars, a group of mainly young singers was molded into a flawless ensemble, held together by an experienced producer-director, achieving beautiful, convincing effects through stunningly simple means. Unlike Goldovsky, a government subsidy allowed infinite pains to be taken to stretch the limits. Months of arduous rehearsal were spent to solve innumerable problems (e.g., performers at the Komische Oper were expected to be so synchronized that they were not permitted to look at the conductor).

It was a concept that ruled out displays of vocal bravura or operas filled with applause-drawing numbers. A singing actor of *Musiktheater* must not sing at his partner (or to the conductor) but react in psychologically meaningful ways. For that reason, Felsenstein's concepts cannot work or are of little value when the singing in a particular opera is artificial, such as singing as a "presentation," as is experienced in a concert. If the singing lacked inevitability, his method assumed that there was no possibility of a total theatrical experience. It was said that Felsenstein viewed his final product as a failure if his audience paid more attention to what was transpiring in the pit rather than being absorbed in what was shown on stage.[15]

From this emerged a stronger sense of theater than Sarah had yet experienced. In ten years of visits witnessing intendant Felsenstein's productions, Sarah absorbed new standards that nurtured her sky-reaching dreams. She was particularly impressed that his productions seen the previous year were not allowed to sink into routine when they returned to the repertory, as opposed to revivals she had witnessed at the Met where there was an overall slackening of the original stage directions. She vowed to keep her own productions fresh by adding new details and adapting to new personalities as casts changed.

Returning to Boston, Caldwell resumed her two-track schedule of conducting the BU Opera Workshop and assisting Goldovsky. He was then preparing the American premiere of an abbreviated version of Hector Berlioz's epic *Les Troyens* to be mounted at the old opera house in March 1955. During the closing scene of the capture of Troy, when the Trojan virgins prepare to kill themselves rather than yield to the Greeks, Sarah recalled, "Boris had them all dressed in freshly starched white attire which did little to convey to the audience the deprivations they must have endured during the long siege, and the whole point of dread and foreboding in the first half was lost." She had started to realize she had grown beyond her first mentor.

Between Felsenstein and Goldovsky, Sarah Caldwell had "two white knights of opera," (although she often referred only to Goldovsky), but she harbored the growing conviction that she could make her characters more recognizable and more accessible to her audiences than either of these accomplished men had managed to do. While each approached his craft differently, Goldovsky and Felsenstein were similar in one important respect: that nothing should be done in staging that would go against the spirit of the work, a maxim that Sarah was to follow throughout her career. She had learned and retained from them what she felt was important, but she knew what she had retained was a launching pad to push the envelope. She was increasingly confident of her own innovations.

By February 1956, she had obtained Paul Hindemith's permission to mount a nonprofessional U.S. premiere of his *Mathis der Maler*. Caldwell again proved herself able to overcome hurdles, this time the limitations of an undersized orchestra pit at the Boston University Theater. How she achieved her solution was a miracle unto itself. She situated her seventy-piece orchestra at stage rear, behind a scrim beyond the view of the audience. In front of the scrim, singers and chorus gave their performances without prompter or visible conductor. Amplification was used to bring the orchestra's sound forward for the benefit of both singers and audience. Hidden microphones transmitted the singers' voices back to Sarah, at the podium. *Opera News* reported,

"Although the scenery could not be called lavish, it was planned with such taste, equipped with such fine properties and lighted with such cunning that the effect outranked many more prodigal productions." *Musical America* added, "Nothing so big and impressive as *Mathis* has been attempted here [in Boston] in a generation."

Other works staged by Caldwell during her nine-and-a-half-year stint at BU were Puccini's *Madama Butterfly*, Bizet's *Carmen*, Mozart's *La Finta Giardiniera*, Vaughan Williams's *Sir John in Love*, and Weill's *The Threepenny Opera*. Also performed were the following short operas: Puccini's *Il Tabarro*, Bohuslav Martinu's *Comedy on the Bridge*, Manuel de Falla's *El Retablo de Maese Pedro*, Jacques Ibert's *Angelique*, a Boris Blacher triple bill consisting of *The Tide, Romeo and Juliet*, and his *Abstrakt Opera #1*, Ernst Toch's *The Princess and the Pea*, and two pieces by an old chum from her Tanglewood days, Robert Middleton's *Life Goes to a Party* and *The Nightingale is Guilty*.

For her *Butterfly*, Sarah was intrigued with the idea of an Asian singer in the role of Cio-Cio-San and cast a Japanese soprano, Taeko Fuji, in the title role. Her voice was adequate within the confines of the small BU theater, and the experiment emboldened Sarah to consider casting other Asian singers in Japanese roles the next time she got around to doing Puccini's opera.

Sarah's workshop had attracted an eager group of young pupils, leaving Sarah feeling frustrated by the lack of a permanent professional opera company that they could graduate into. To beef up the scholarship fund, Sarah mounted a fund-raiser on March 12, 1958, a black-tie affair called "A Maske in the manner of the 17th Century" at Boston's Isabella Stewart Gardner Museum, whose interior spaces echoed the ambience of a Venetian palazzo. While museum guards stood by nervously, musical "happenings" were presented in various rooms of the museum. The divertissements included madrigals and an abbreviated version of Scarlatti's *Il Trionfo dell'Onore*, reprised from Sarah's earliest effort at BU.

Sarah's BU Opera Workshop had attracted the interest of WGBH-TV, Boston's educational channel, to coproduce a short work written for the television medium, still in its relative infancy in 1957. With this venture Caldwell would make a whole new audience aware of her innovation and invention and prove by her many imaginative touches that opera could draw an audience for telecast on the small screen. The work, *Sterlingman*, by Klaus George Roy, a professor at BU, would be simulcast.

Its plot involved a querulous and poverty-stricken older couple, the intended victims of scam artists. Sarah heightened the dramatic tension with the camera catching only the hands, never the faces, of the characters.[16]

In 1958, Boston's movers and shakers chose Sarah to provide the annual summer festival centerpiece, to be held outdoors in the Boston Public Garden. Faced with the limitations of her BU workshop, the prospect of forming her own group to perform to a larger audience was a heady one. When the telephone call came late one afternoon from the Boston Summer Arts committee at her BU studio, her answer was an immediate "yes," given without calculating the financial consequences. Fiscal realities would demand consideration later, but that night, Sarah would barely sleep, and by morning she was ready to shout her excitement from the rooftops. On the floor of her apartment that day lay newspapers, dropped where they were read, on her kitchen table a loaf of moldering bread, ripped from its cellophane packaging in the middle by a ravenous hand, with chunks torn out of it. Tidying up would have been the last thing on Sarah's mind, as would either washing or primping. Instead, she quickly donned one of several black wrinkled dresses from the closet of her Back Bay apartment, then set off to organize her colleagues with the rallying cry, "Let's go do some opera."

NOTES

1. The Missouri State Teachers College was renamed Northwestern Missouri State University.
2. "Music's Wonder Woman," *Time*, November 10, 1975, 52–65.
3. Ibid.
4. Charlton Henry Alexander died suddenly of a heart attack before Senate confirmation. Alexander was the first Southerner to be nominated for the Supreme Court since the Civil War.
5. "Music's Wonder Woman."
6. James Billings, interview by the author, October 10, 2001.
7. "Music's Wonder Woman."
8. Alan Rich, "Music and Dance," *Boston Magazine*, February 1976, 64.
9. Interview with *Boston Globe*, March 28, 1976, 14.
10. "News," *Opera*, November 1950, vol. 1, no. 6, 39.
11. As of 1954 the department was renamed the School for Applied and Fine Arts.

12. Harold Rogers, "Miss Caldwell gives 'Rake's Reform' at BU," *Christian Science Monitor*, January 16, 1953, 8.

13. Cyrus Durgin, "Opera, Stravinsky conducts 'The Rake's Progress,'" *Boston Globe*, May 18, 1953, 12.

14. Jules Wollfers, "Opera Group sets new sights," *Boston Herald*, August 21 1960, 10.

15. Peter Paul Fuchs, ed., *The Music Theater of Walter Felsenstein* (New York: W.W. Norton & Co., 1975), xiv.

16. On August 5, 1965, Caldwell returned to WGBH-TV's Aaron Copland–hosted series, "Music in the '20s: New Faces/New Movements in Opera, Neo-Classical Music," to conduct (but not direct) the thirty-minute opus *Hin und Züruck* by Paul Hindemith.

3

SARAH THE IMPROVISER

In the fall of 1957 Sarah set to work negotiating a nest egg of capital funds pledged by potential backers around a coffee table in a friend's suburban Boston home. The result was a modest sum of $5,000. A substantial shortfall remained. To close the gap, she approached two wealthy supporters of Boris Goldovsky's New England Opera Theater without Goldovsky's knowledge. Because she was successful in getting their support, Sarah and Boris became estranged and did not speak for years. But by April 11, 1958, the Opera Group of Boston was incorporated as a nonprofit cultural and educational corporation. In order to give added heft to her fund-raising efforts, Sarah enlisted Igor Stravinsky, who agreed to act as honorary chairman.

Financially sustained by her salary at Boston University, Sarah would attempt to serve two masters as she also nurtured her risky new enterprise, the Opera Group of Boston. Her entrant for the 1958 summer festival, an 1875 operetta by Jacques Offenbach titled *Le Voyage dans la Lune* (Voyage to the Moon), inspired by Jules Verne. Sarah claimed she found the score languishing in the Boston Public Library stacks and fashioned her own English translation.

Despite Sarah's new company's debut on the local scene, Boston remained a symphony town, and at its core was the Boston Symphony Orchestra, the hub for classical music for all of New England. The symphony was deservedly famous and had been for nearly a century. Whether Boston wanted another opera company was an open question.

The opening night for *Voyage to the Moon* on June 18 was yet another opportunity for Sarah to further raise her own profile in a free municipal event of wider attendance than the limited number of those drawn to her innovative but circumscribed BU Workshop. She and her set designer, Robert Fletcher, found their first obstacle in mounting the Offenbach work. The outdoor venue would not allow any overhead rigging, which was customary for use in hanging scenery. To provide the backdrops they wanted, they devised an ingenious group of sliding panels that were freestanding and could easily be maneuvered. Three weeks prior to opening night, Sarah's cast assembled for rehearsals in New York, with a final dress rehearsal in Boston.

The weather was less than cooperative that fateful night. An unlikely fifty-four-degree chill with intermittent drizzle descended on Boston. Sarah continued unfazed, wrapped in an ill-fitting overcoat, while her musicians huddled under umbrellas. In her staging, she'd emphasized Offenbach's satiric drollery whereas Boston had been used to cute slapstick marking its comic presentations. The production was a success. In the words of the Boston Arts Festival Committee, Sarah's Opera Group was "the outstanding feature of the 1958 season."[1]

With her Opera Group launched, she had assembled a first-rate cast, and to beef up the musical quality, she arranged for the participation of musicians from the BSO as well as other freelancers in the area. Along with her dream of providing a venue for young, talented artists, Sarah would also hire the best artists available on the national and international scene and forage between two excellent musical conservatories in the area to flesh out minor parts and, in time, to build a first-rate chorus. To ensure an excellent product, Sarah explained to one of her associates, "Artists would have to submit to a regime of two weeks' rehearsal prior to performance, rather than having a major artist arriving for only a cameo appearance that would not be integrated into the ensemble."

Meanwhile, a summer-long search for a home for the Opera Group was in progress. By October, the Fine Arts Theater, a cinema house on Norway Street, was obtained, renovated, and renamed "The Little Opera House." Originally, this space was nothing more than an upstairs hall with its own street entrance, in the same structure as the Loew's State Theater. On January 9, 1959, the unlikely venue saw the curtain rise on Puccini's *La Bohème*, in a space that accommodated only four hundred spectators, requiring yet again Sarah's resourcefulness and ingenuity. In staging the opera, Sarah was up against another obstacle in the form of Lois Marshall. William Judd, an artist manager from Columbia Artists Management Inc. (CAMI) had suggested the Canadian soprano for the role of Mimi, which would be her operatic stage debut. Though possessing a voice with undeniable evenness and luster, Ms. Marshall had suffered a bout with polio as a child, and was left with a withered leg and a noticeable limp. As a consequence, her main work had been in recitals. In overcoming this problem, Sarah so artfully contrived Ms. Marshall's entrance in Act I that few in the audience were aware of her physical impairment. She was seen leaning on a balcony railing. If Lois Marshall had qualms about performing in opera, that would have been understandable. However, Sarah did her best to put her at ease and reassured her, "Don't worry, honey, you'll be in bed the entire last act."

Although Sarah invested most of her budget for the season's three operas on the opening *Bohème,* it did not have the look of an expensive production. In fact, the first act was thought to resemble a toolshed rather than an artists' garret. Her designer, David Hays, espoused the fashionable conceit at the time of exposing the back brick wall of the theater. It was not understood by the Boston audience, and Sarah was not particularly pleased with the result, exclaiming, "The designer wanted an ugly back wall, and this theater had the ugliest."[2] Still, public reaction to the opera was so strong that to satisfy the demand, she was obliged to arrange for a dozen performances beyond the original three. Her new enterprise had flowered into something she dared not anticipate, a brilliant success, a *Bohème* of fire, persuasion, and glorious singing.

With her second offering that 1959 season, Sarah and her set designer Robert O'Hearn were put to the test. Rossini's *Barber of Seville* was brought in on a limited budget to compensate for the overspending on *La Bohème.* Sarah never delegated responsibility well and demanded control of every part of her company, including financial management. However, with each challenge, Sarah enlisted O'Hearn's assistance in finding a solution. Unable to pay for more than a basic unit set, she had Rosina singing her aria from one of the side loges in the auditorium at the Boston University Theater. A series of stylized latticed structures on stage were attached to moveable walls that appeared to be covered with satin brocade. On either side of the set, doorways led to Dr. Bartolo's sitting room and to Rosina's boudoir. With the walls hinged, each could be swung toward center stage to reveal the room in question. Action could be moved from one scene to the next rather than have the audience presented with just one room. Robert Trehy exhibited the requisite suave singing and stage deportment for the title part while Phyllis Curtin was a captivating Rosina in a role shorn of its usual variations. As with the earlier *Bohème*, performances alternated between Italian and English.

John Gay's *Beggar's Opera*, with sets by Lester Polakov, concluded that first season. Sarah had worked with Lester on a few of her productions and was stimulated by his bold ideas and interesting concepts. To create the right atmosphere and to bridge the gulf between modern-day and eighteenth-century audiences, Sarah's orchestra included a lute, a harpsichord, and a recorder, which conveyed an authentic feeling to the ballads, which was not always the case in performances given of this work. She then set out to cast the piece with singers who could act, rather than actors who could sing. When she found herself short in casting of the roles of Mrs. Peacham and her daughter Polly, Adelaide Bishop was persuaded to sing both roles. Sarah suggested a different voice for each character and Ms. Bishop obliged. It was a novel approach that delighted and amazed the critics. Fortunately, both characters do not appear simultaneously, but "Addie" (as she was known to her colleagues) proved to be a quick-change artist in the bargain.

Sarah's involvement with her new company seemed all-engulfing, leaving little time for anything else. The floorboards of her Back Bay apartment began to groan under the weight of her expanding collection of operatic scores, the excess stored in her bathtub. "I'm afraid I do not relate well to possessions," Sarah told *LIFE* magazine. There were occasions when she could not recall where she had parked her car (often impounded), and misplaced several handbags. When her colleagues observed her carrying around her personal items in a brown paper bag, they assumed she had again locked herself out of her apartment.

Upon returning to her Back Bay apartment one night, she could not remember where she had left her latch key. The problem was easily solved. One of her neighbors had placed a large decorative faux-rubber plant in the common area. It so happened that the bolt of Sarah's apartment door could be jimmied to free the lock if one of the leaves of the plant was inserted between the bolt and the keeper. In a matter of days the denuded plant stood as a lonely sentinel in the hallway of her floor as an example of Sarah's uncanny ability to solve yet another problem by way of an improvisational touch.

Her excitement in what she had accomplished that first season found a counterpart in the enthusiasm of William Judd and others in the New York scene. Sarah's first season had successfully shown what an opera company should and could be in America. Now she had attracted a coterie of admirers, whose numbers included the well-known set designer Oliver Smith. Sarah was employing designers and lighting technicians who were on the cutting edge of what could be accomplished theatrically. Judd became one of her biggest boosters and flew to Boston to see *Voyage*. Before he returned to New York, the two dined at Joseph's restaurant on Newbury Street. Between courses of turtle soup and veal scallopine, various possibilities were discussed, with Judd telling Sarah, "I think we can offer this piece as an entrant for Brussels, perhaps in September?" Sarah's typically affectless stare was hard to fathom, as she buttered a piece of bread. However, in a moment of ardor, she reached a second time for a butter patty, placed it directly in her mouth, and swallowed it whole!

The 1958 Brussels Fair was going on at the time, but time constraints did not allow Sarah's participation. Still, a nationwide tour with CAMI sponsorship was a distinct possibility. Judd told Sarah that cities across the country had presold subscriptions that would allow the insertion of *Voyage* into their schedules and that would open up other booking possibilities.

With her 1960 projected tour in place, Sarah began to choose other works to offer her second-season subscribers. She was also busy on the telephone organizing her board of trustees. As with her New York admirers, Caldwell drew the attention of effective people in Boston, such as Cardinal Cushing's right-hand man, Monsignor Francis T. Lally of the archdiocese. As one of Boston's most influential clerics, Monsignor Lally was someone who made things happen. He had been successful in tapping fund-raising from area sources and spearheaded many worthy projects that no one else seemed able to get off the ground.

However, there was a rival entity called the Boston Opera Company, whose board consisted of a cadre of wealthy patrons, and whose purpose was to fund the Metropolitan Opera's annual tour of Boston. While Sarah's subscription-based company was done on a shoestring budget, the Met productions were quite expensive. Sarah wanted opera for everyone, not just for the wealthy. She expressed her view rather emphatically, "They see these events as more a social than a musical occasion."

At her board of trustees meetings, Sarah quickly became inured to the superlatives that often passed for sentiment. One particular board member would start off the meeting by offering a motion of "appreciation" for Miss Caldwell that was to be spread across the minutes. It got to the point that Sarah knew what her board members were going to say even before they said it. Eventually this led to her closing her eyes on occasion, giving others the impression that she was asleep. Quite often she was! On a few occasions when non-board members were present, it was often difficult for them to repress laughter at the way in which Sarah would respond to some situations.

In the end, Sarah was determined that her board would reflect a cross section of the Boston commercial community, including merchants, corporate heads, arts enthusiasts, and even longtime personal friends. Furthermore, substantial contributors and their families might be invited to what were otherwise closed rehearsals. On some occasions, children of family members of these backers might find themselves onstage, appearing as supernumeraries, in a gesture of cuteness.

"Mom, there's a tooth fairy at the door!" Sarah couldn't help noticing a child's toy pistol out of the corner of her eye on her last visit to a board member's suburban home. Upon learning that the tiny tot had just lost his last baby tooth, she went into action, dispatching one of her supernumeraries to deliver a gift, while dressed in a costume worthy of the dew fairy from Tchaikovsky's *Sleeping Beauty*. Inside the brightly wrapped package, rows and rows of gun caps. It was just another example of Sarah's calculus in finding ways to bond with her wealthy and influential backers.

With the demise of the opera house, Boston was left with fading vaudeville houses and movie palaces, all with shallow stages and small orchestra pits—none ideal for opera. If her biggest problem was where to hold it, then she would have to content herself with what was available. Through Monsignor Lally's intervention, Caldwell was able to obtain permission from the archdiocese to rent its three-thousand-seat Donnelly Memorial Theater, which would help meet the economic needs of theatrical presentation. Its location in the Back Bay section of Boston (Norway Street and Massachusetts Avenue) was felicitous. The archdiocese had bought what was once known as the Loew's State Theater, an old vaudeville movie palace, renamed it the Donnelly Memorial Theater, and used it for showing religious films. The film title that blared from the marquee that fall of 1960 before Sarah and her motley crew moved into the cold, empty theater was *The Joyful Mysteries of the Rosary*.

With her first season and its prologue, Caldwell had seized an opportunity to make an indelible mark as a creative, innovative force in American opera. To the extent that her innovation remained the hallmark of subsequent seasons, Sarah and the company would thrive in public opinion. As other aspects of this remarkable persona came to the fore and as conflicting demands deprived her of the time needed to exercise her creative talents, the luster wore off and the limitations of the real world reduced the company to more conventional, regional status. But this was the glorious beginning, and inspired innovation had triumphed.

NOTES

1. Linda Cabot Black, Secretary of the Boston Fine Arts Committee, June 18, 1958.
2. Herbert Senn, interview by the author, August 18, 2000.

4

GETTING THE SHOW
ON THE STAGE

In less stressful moments, Sarah was capable of high spirits and a loud, infectious laugh. "Ha! That small playhouse was the best way to lose money ever invented," she told Monsignor Lally, referring to her very first *Bohème*, held in the four-hundred-seat cinema house. It was her way of thanking him for the use of the larger three-thousand-seat Donnelly Memorial. Now she would have to juggle the rising costs of opera presentation with the needs of a growing subscriber base. Since subscription income only paid for one-third of the cost, much more would be required to keep the wolf from the door while getting the show on the stage.

To get her very first season up and running in 1959, a fund-raising effort dubbed "Operation Opera" was launched with some fanfare with a kickoff banquet at the Sheraton Plaza Hotel ballroom. The event was hosted by Boston mayor John Hynes, who proclaimed "Operation Opera Week." Although Caldwell received excellent support from the local media, she was suddenly thrust into a new arena that would require bold action. Subscriptions sales were only trickling in. "Getting involved in fund-raising was not a matter of instinct, but a matter of necessity," Sarah told a reporter. Applying her mathematical gifts, she calculated she needed a return of $10 per head and dispatched cadres of her volunteers, fanning them out as far west as Worcester and as far north as Portland to secure funds. They returned with 8,500 subscribers, a respectable number for Boston and its environs. As later surveys would show, an overwhelming majority of her subscribers had zip codes identifying them as residents from areas lying outside Boston rather than from within the city itself.

Sarah had used her theatrical wizardry for the artistic side of production; other assets would be needed for the distasteful job of begging. She later discovered that her voice, a deep resonant contralto, could be persuasive when seeking money from would-be contributors, particularly in telephone canvassing. Sarah was quick to learn that where a man might be hesitant to ask for money, a woman should feel no such qualms and might use her feminine wiles to greater advantage. An advertising executive Sarah had invited onto her board marveled at her salesmanship and the numbers proving it, telling her, "You could sell green toothpaste." Later, Sarah got back to him with the reply, "Why didn't someone tell me how easy it was to raise money? . . . All you have to do is *ask* for it."

To prospective donors, Sarah presented herself as a visionary interested in the developmental and educational side of opera, stressing that certain performances or dress rehearsals would be reserved for children and students. To counter any residual Calvinist influence that still prevailed in Boston, Sarah was careful to emphasize the educational aspect of opera that helped put the best media spotlight on her fund-raising.

To keep expenses from outstripping the funds raised, the costs of opera production would have to be reduced still further. In her trips to European opera centers, Sarah had seen how much more economical abstract productions could be than the realistic stagings then fashionable in the United States. Her first and second seasons had featured realistic sets. With her third, she introduced Wolfgang Roth as a set designer at a press briefing at Joseph's Restaurant. She explained to the assembled group how Roth's sets for *Otello* and *Falstaff* would involve photo projections on flats and thereby save on the expense of building, transporting, and storing bulky scenery and props. To some, this might have conjured up an idea of projections on painted bed sheets, but Sarah saw exciting and dramatic possibilities. She would command productions with style while hoping to achieve the impact of what Wieland Wagner had accomplished in post–World War II Bayreuth on a limited budget. Her vision was confirmed by reviews like Louis Chapin's in the *Christian Science Monitor* for her third-season *La Traviata*: "Wolfgang Roth . . . by using basic units, gauze drops, and stylized partial ceilings . . . realized far more space and focus than is possible with conventionally palpable interiors." Robert Taylor of the *Boston Herald* added,

"Violetta's banquet rooms in Act I, for instance, resembled a dinner *intime* rather than an opulent ball. The costumes and scenery are striking, though clean and spare."

Writing about Roth's work on Sarah's production of *Otello*, William Storrer of *Opera* wrote, "Mr. Roth was able to create a remarkable projection of grandeur, the crowd swirling about the dark stage against a setting of clouds hurrying across the sky, lightning flashing in the distance, and pennons waving in the strong breeze."

With an eye on money problems that could only be solved by drawing in additional audiences and galvanizing community interest to buttress her fund-raising base, Sarah offered such ploys as hiring Arthur Fiedler, the much-celebrated conductor of the Boston Pops concerts, to conduct his first opera, even placing his name on the marquee in her third season's *Die Fledermaus*. (The theater marquee read "Fiedler-maus," a play on the conductor's name.) She also invited the prize-winning entrants of a local ballroom dance contest to appear as guests in Act II, thereby transferring any public interest in the competition to her own enterprise. Additionally, the showcasing of Sarah Leland and Earle Sieveling, soloists of the New York City Ballet, drew the attention of area balletomanes. Critics acclaimed the *Fledermaus* as the most polished production of that season. Fiedler's conducting satisfied the audience, but not the company, who found his first venture into opera to be at a faster tempo than they could sustain. The well-loved conductor later returned for a gala concert but not for a full-length work, but Sarah had achieved her purpose with a coup: his name filled the house with paying customers.

Contrary to the wisdom of her mentor Walter Felsenstein, who once stated he would not permit extraneous effects or gags, future seasons found Sarah demonstrating her keen awareness of popular entertainment values in satisfying whatever appetite her audience might have for pure amusement.[1] One such flourish in her 1961 *Fledermaus* had her singers actually cooking cherries jubilee in chafing dishes onstage during the party scene. In 1977 during her nineteenth season, a Boston Red Sox team member made headlines (he was picked up for marijuana possession). Sarah had him appear as a guest in a party sequence, in his uniform, in Offenbach's *Orpheus in the Underworld*. In addition to sports luminaries, Sarah engaged show-business personalities such as Victor Borge, Kitty Carlisle Hart, Margaret Hamilton, and Fred Gwynn, as well as Sid Caesar and Imogene Coca, who would have the audience roaring with laughter.

CHAPTER 4

The ability to wield the levers of publicity to enhance her agenda may have been passed to Sarah from her father, Edwin Fletcher Caldwell, a raiser of Black Angus cattle. When one of his outstanding steers failed to fetch a price he felt satisfactory at a local auction, he withdrew the animal and devised another strategy. He alerted a reporter he knew at the *Kansas City Star*, suggesting they dispatch a photographer to Kansas City's top hotel at noontime the next day. As if on cue, Caldwell appeared with his prize steer, leading it through the hotel entrance and into the dining room with flash bulbs popping. With the picture gracing the front page of the *Star*, he returned to the auction, where he realized his price.

The problem of fund-raising appeared as early as the planning for the second season and was to hobble the company inconsistently but inevitably for decades. Money problems frequently led to delays in starting rehearsals until Sarah could pull a cast together and sometimes meant that there was nothing left over in the coffers for the sets. Entire scenes in operas would be eliminated. For example, the Transylvania scene in her 1962 production of Massenet's *Manon* would have to be dropped. Likewise, in her 1963 *Faust*, the Walpurgis Night scene was cut and Valentin's funeral would be played in the church scene. Money could not be found for the peasant dances in the Kermesse scene; instead, the dances would be performed gratis, courtesy of a group of local Lithuanian folk dancers. Such arrangements normally required the consent of the American Guild of Musical Artists (AGMA), the union of the soloists, choristers, and dancers. When this was pointed out to Sarah, she gasped, eyes wide and innocent, "Lithuanian? I didn't know they were Lithuanian."

Sarah saved by appropriating to herself all tasks, large and small, that could not be handled by existing staff and volunteers. Writing checks, paying bills, monitoring lighting rehearsals, and providing the last word on almost every detail of operation, Sarah was the one to answer every question, to satisfy every need. As a result, she was putting in twenty-hour days, surviving on cups of coffee, doughnuts, Cokes, and hamburgers. In those early years, Sarah was often summoned to New York by officials at AGMA. They threatened to close her down for not furnishing withholding taxes and dues payments. For each such crisis, Sarah used all of her considerable persuasive skills and was allowed to buy time by consenting to time-payment protocols requiring evidence of the receipt of monies, validated on the spot by a shop steward before the union would allow the night's curtain to go up.

At one point Sarah learned that IRS auditors were expected momentarily—too soon for her to reach her accountant and attorney. Fearing that an audit might jeopardize the company's continued existence because of unkempt record-keeping, Sarah reportedly ran to a window, flung it open, then turned on a large fan to "circulate" her records out the window and down the street.

Sometimes she got lucky, her own ingenuity seemingly attracting outside forces to help her. Vassar College came to her rescue when her fourth season was imperiled by an especially dire insolvency, promising an infusion of cash if Sarah would mount an opera the college had commissioned for its centennial, *Command Performance*, by one of its own professors, Robert Middleton. She had already produced two Middleton operas in her Boston University workshop days. His latest effort, one modestly scored for seven instruments (including the composer banging away at the piano) revolved around a gift of an ornate baroque pipe organ by Queen Elizabeth I to the sultan of Turkey.

Sarah and her company opened *Command Performance* in Poughkeepsie and later moved the production to Boston. *Globe* critic Cyrus Durgin thought it to be the finest and most unified production to date while others complained that Middleton drowned out the singers. With Vassar carrying a sizeable portion of the cost, Sarah was able to bask in the glow of a world premiere to her Boston audience.

It was not the custom for regional opera companies to have their own costume shops, and Sarah had to weigh two options: either rent them or order them made at a considerable cost from a purveyor. For her *Manon* with Beverly Sills, she went the route of ordering new costumes from a costume shop. Rehearsals were well under way when she learned that the costume shop's rental truck was at the rear stage dock with a COD request for payment. Hoping to avoid a confrontation (and defer payment), Sarah sent one of her runners to haggle with the shop's owner. But he insisted on payment in cash. At a loss, the runner summoned Sarah, and by the time Sarah was brought to the scene, the owner was waving a threatening pair of scissors, implying he would cut the costumes to rags if he was not paid immediately. Realizing that he would not be as easily swayed as her donors and knowing she had no alternative, Sarah reached into one of the voluminous pockets of her dress to retrieve the required sum in cash.

The money situation grew especially nerve-wracking during rehearsals for *Die Meistersinger von Nüremberg*, when a large number of cast members assembled at the company's Newbury Street office clamoring for their pay. Sarah suddenly appeared, heading for the inside office. She had been neglecting herself again, working around the clock with rehearsals, her hair stringy and matted. The "atmosphere" around her was so bad that it was not possible to come near her. She wore a raincoat, and, as far as anyone could determine, little else underneath. Without acknowledging anyone, and the way cleared by her effluvium, Sarah strode into the back office where a voice inside was overheard to say, "We are not able to make payroll: we're out of money."[2] Denying the assembled throng that parted on each side as she passed, Sarah headed straight to the street exit. She reappeared within an hour with bags of money to make payroll. She had successfully turned to a donor for help; she'd then cashed the check in the office of Stanley Rabb, owner of Boston's "Stop and Shop." The crisis was deferred for the moment, as it was to be time and again.

Local skeptics were confounded when her little company dared to take on a work as challenging as Wagner's *Die Meistersinger von Nüremberg*, just after the production of *Manon*, which seemed to eat up all her company's resources. The overspending on *Manon*, particularly its lavish cash-only costumes, had a telling effect: old Nüremberg looked more like a housing project than like sixteenth-century dwellings. When her newly acquired skills at fund-raising were not enough, Sarah fell back on innovation and scored a triumph over hard reality. Her *Meistersinger* was, according to Kevin Kelley of the *Boston Globe*, "ingenious and hilarious in treatment." The company then lacked a chorus, so crucial to this opera, but in a spate of improvisation, Sarah managed to coax the participation of the local Lexington Choral Society, as well as the Children's Chorus from St. Peter's Church in Cambridge, bringing down the cost greatly compared to what it would have incurred with professionals. That her fledgling company succeeded in mounting *Die Meistersinger* was a source of awe and amazement to those who knew the costs of operatic production.

When her Boston premiere of Schoenberg's *Moses und Aron* was on the verge of being canceled for lack of funds, Sarah boarded a plane for Washington to seek the aid of Roger Stevens, chairman of the National Endowment for the Arts, whom she barely knew, but she pled her case persuasively.

To keep her Boston company going, Sarah was constantly fighting an uphill battle. Surveys showed that San Francisco, with a smaller population than Boston, had a much higher proportion of contributions to its homegrown opera company. San Francisco also had a symphony orchestra, a ballet, a repertory theater, and other arts institutions seeking their share of federal, state, city, and corporate funding, whereas Boston was more of a blue-collar town, despite Boston's impressive museums and large number of institutions of higher learning. With the passing of time, competition would intensify among various performing arts groups and other institutions that required funding for their very survival. It was often the case that the cash flow of Sarah's Boston company was so slim that advance ticket sales were paying the salaries of those now performing. Under these circumstances, Sarah found herself hobbled in an uphill battle to make ends meet.

In spite of the financial constraints plaguing the company, running a tight ship seemed to be beyond Sarah's compass of understanding. Great wads of bills and even uncashed checks were often found beneath seats, sofa cushions, or even on the floor of her car. At the same time, her company was garnering the reputation as a debt-ridden institution, a hinderance that hobbled fund-raising from corporate entities and foundations. Before granting funds, sources such as the National Endowment for the Arts and state arts councils looked for solvency. They, like private foundations, demanded budgetary constraints and fiscal discipline on the part of performing arts organizations. Sarah's enterprise was more often run like a mom-and-pop store, borrowing heavily as the need arose without any regard or plan for repayment. Oftentimes the notes were forgiven. Sarah's most promising prospects were wealthy individuals. Sarah always seemed to survive through the help of generous patrons who loved music. They knew what it would cost them, but she was such a force of nature that they gave in willingly.

NOTES

1. Peter Paul Fuchs, ed., *The Music Theater of Water Felsenstein* (New York: W.W. Norton & Co., 1975), 174.
2. Christopher Mahan, interview by the author, March 15, 2000.

5

SARAH THE MUSICOLOGIST

From the beginning, Sarah used creativity to get her ambitious programs onto the stage. With her second season, the realities of funding forced her to acquire the skills of a grassroots financier. By her fifth season, the need for uniqueness (and paying audiences) had inspired her to examine musical innovation. Surely, in the vaults of libraries and opera houses, there were new and old approaches to standard works and opportunities as rich as Offenbach's *Voyage to the Moon*. Her research had identified two rare volumes of *Voyage* in the stacks of Boston's public library that revealed numerous costume plates in watercolor, as well as scenic sketches of the original Paris production. In the course of time, it was only logical that Sarah the improviser, Sarah the fund-raiser, would become Sarah the musicologist.

Sarah espoused the view currently in fashion among other musicologists that original versions of works should be favored over subsequent editions. If a composer's work failed, it did so owing to inadequate performance, or perhaps the piece was ahead of its time or suppressed by censors or possibly misunderstood by an uncomprehending public.

On one of her many trips to Germany in the 1950s, Sarah witnessed an earlier version of Puccini's *Madama Butterfly* produced by Joachim Herz that inspired her to strike out on her own. Her new production was intended to surpass her prior Boston University workshop endeavor. After much reflection, she would follow through with new thoughts she had been mulling over, but again casting Asian singers in the roles of Japanese characters. But first, she traveled to Italy with

Osbourne McConathy as her music librarian. In Milan, the two visited Casa Ricordi, Puccini's publisher. They were shown the original score and other materials. With several versions to choose from, they were drawn to the two-act La Scala premiere that displayed a more negative side of Lieutenant Pinkerton.

Subsequent editions eliminated about twenty-five pages of the vocal score, involving Pinkerton's rude behavior toward the Japanese servants, that lead up to the wedding scene. Earlier, Puccini had gone to some length to cast an unfavorable light on Butterfly's relatives. Uncle Yakuside is depicted as a leering drunk who nearly spoils the festivities. Sarah reasoned that the more Navy Lieutenant Pinkerton is seen as insensitive and uncomprehending, the more it played into the clash of cultures. In later revivals, Sarah had Pinkerton playing with a football in Act I. Subsequently, it was conspicuous as a prop, seen on a shelf of bric-a-brac, a solitary football among Cio-Cio-San's most treasured possessions.

In an effort to again find the right singers with sufficient vocal heft to fill the cavernous Donnelly Memorial Theater, Sarah flew to New York for auditions but was unable to find any to her liking. Undeterred, she reengaged Taeko Fuji, the Cio-Cio-San of her earlier BU studio effort. She would appear under her married name, Taeko Tsukamoto, while Sarah sought a small venue, finally choosing an "under the radar" location. Two area high school auditoriums, Winchester and Wellesley, would serve her needs, plus a performance at a small theater off Harvard Square in Cambridge.

She commissioned a handsome production with sets by Ming Cho Lee, which opened in December 1963. But it was not the urtext *Butterfly* that would have satisfied the longings of scholars or musicologists. Instead, it was performed in two acts, with those in attendance recalling the second and third act played "without pause." Years later, Osbourne McConathy mused, "Sarah and I did not always agree. My preference would have been for the ur-Butterfly, which to my mind was more powerful than those revisions that followed. Instead, Sarah would add bits here and there, sometimes combining Puccini's early and late thoughts, and if the tenor in question wanted to sing the aria Puccini later inserted, she would throw it into the bargain." McConathy was referring to the famous but short "Addio, fiorito asil." With a tone of dismay, McConathy added: "Sarah would let the tenor sing it."[1]

To bring her audiences closer to the piece, Sarah used an English adaptation by Ruth and Thomas Martin. Seeking authenticity, she insisted on the use of bamboo. Although the bamboo made an authentic appearance, the heat from stage lighting oftentimes caused the bamboo to crackle noisily and splinter. One participant recalled that it would occasionally go off with the sound of a howitzer.

After a long day of rehearsals, Sarah was still up on stage. She had just introduced a Japanese consultant she had brought in to help with the cultural authenticity of the production. Her eyes looked glazed as if from lack of rest; occasionally she would close them while appearing to be fully cognizant of what was being said to her. Sarah had suggested that instead of having Butterfly and Suzuki strewing the stage with flower petals, she would have them construct numerous miniature flower arrangements. Her consultant was having none of it. Suddenly, Sarah's eyes snapped open as he flew into a rage and actually screamed at her in front of the entire company, "Is this what you call democracy?" With that, he stormed out into the night in the middle of nowhere in suburban Boston.[2] Sarah's determination to impose her will demonstrated that producing an opera was not necessarily a collaborative art.

In the course of thirty-two seasons of Sarah's company, Ming Cho Lee's *Madame Butterfly* was offered more than any other work. Yet, always mindful of the lessons learned from Felsenstein, Sarah would infuse new details with each revival, thereby ensuring that each audience would experience something novel, even in an old production seen many times.

Operas left incomplete at the time of the composer's death, or those with several different editions, were fertile ground for Sarah's tinkering, such as Jacques Offenbach's *Les Contes d'Hoffmann*. Although it was not clear that Sarah had any individual thoughts about the work, in a gesture of affection toward Felsenstein, she did yeoman's service in bringing his Komische Oper production to her Boston Donnelly Memorial stage in her 1965 season. To ensure the authenticity of her endeavor, Sarah even imported Felsenstein's set and costume designer, Rudolf Heinrich, to re-create his production in all detail, including costumes and lighting. Felsenstein even dispatched one of his assistant directors to ensure that his version would be completely faithful in all respects.

There was one unusual departure. During the final dress rehearsal, three chorus members were singing the Barcarole in the pit. Beverly

Sills, who had taken on all of the roles of the various heroines, stepped to the edge of the pit and stopped the orchestra. "What are they doing? This is the big hit of this show, and if I don't sing it, nobody does."[3] With that rebuff, Ms. Sills would sing the most famous tune in the opera as an opera star turn—written for her or not! Otherwise, the musicology of this version was borrowed and not one of Sarah's own invention. However, it was still her choice and realization of it that permitted an American audience, who would have otherwise had to travel to Europe, to experience it.

Felsenstein's five-act version, sung in English, differed in many respects from productions familiar to U.S. audiences. The biggest change, now common, was to have the Munich scene precede the Venetian one. In that sense, Sarah's import was ahead of its time, with spoken dialogue replacing the customary recitatives. Also, there were many musical repetitions. The famous Barcarole was used as a background for the Hoffmann-Schlemil duel, and a new ending found Hoffmann on his feet singing (rather than dissolving in a drunken stupor), with Stella and Lindorf left to vanish from opposite sides of the stage.

Unfortunately, Sarah's efforts were misunderstood and not well received by the local press. Michael Steinberg of the *Globe* praised designer Heinrich for the evocative visual setting, beautiful costumes, and atmospheric lighting but carped that the version was "too talky . . . and a first class stupidity."[4] Nevertheless, Sarah's mounting of *Hoffmann* aroused wide interest and comment far beyond Boston.

Also for the 1965 season, Sarah told her board of trustees, she would bring Modest Mussorgsky's original *Boris Godunov* to an American audience for the first time. She meant no Polish act, no Forest of Kromy scene. Previously, Sarah had traveled to Leipzig in search of the original score and, having found it, carried it home under her arm to protect against the slight risk that it might be lost or misplaced among airline luggage.

Concurrently, the Metropolitan Opera had been moving toward the original Mussorgsky version as prepared by Karl Rathaus, which retained the Polish act and the Forest of Kromy scene. Other opera companies were beginning to rethink their versions along the lines of Shostakovich's reworking of the score away from the Rimsky-Korsakov standard. Sarah was the first in America to offer her audiences the complete original version of the opera. *Boris* was seldom heard on the regional circuit beyond New York, Chicago, and San Francisco. That this original version was taken up by a small company with limited resources was a true milestone in American opera. Key to the success of the evening for Sarah was the planned appearance of Boris Christoff, the well-known bass who had made something of a career performing the title role. His renowned interpretation was seen in Chicago but not on the East Coast. Unfortunately he canceled and was replaced by George London, who was experiencing vocal difficulties at the time. In spite of this handicap, Sarah assembled an excellent cast, and the work was repeated the following season with Christoff, now recovered from brain surgery, assuming the title role.

Though he did not fall down the stairs from the throne at Boris's demise—as did George London and Jerome Hines—at one point Christoff amazed his audience by an insane leap from the stairs into the arms of several members of the chorus. In the throne scene, he became confused offstage and was not seated on the throne when the curtain went up. One of the critics, not realizing the real reason, commented that Sarah had found new meaning in the piece by showing the empty throne as a brilliant symbol that the opera was really all about the Russian people, and not just the story of Boris. Sarah's "brilliance" was in fact only Christoff's forgetfulness, brought on by his brain surgery of the previous year.[5]

Sarah's production of the first version of Mussorgsky's masterpiece was an effort by a regional opera company to pick up the challenge and present the work in its more powerful form, more taut, more grim than the familiar one. Subsequently the Spoleto Festival in 1971 took up the cause of this earlier edition, as would other opera companies thereafter.

The 1966 season saw the U.S. staged premiere of Rameau's *Hippolyte et Aricie*. Sarah and Osbourne McConathy inserted music garnered from various performing editions, including arias written by the composer for different performances, tailored to display the strengths of various artists of the day. Sarah claimed that after lengthy and delicate negotiations, Osbourne McConathy was allowed into the stacks of the Paris Opera Library, where uncatalogued sections of the score were retrieved.[6]

The pastoral quality of the piece was highlighted by Sarah's new design team, Helen Pond and Herbert Senn. Their use of dry ice, sparklers, tumbling waves as produced by a baroque-inspired wave machine, airborne furies, and a terrifying sea monster contributed to the aura of theatrical magic. As appropriate for any baroque opera, the ballet was enhanced with a stellar performance by Neils Kahlet of the

Royal Danish Ballet and Eleanor d'Antuono of the American Ballet Theater. Singing honors were shared by Beverly Sills and Plácido Domingo in the title roles.

Sarah's 1969 season found her exploring Verdi's first thoughts on his adaptation of Shakespeare's *Macbeth*, whereas most opera companies showcased the later 1865 Verdi/Boito revision. It is doubtful that even Sarah believed the original was superior in any way, but the insight audiences would gain from seeing a production of the original would more than compensate for any theatrical deficiencies.

Her groundbreaking 1973 production of an all-French *Don Carlos* was a musicological high-water mark for the opera company, well ahead of its time. Andrew Porter, writing for the *New Yorker*, noted, "Sarah and her colleague Osbourne McConathy prepared their own edition afresh from Paris materials and reconstructed as complete a performing edition as possible."[7] This version was the original Verdi score that contained twenty-one minutes of music cut from the original rehearsals, music that Andrew Porter had found in the archives at the Paris Opera.

The *Don Carlos* sets as designed by Donald Oenslager were borrowed from the San Antonio Grand Opera Festival. They were oversized for the twenty-three-foot limited stage depth of the Orpheum, the performance venue at the time, but conveyed a wonderful sense of atmosphere, highlighted by Duane Schuler's lighting that helped create illusion. The Orpheum stage lacked wings for a waiting chorus as well as space for scenery storage. Always quick with the illustrative anecdote, years afterward, Sarah's head shook with laughter as she recalled the difficulties in mounting the work: "The props had to be carried out the back door to get them off stage."[8]

Her *Don Carlos* boasted one of her better casts. Donald Gramm dominated as Philip II, while Sarah brought in Michele Vilma from Paris, a fine Princess Eboli. French Canadian Edith Tremblay, at twenty-one years of age, was a very young Elisabetta for a role normally assigned to more experienced dramatic sopranos. As Posa, Willam Dooley was fighting a cold and suffered pitch problems from time to time. John Alexander was his usual reliable self, if a bit wooden in the title role and downright awkward when Sarah had him play up the indecisiveness of Carlos's behavior as shown in bouts of epilepsy.

Except for a couple of rough spots in the performance, those fortunate to attend *Don Carlos* were able to judge for themselves what had been suggested only by scholars and Verdi enthusiasts: that an all-French *Don Carlos* presented the work in an entirely different hue, with some judging it superior to the standard Italian version.

With a particular artist willing, Sarah would eagerly insert a longer, more difficult, and more demanding aria, thereby giving her audiences arias that were rarely performed. At a concert with the Boston Symphony Orchestra, Beverly Sills sang a more difficult rendition of the already exacting aria "Marten aller arten" from Mozart's *Die Entführung aus dem Serail*. Upon learning of this feat, Sarah had Ms. Sills repeat it when she sang as Constanze in her 1965 season.

The insertions of various arias often grew out of the needs of a specific performance, such as a long-forgotten aria for *Norma*'s Oroveso composed by Richard Wagner at the time he took up conducting duties in Riga, Latvia. It was an aria Donald Gramm would assail (high-lying for a bass). It incited the Druids to action in throwing off their oppressors. Sarah sought to connect it to a historical movement, in this case, the pre-Risorgimento Italian movement of Bellini's day. Sarah went to the trouble (and expense) of having the theater balconies decked out in bunting in the colors of the Italian flag to create a festive air. As an added touch, she had the house lights raised while Gramm delivered the Wagner aria, a gesture perhaps only she understood.

And so it went—disused caballetas were revived and arias written for forgotten performances resurrected, even if they tended to stop the dramatic flow of the action. Sarah was later to present the one-act version of Wagner's *Flying Dutchman*, omitting the final redemption-through-love motif long before it was customary for major American opera companies to do so.

Existing performance practice meant little to Sarah if she had her hands on the autograph score and had determined that a one-time copyist had erred in recording a notation. For *The Barber of Seville*, Sarah's reading of a manuscript she located in Italy led to a questionable determination that Rossini had written a syncopation in the "Fredda ed immobile" ensemble, with the syncopation occurring right before the word "restami." When Sarah's cast performed the ensemble with that syncopation, a highly comical and breathless effect was created. Thus, Sarah had Beverly Sills and Ruth Welting performing it while some scholars began to question Sarah's reading of the score, suggesting she had misread the syncopation. In their view, it was an example of Sarah's hasty pudding.

Later, in 1974, Sarah mounted a new production of Rossini's *Barbiere*. She would prevail on Ms. Sills to offer the extended variations of "Ah vous dirai-je, maman," as written by Adolphe Adam. The fiendishly difficult aria and variations were inserted in the famous lesson scene. Apart from Ms. Sills's spectacular pyrotechnics, Sarah had the inspired idea to present the lesson scene as a musicale chez Bartolo. Her inspiration may have come from basso buffo Donald Gramm's skill as an accomplished pianist, who was also equally proficient on the harpsichord. The trio of musicians also included Nicholas Muni (Ambrogio) miming the flute part and Jan Curtis (Berta) playing the triangle.

In her 1977 season, funds failed to materialize for a planned production of Bellini's *La Sonnambula*. Instead, Sarah would fall back on a new production of *Rigoletto* for Ms. Sills. In Act I, there was a cameo appearance by "Diane de Poitier" (Monterone's daughter) from Victor Hugo's play *Le Roi s'amuse*, played by one of Sarah's motley circle. Fellow performers recall a hanger-on who occasionally fulfilled various minor roles, though ones with higher profile than a mere supernumerary. More curious still was Sarah's choice to insert in Act IV an aria for Maddelena, sometimes referred as "Maddelena's aria," that tended to slow down the action.

But for Sarah, the inclusion of the aria was as topical as the latest news flash that had the entire rarified circle of Verdi scholars astir in the late 1970s. A Belgian musicologist came forth claiming possession of a copy of the *Rigoletto* score (in French) from the year 1858 on the occasion of its Brussels premiere, one that included "Maddalena's aria." The controversy was put to rest with the revised 1981 edition of Julian Budden's exhaustive three-volume *Operas of Giuseppe Verdi*. It was a "salon piece" composed by Verdi but had nothing to do with *Rigoletto*. Budden described the claim based on the French score as a "false trail," one on which even the most careful of scholars may sometimes be led.[9]

With the passing of time, Sarah's attention was drawn elsewhere, with fewer and fewer opportunities seized for joint exploration with her audiences. Despite the "Maddelena aria" fiasco, her trademark informed scores demonstrated how practices or inserts had cropped up over time to the detriment of the work in question. But it also spoke to the prodigality of her inquiring mind, not to mention her zeal to delve into operatic dustbins. Her passion in these areas knew few limits, thus earning her the gratitude of scholars and a wider community of connoisseurs, thereby raising her company from one of regional striving to that of international stature.

NOTES

1. Osbourne McConathy, interview by the author, October 27, 2000.
2. James Billings, interview by the author, October 10, 2001.
3. David Lloyd, interview by the author, February 18, 2002.
4. Michael Steinberg, "Boston Opera: 'The Tales of Hoffmann,' Sumptuously Produced," *Boston Globe*, March 11, 1965, 47.
5. Norman Kelley, interview by the author, January 5, 2000.
6. Osbourne McConathy, interview by the author, October 27, 2000.
7. Andrew Porter, "Musical Events, Proper Bostonians," *New Yorker*, June 2, 1973, 102–105.
8. Herbert Senn, interview by the author, August 18, 2000.
9. Julian Budden, *The Operas of Verdi*, vol. 3, *From Don Carlos to Falstaff* (New York: Oxford University Press, 1978), ix.

6

THE GOLDEN YEARS

Sarah's daring efforts in musicology, innovative stagings, and newly earned fund-raising prowess helped catapult her image beyond Boston. But her paying subscribers were clamoring to see established international artists. She had done her best to attract important artists by offering them unusual repertory and productions, but more was needed. Two problems stood in her way. The higher fees demanded by major artists required even more in the way of fund-raising, and secondly, when she attempted to negotiate the treacherous shoals and reefs of casting, she did so without the aid of a compass. However, from time to time she found herself relying on others whom she had come to trust.

Sarah's focus was that of what we now call a dramaturg, primarily concerned with exploring the psychological underpinnings of the characters in the operas or looking into the social, political, and economic milieu of the time. She was never one to idly dream of great casts that she could present to her audiences. Her early training as a musician, first as a student of the violin and then the viola, may have influenced her views. According to her reasoning, a violinist or violist was capable of playing virtually all of the literature written for that instrument. In the same way, she believed that every baritone, tenor, soprano, and mezzo-soprano was surely capable of singing any role in the repertory within the range of that voice. That the human voice was a delicate instrument seemed lost on Sarah, who often asked singers to take on roles heavier than their voices would allow. It was as if she did not understand that you cannot ask a singer to sing like a clarinet or a flute.

The American tenor John Alexander probably possessed, more than any other artist who appeared with Sarah's company, the capability of a particular voice type to take on just about any role, light or heavy, in the standard repertory. Alexander was equally at home with the lighter and heavier roles written for the tenor voice, such as Alfredo in *La Traviata* or the Duke in *Rigoletto*. Heavier roles, such as Lohengrin and Pollione in *Norma* also lay within his grasp. All of these roles, except Lohengrin, he performed for Sarah.

Sarah often relied on the wisdom of others, such as William Judd of Columbia Artists Management Inc., or even recommendations of other artists for casting suggestions. John Alexander pressed Sarah to hire coloratura Beverly Sills, whose close associates referred to her as "Bubbles." They were a team as far back as the early 1950s with the Charles Wagner touring opera company and later with the New York City Opera. On the occasion of Ms. Sills's postperformance backstage visit with John Alexander in the role of Alfredo in the 1961 *Traviata*, Ms. Sills was introduced to Sarah. After an exchange of pleasantries, it was suggested that Ms. Sills join the company at a future date. However, when Sarah telephoned her the following day at her home in nearby Milton to discuss certain roles, Ms. Sills seemed less enthusiastic, curtly informing Sarah that she was six months pregnant. Sensing that "Bubbles" was giving her the brush-off, Sarah tartly replied: "You weren't six months pregnant last night!"

Sills was not known in Boston when she finally appeared with the company the following season, although she had lived in Milton since 1956 when her husband, Peter Greenough, scion of a wealthy Cleveland family and now *Boston Globe* financial columnist, moved the family to Boston. From the fourth season on, when she first appeared as Manon, Sills went on to sing nineteen roles with the company, building a significant portion of her career in Boston, being highly successful in those that lay within her range. She was less assured in heavier roles such as Norma. But with her winning stage presence, distinctive voice, and on-point staccati, plus the confidence she radiated while performing soubrette roles, Sills was capable of communicating a sense of fun that did much to enhance audience enjoyment.

Joan Sutherland was another artist who gave significant glitter and credibility to Sarah's star roster. Unlike Sills, Ms. Sutherland was already an established star on the international circuit by the time she appeared with Sarah's company. Back in the fourth season, Sarah was in a quandary. Out of uncertainty, she failed to book any singer for the role of Gilda in her upcoming *Rigoletto*. One of her assistants, Christopher Mahan, finally suggested Joan Sutherland but cautioned Sarah that her husband, Richard Bonynge, would have to conduct since they booked as a team. Not at all put off by the requirement, Sarah replied, "Do you think they would come?"[1] A subsequent telephone call located Richard Bonynge. He regretted that prior engagements precluded their participation but promised to consider a future booking.

During the 1963 season at Carnegie Hall, Joan Sutherland sang Elvira in Vincenzo Bellini's *I Puritani* for the American Opera Society to considerable acclaim. Sarah engaged the Bonynges for her 1964 Boston lineup in a new production of the Bellini work. It was one of the first occasions that drew the attention of out-of-town critics and reporters from national newspapers to Boston. The *New York Times* critic Harold Schonberg wrote, "It was an exciting evening, and it is no disservice to the other participants to give Miss Sutherland most of the credit. For, where most of them were good, she was spectacular. And it must be said that when she sings, it is an event and realized as such by the audience. Something of the glamour and electricity of a vanished age of prima donnas stalks the house when she is in action."[2]

In the rehearsal phase Sarah presented Ms. Sutherland with a number of suggestions thought to invest the role of Elvira with greater feeling. At a postperformance cast reception, Sarah's artists mingled with board members and wealthy contributors. Joan Sutherland graciously acknowledged many insights she had gained under Sarah's direction, even though she had previously undertaken the role for Barcelona and Glyndebourne. "Working with Miss Caldwell has allowed me to find a greater depth to the part that was not apparent to me in my previous performances."

Time magazine now hailed Sarah as "the best opera director in America," and for the first time in the company's history, a chorus was engaged on a seasonal basis, specially trained in a preseason workshop that gleaned many fine solo-quality voices recruited from local conservatories. While in rehearsal in an abandoned synagogue, Richard Bonynge was quick to affirm that the chorus was one of the finest he had encountered.

By the 1965 season, Sarah set up her own scene and costume shop, a notable departure from other regional companies that were obliged to rely on expensive workshops in New York and elsewhere for their needs. The new scene shop allowed her productions to be tailored to the specific needs of the shallow stages of former vaudeville houses, making maximum use of limited space. As a result, what was seen in Boston would reflect her own imprimatur, distinctive in identity and style. At the annual meetings of the Central Opera Service, an arm of the Met Guild set up to assist U.S. and Canadian opera companies in coping with various problems, news of Sarah's costume shop made her the envy of her regional opera colleagues.[3]

Another singer who helped build artistic capital for Sarah in those early years was bass Norman Treigle. When he appeared in Sarah's 1963 season as Mephistopheles in Gounod's *Faust*, William Allen Storrer of *Opera News* remarked, "Norman Treigle commanded the stage at all times and revealed a rich bass-baritone of apparently limitless volume."[4] The general sentiment among many was that Sarah's company had Treigle, while the Met did not. Among Boston audiences, there was a growing recognition that the casts offered by Sarah's homegrown Opera Group were often of equal strength, if not superior, to the Met tour performances seen every April.

In her 1965 season, Sarah mounted Rossini's *Semiramide*, a work not seen in Boston since 1918 and one very seldom revived. Joan Sutherland and Marilyn Horne were featured in one of the most glamorous casts ever offered by the company, with Ms. Horne making her company debut as Arsace, already six months pregnant, a fact for all to see. Being considerably shorter than Ms. Sutherland, Sarah had the mezzo wearing a goatee and a little fez-type hat to raise her stature, but in the end, she looked like nothing so much as O. Soglow's "Little King" from the funnies.

Sarah often tried using animals in her productions and had pigeons released for Semiramide's entrance, creating a startling effect. Doves rather than homing pigeons were originally scheduled. But when Sarah found out how much it would cost to rent them, she decided to substitute pigeons at a substantially lesser cost. During the performance, backstage technicians became alarmed when one of the pigeons strayed and walked under the lighting control board. Sparks flew! To everyone's amazement, the errant pigeon walked out unharmed while the rest flew up into the rafters of the theater and would not come down. Gradually, many but not all were captured. After a month of pigeon poop falling on the shoulders of audience members who attended events when other presenters rented the theater, Sarah received an ultimatum from the theater owners: either promptly arrange for the removal of the pigeons or her contract for use of the theater would be terminated. At a cost of $800, a bird handler was brought to the theater in an effort to capture the remaining birds for a sum that far exceeded any savings she had realized by not using the more expensive doves.

However, nothing could be done with *Semiramide*'s absurd plot, which involved a queen who has presumably killed her husband, then falls in love with her general, only to discover that he is her son (sung by a woman in male clothing). The singing was glorious, but some had to avert their eyes during the love scenes.

Sarah had hired the set designer Raymond Sovey, by then a very old man. Unfortunately, he resigned on short notice, leaving her stranded. The preceding production of Mozart's *Abduction from the Seraglio*, a production much admired, introduced Boston audiences to Sarah's new design team, Helen Pond and Herbert Senn. On short notice, they agreed to grind out a production to avoid disappointing her subscribers. Given the time constraints, they commandeered a raked stage already set up in an abandoned synagogue for the season's next production, *Intolleranza* of Luigi Nono. The hasty manner in which *Semiramide* was mounted caused conductor Richard Bonynge to exclaim, "Why is Sarah always so far behind?"[5]

For *Semiramide*, both Sutherland and Horne were repeating roles they sang so spectacularly in a concert version at Carnegie Hall the prior year. It was even suggested Horne had temporarily eclipsed Joan Sutherland's brilliance in the title part. Michael Steinberg of the *Globe* noted, "With her forceful diction and the dramatic projection of her singing, she [Horne] would seem to be a more imposing mistress of the bel canto style than Sutherland."[6] After the performance, the phrase uttered by Harold Rogers in the *Christian Science Monitor* was on everyone's lips: "A Golden Age of Opera" had returned.[7]

The many fine scenes with Joan Sutherland and Marilyn Horne strengthened Boston's confidence in Sarah Caldwell's choice of repertory, contrasted with the Met's week-long annual visit, which demonstrated cautiousness in repertory and oftentimes undistinguished achievement. Sarah's financial constraints limited each opera to one or two performances, which failed to satisfy demand. Invariably, sold-out houses meant many hopefuls were turned away. Sarah so deplored the situation that she would sometimes sneak out the front door and allow entry to disappointed standees.

It was not only the bel canto works that drew attention to the company; Sarah was determined to challenge her audiences with avant garde fare, such as Alban Berg's *Lulu*. In the summer of 1963, she traveled to Santa Fe and witnessed the U.S. premiere, performed as a two-act version. Sarah's distinguished cast would feature Joan Carroll (who sang the title role for Santa Fe), and Ramon Vinay, a former heldentenor now reclaiming his baritone roots, as Dr. Schön. Frank Poretta played his son Alwa, with Joshua Hecht as Schigolch, David Lloyd as the painter, and Blanche Thebom as Countess Geschwitz. Joan Carroll's husband, Rudolf Heinrich, was responsible for the sets, a series of slides and projections as well as a wonderful curved staircase for Act II. *Lulu* was performed in an unidentified English translation. Heinrich was praised for creating wonderful effects, each scene a series of monochromatic photographs as slide projections that created a feeling of fluidity. Caldwell had a triumph on her hands.

If her genius was attracted to the complexity of seminal twentieth-century works, such as Alban Berg's *Lulu*, it would only be a matter of time before Sarah set her sights on even more ambitious fare. With *Lulu* as her calling card, she hoped to offer the American premiere of Arnold Schoenberg's *Moses und Aron*, which she had recently seen in Europe. Sarah was startingly thwarted by none other than Schoenberg's widow, Gertrude Schoenberg. She tried several times to approach her but found her behavior both inflexible and bizarre. Gertrude once confided that she spoke nightly with the shade of her departed husband. But Sarah had a plan. She would offer the American premiere of *Intolleranza*, an opera written by Gertrude's son-in-law, Luigi Nono, for her 1965 season. It would serve to bring family members to Boston.

Luigi Nono was invited to assist in the premiere, but further complications arose when the U.S. State Department refused him a visa, alleging his membership in the Italian Communist party. Sarah was on the telephone to several distinguished American composers (including Walter Piston, Lukas Foss, and Aaron Copland), pleading with them to come to Nono's defense. Finally, the State Department reversed its decision, but not before a veritable media frenzy erupted, putting Sarah and her company in the center of a publicity blitz. The controversy surrounding the composer not only attracted the curious, but suddenly a lone protestor with picket sign appeared in front of the Donnelly Memorial, drawing more public attention. Fearing that this solitary individual might become discouraged and abandon his vigil, Sarah looked at her assistant stage manager and said, "Do something!" That something was for him to slip outside the theater and provide free coffee and doughnuts.[8] *Intolleranza* was a *succès d'estime* for Sarah and little else. It did signal the first American production of the famed Czech designer Josef Svoboda, who had been much heralded in Europe but virtually unknown in the United States.

Gertrude Schoenberg traveled to Boston with her daughter to attend the performances but was still evasive about any commitment. She was not particularly impressed with Sarah's presentation of Nono's opera, though it was not clear whether the composition or the production was the problem. Later, in an interview with the *New York Times* from her home in West Los Angeles, Gertrude Schoenberg said that practically every conductor in the United States had approached her for permission to mount the American premiere of *Moses und Aron*. She had not acceded to any of the requests because, on investigation, she found they could not guarantee all the rehearsals she felt the opera needed. Also she found there was not sufficient financial backing to present the large-scale work.

After the close of her 1965 season, Sarah and her managing director, John Cunningham, encountered Gertrude in London on the occasion of the British premiere of *Moses*. The two sleuths set out on a merry chase, finally locating Gertrude in Berlin at the Hotel Berliner Hof, where they checked in. A chance meeting between the two redoubtable women occurred in the hotel lobby. Drinks were ordered. Conversation was awkward. In a matter-of-fact manner, Gertrude announced it was her birthday. With an urgent look, Sarah turned to Cunningham and said, "Do something!" That something was a special birthday dinner in the lounge (the guest of honor would not move from her chair). Generous cocktails and toasts lubricated any remaining friction. Affably the widow acceded to Sarah's wish to stage the U.S. premiere of Schoenberg's *Meisterwerk*.[9]

With the American premiere for the Schoenberg work set for her 1966 season, Sarah also offered her audiences an imposing lineup of other works, one that greatly strengthened the Boston public's assessment of her abilities. She was beginning to receive the vote of confidence she had so long sought from her Boston public, or at least the Boston public that may have existed in Sarah's mind. First, set designer Oliver Smith's debut production with the company, Mozart's *Don*

Giovanni, was followed by *Boris Godunov* in an original version, then by Beverly Sills and Plácido Domingo in a baroque rarity, Rameau's *Hippolyte et Aricie*. Afterward, Renata Tebaldi made her company debut in Puccini's *La Bohème*, featuring Mr. Domingo's first Rodolfo. The planned *Moses* would wrap up a spectacular season.

During the *Bohème* rehearsals, Renata Tebaldi summoned Sarah, John Cunningham, and designer Rudolf Heinrich to her suite at the Ritz-Carlton Hotel. Tebaldi was a tall, solid woman, handsome rather than beautiful, and by this date no longer young. The original Heinrich costume made that reality all too evident. Later on, the wonder worked by Heinrich with a new dress, shawl, and hairpiece allowed her to shed years and inches, so effectively representing the frail young seamstress that a stage manger tried to have the "stranger" bustled off from the wings so that Madame Tebaldi could take her place for Mimi's entrance.

Sarah hesitated in casting the roles of Marcello and Musetta. Prodded by her manager, Edgar Vincent, she replied, "Don't worry—at the last minute everyone is available!"[10] Weeks passed, and Sarah continued to dillydally. With a matter of days left before the scheduled performance, her default obliged the company the expense of importing British baritone Peter Glossop and, later, Adele Leigh, at a cost that far exceeded what was paid to Renata Tebaldi and Plácido Domingo. If only Sarah had planned more effectively, capable artists could have been engaged at a far lower cost. This pattern was to continue throughout the history of the company.

Renata Tebaldi's appearance in *Bohème* was the primary draw. The young Domingo and Tebaldi interacted in a most convincing manner. Sarah's first-season *Bohème* had won her wide acclaim. She could very well have trotted out her former production from the warehouse, but Sarah seldom did that. Instead, a new production would try out several ideas she had been considering for some time.

Working closely with her designer, Rudolf Heinrich, Sarah devised a most unusual take on Act III of Puccini's opera, reasoning that if Mimi was ill with tuberculosis, it was excessively cruel that she should be seen shivering out in the cold, as is normally the case. Instead, Act III would show a set divided in half, a snowy landscape on the left and an anteroom of the inn on stage right. Stage action would now flow quite naturally from outdoors to the less chilly inn where the couple decide they must separate.

Looking back after a lifetime of performing, Plácido Domingo recalled,

> I've sung the farewell duet many times, and I always found it strange that Rodolfo should be so inconsiderate as not to insist on saying goodbye inside the warm inn. Only once was this problem solved for me. Sarah Caldwell . . . divided the stage in half, one part snowy landscape and the other the inn's anteroom. I dragged Mimi [Renata Tebaldi] into the inn, just before her aria, I felt Rodolfo's character finally and completely realized.[11]

With innovative musicology in mind, Sarah had promised her audiences a *Bohème* different from the standard version, claiming that during her visit to Puccini's publishers, she was allowed access to the composer's original documents. However, Sarah neither addressed nor disclosed the results of her sleuthing, and none were noted by the critics.

The scheduled May 1966 American premiere of *Moses und Aron* was delayed until the end of the year. First, the tenor Sarah wanted withdrew, and later George London canceled (the bass-baritone was having vocal difficulties). Sarah's second choice for the sprechstimme role was John Gielgud, but, having failed to interest him, she continued to dither until two weeks before the performance. At the last minute, she convinced bass-baritone Donald Gramm to take the role. Welsh tenor Richard Lewis would be his Aron, with Eunice Alberts, Robert Trehy, Maxine Makas, and Harry Theyard filling out the rest of the cast. A chorus of 120 singers drawn from the New England Conservatory Chorus had been rehearsed for the earlier performance dates in May, but the delayed move to November found the chorus on tour in Russia, necessitating the training of a new chorus. As a result of the postponement and other factors, costs increased from $200,000 to $300,000, making *Moses und Aron* a real money eater. Sarah found out for the first time how costs could spiral out of control. Also expensive was the use of the theater since it was only leased when the company was performing. Other outlays were incurred by renting rehearsal space. Storage for sets at yet another location necessitated transport expenses. The company's contract with American Guild of Musical Artists had expired, and the new contract cost was up 25 percent. A fee of $10,000 was due Gertrude Schoenberg to cover performance rights for *Moses* for the next three years. Irving Kolodin of the *Saturday Review of Literature* recalled, "That the work ever opened at all was greatly to her credit."[12]

Despite the cancellations and recasting, *Moses und Aron* was thought to be the triumph of Sarah's eight-year-old company. It was a handsome, stunning production with sets by Oliver Smith. He had the bare bricks in the back of the stage painted gold and made exciting use of scaffolding. Sarah was credited for not having overstaged the piece and for leaving a great deal to the viewer's imagination.

Donald Gramm and Richard Lewis were seen in matching beards and bathrobes. Harold Schonberg, writing for the *New York Times*, noted, "Both were superb. . . . the choreography of Claude Kipnis was not overdone but it left its mark, causing a handful of proper Boston ladies to flee the theater during the orgy in the second act, with its fairly lurid bacchanalia." Osbourne McConathy conducted the orchestra of mainly BSO players and a few contract musicians. Sarah wanted the supernumeraries, who were really more actors than anything else, to be scantily dressed for the purpose of the second-act orgy. In order to achieve a convincing appearance of male pulchritude among the supernumeraries, Sarah sent one of her runners to local body-building gyms, where a flyer was posted seeking volunteers. It read: "You should be 6 foot, 2 inches, and well built." Another possibility for realism led Sarah to interview female strippers for possible use in the orgy scene. However, this was soon abandoned in favor of singers and dancers in body stockings.

Sarah liked using animals when appropriate. For the last rehearsal, Sarah had sheep brought to the theater, temporarily housed in pens beneath a lateral front platform that ran the width of the stage and around the pit with connecting ramps from the front boxes to the stage. When the sheep began to bleat during rehearsals, conductor McConathy protested, "Either they go, or I go."[13]

While the ramp gave more room for maneuvering for the two hundred choristers, Sarah's next daunting task was how to order her diverse forces in a coherent fashion. In a burst of inspiration, she amazed her colleagues with her ability to marshall large groups. One of her runners was dispatched to scour various toy stores. He returned with some two hundred two-inch dolls in red, blue, yellow, and orange, all wearing little derbies. One night, after everyone left the theater, Sarah gazed interminably at these miniature figures set on a mock stage (36" x 18"). Little by little she began to move them about to cohere with the action and music. In a later rehearsal, the live participants were fitted out with paper derbies in matching colors, allowing Sarah to achieve fluidity of movement while averting a potential traffic pileup.

Before the December 1, 1966, premiere, the company gave a "student performance" of the work, which was itself an act of generosity. When one of the unseen chorus men, Jim Curran, intoned, "Moses is coming down from the mountain," just as Donald Gramm was to descend, the students shrieked with laughter, but Gramm took his time and somehow the dramatic moment was not broken. To avoid further embarrassment, this mirth-provoking line was excised from the subsequent performance.

"Sarah Caldwell's staging was clever, with just the right mixture of symbolism and naturalism," commented Harold Schonberg of the *New York Times*.[14] Irving Kolodin worried that the ramp around the orchestra had blocked off the quality of sound it produced, which he described as "dead and distant."[15]

Allen Forte's English translation was faulted in not measuring up to what Schoenberg was trying to suggest. Irving Kolodin said it best: "It destroyed the pattern of alliteration to which the composer had attached so much importance. 'Einziger, Eweger Allgegenwärtiger' (hardly matched by 'One, infinite, thou omnipresent one') to his final 'O Wort, du Wort, das mir Fehlt' (O word, thou Word, that I lack!)."[16] Harold Schonberg summed it up, "Congratulations to all concerned. At last we in America have had the chance to see and hear the opera that all Europe has been talking about for the past ten years."[17] Sarah had drawn people from all over the country to see *Moses und Aron*. Michael Steinberg, writing in the *Globe*, added, "With Sarah's company, we have something highly significant, of which the city can be very proud."[18]

Now Sarah's homegrown company was basking in a national spotlight, with Sarah, its driving force, becoming a national personality. The Associated Press labeled her "Boston's indefatigable miracle worker," while Andrew Porter of the *New Yorker* hailed her as "the single best thing about opera in America." "Boston genius," trumpeted a *Boston Herald* Sunday headline, while *Time* magazine called her "music's wonder woman." An editorial in the *Globe* chortled that Sarah and her Boston Opera Group had single-handedly recaptured Boston's long-lost cultural crown as the onetime "Athens of America"—referring to Boston's self-bestowed title coined back in the mid-nineteenth century when the city was the seat of American book publishing and boasted a circle of men of letters, such as Longfellow, Thoreau, Emerson, and Alcott in nearby Concord.

CHAPTER 6

With these newly placed laurels resting firmly on her head, Sarah was even attracting the attention of not only Beacon Hill spinsters, but also Brahmin elitists. They gave needed heft to Sarah's fund-raising Founder's Campaign under the direction of no less than John Godfrey Lowell Cabot. Sarah's Opera Group had its own outreach opera guild aimed at enlarging the ranks of new subscribers.

With Sarah's fame growing by leaps and bounds, Boston began to feel that it did owe her something, but was unsure as to what that was. Not shy in the least, Sarah spoke boldly about her overarching vision— a twenty-five-week performance schedule and an opera complex of no less three theaters: a small theater suitable for baroque works, a larger hall for experimental pieces, and yet another theater for regular operas. "For the first time I've been able to assemble a group of people who can ultimately function as a company," Sarah told *Musical America*. The ranks of her subscribers had swelled to the highest number yet.

Her 1967 season began rather smoothly with a repeat of Oliver Smith's production of Mozart's *Don Giovanni*. Smith accompanied Jacqueline Onassis to the theater. Her presence created quite a stir. Mrs. Onassis even allowed the company use of her name in connection with fund-raising.

The Bonynges were back with their entourage, their friend and fellow Australian, "Greta," (Margarita Elkins) as Elvira and Canadian mezzo-soprano Hugette Tourangeau as Zerlina. Greta and Hugette were regulars when it came to the Bonynges' "traveling road show." Ms. Sutherland was Donna Anna. Sarah had failed to enlist a "Don" until the last minute and had to settle for Justino Diaz, a very young performer at the time. Bass-baritone Donald Gramm repeated his much-admired Leporello. Robert Trehy was Massetto.

Sarah enlivened the production with touches gleaned from her research into original materials. Among them were two dwarfs, male and female, in Don Giovanni's coterie, similar to those seen in the famous seventeenth-century Velasquez canvas "Las Meninas," depicting life in the Spanish court. Sarah reasoned that if such figures were prominent in the court, they would also have found favor among Spanish nobility. The original "Don Juan" play, Tirso de Molina's "The Trickster of Seville," had two servants with dialogue.[19] In the finale, Sarah had them leaving carrying their suitcases.

Sarah fancied the use of a pair of greyhounds. Unfortunately, they began to bark when the Don tried to rape Zerlina! Although not mentioned in any reviews, Ms. Sutherland fell in the first scene and later complained of a strained back. Still, according to *Opera News*, "Joan Sutherland managed to spin out phrases with tonal purity, technical accuracy, and emotional warmth."

Soon, there were troubling signs on the horizon. The old vaudeville house, the Donnelly Memorial, was sold to the Christian Science Group and rechristened the Back Bay Theater. Despite the new name, the intention of the Christian Science Group was to demolish it. At the same time, Sarah's glittering star register was beginning to diminish to a nadir when it became clear that the Bonynges would not return. They were displeased with the chaos that seemed to constantly swirl around Sarah. To appease them, and knowing of their fondness for Franco Zeffirelli, Sarah arranged to borrow, at the expense of $10,000, Zefferelli's *La Traviata*, created for the Dallas Civic Opera. Unfortunately, the Bonynges' tight schedule would allow for only one performance, and to keep them on the company roster for yet another season, the contract provided that the orchestra would already be rehearsed before Bonynge arrived. Regretfully, due to a shortage of funds and because the rehearsal conductor (McConathy) was unreliable because of his bouts with alchol, there were no orchestra rehearsals preceding Richard Bonynge's arrival to take over the baton. When he first mounted the podium, that fact became immediately apparent. He dropped his baton, then stormed out of the theater and had to be talked into coming back.

Since one performance of *La Traviata* was hardly enough to satisfy the demand of Sarah's growing audience, the Bonynges were stunned to arrive at the theater some days later and find a fully packed house for the final dress, as if it were a regular performance. It was claimed that Sarah had even sold tickets (listed as Series B on a brochure). The Zefferelli production was another problem for Sarah. He was a director whose style was totally different from hers and an anathema of what Sarah had set out to accomplish.

As a result of her increased fund-raising activities, Sarah was out making her mendicant rounds and was absent from some of the rehearsals with Joan Sutherland and the cast, leaving the blocking to the performers. At the final dress, Ms. Sutherland was visited backstage by an admirer who wondered why she was only "marking" and not singing out before a group of students and others, since there were important backers in the theater. "Of course, I will sing out and would have done so had I known there were contributing members of the company in the audience," Joan commented. The Bonynges felt they were being ill used and vowed not to return to the company.

A stage mishap in Act III of *La Traviata* reflected poorly on the missing Sarah and heightened the growing sense of confusion that seemed to attend her. Anastios Vrenios (Alfredo) thought he had worked out a bit of blocking with Ms. Sutherland. He was supposed to throw money into her face, with Joan positioned to collapse as if in a fainting spell, falling into a convenient chair. As it turned out, Ms. Sutherland was nowhere near the intended chair, lost her balance, and fell to her knees, raising a cloud of stage dust. Thanks to her professionalism, she quickly recovered and managed to fit the incident into the action so as to make a highly charged moment out of it.

Sarah next began to lose public confidence by promising one thing to her subscribers, then delivering another. In May 1967, a Bartók triple bill announced his one-act *Duke Bluebeard's Castle*, the ballet *The Miraculous Mandarin*, and the pantomime *The Wooden Prince*. No doubt Sarah's research had informed her Béla Bartók once wished all three works—two ballets and an opera—be performed as a triple bill, although none had anything in common thematically. When it came time for the performance, *The Wooden Prince* was canceled, leaving her subscribers with a "triple bill" of two works.

For this production of *Bluebeard's Castle*, Sarah's designer, Dinah Kipnes, created a set of stairs and a bare stage filled with seven stylized doors. Rather than having the doors open as Judith touched them, which in the past had led stage directors to conjure something of dubious shock value, Sarah's inspiration was more abstract. Near the conclusion, when Judith speaks of the tears of Bluebeard's former wives, a cluster of tear-shaped bubbles lowered from the ceiling. Harold Rogers of *Opera News* reported, "When each door was touched, a vision descended from above in the form of contemporary sculpture, providing brilliant patches of color which assembled themselves into a coruscating jewel."[20] The "tears" were plastic globules found in a Boston novelty store, glued together in clusters, and spray-painted with added flecks of luminescent material. Upon viewing the effect at a final rehearsal, Sarah was heard to say, as she often did when she thought she had achieved something special, "It's magic time." Her staging went a long way to confound those who felt the work only worthy of the concert stage and, at least in the next-to-last scene, Sarah managed to realize Bartók's image of "a lake of tears."

Sarah had planned to give the opera in English and had a particular singer in mind for the role of Judith, but that singer was not available. When the intended singer canceled, Sarah was on the telephone, calling every mezzo she could think of to take on the role on short notice. None were available. In the end, she was obliged, at additional expense, to fly in Hungarian soprano Solga Szongi, who knew her role only in Hungarian. Guus Hoekman, the Dutch bass whom Sarah had cast in the role of Bluebeard, knew his role in English. He was forced to learn it in Hungarian in a matter of days! When it came to the performance, his memory was still so shaky that Roland Gagnon and James Billings stood in the wings with large prompting cards to urge him along. Unfortunately, the makeup person put bits of gauze over his eyes to give him a frightening look—an attempt to give him "angry eyebrows." As a result, he could not see a thing and was literally reduced to tears and ended up making up half the text.

Faced with the uncertainties that lay ahead, the defection of the Bonynges, and the impending loss of the Back Bay Theater, which had so accommodatingly facilitated exciting premieres, unusual stagings, and the mounting of rare works, Sarah's newly found "brilliance" was in danger of withering to a dim luster. It was then she took special note of an announcement by the Metropolitan Opera in New York. Rise Stevens and Michael Manual had been running a smaller, cadet touring company for the Met known as the Metropolitan National Company. The Met's move to Lincoln Center had imposed unexpected financial burdens on the parent company. The Met's national touring entity had an annual budget of $2.7 million but had also incurred deficits as high as $800,000, with even higher deficits projected in the future. The Met would be obliged to shed itself of the junior company, leaving open several unfulfilled performance dates in cities throughout the United States in the 1967–1968 season.

Roger Stevens, the chairman of the newly established National Endowment for the Arts, urged Sarah to form a new company to fill the void. Words of encouragement were also forthcoming from Oliver Smith. With Sarah, he saw an opportunity to further burnish his reputation in operatic set design, separate from his usual Broadway fare.

Now there was the glowing prospect of a national spotlight shining directly on Sarah in a new and larger arena, reaching far beyond the narrow confines of Boston's beneficence with two conjoined companies. Sarah was convinced that a turning point in her career was at hand with no time to waste. The prospect of holding and playing a new card in a wider arena was a nourishing one. It would be called ANOC or the American National Opera Company.

NOTES

1. Christopher Mahan, interview by the author, May 15, 2000.
2. Harold Schonberg, "Opera, Joan Sutherland in 'I Puritani,'" *New York Times*, February 14, 1964, 15.
3. Central Opera Service (COS), an arm of the Met Guild, became "Opera America" in 1990 and spun off on its own.
4. William Allen Storrer, "Hub Witchery," *Opera News*, April 13, 1963, 31.
5. Herbert Senn, interview by the author, August 18, 2001.
6. Michael Steinberg, "Sutherland, Brilliant," *Boston Globe*, February 6, 1965, 1, 7.
7. Harold Rogers, "'Semiramide' a Fresh Triumph," *Christian Science Monitor*, February 6, 1963, 7.
8. John Cunningham, interview by the author, December 15, 2000.
9. Ibid.
10. Edgar Vincent, interview by the author, April 10, 2000.
11. Plácido Domingo, "The Magic of Opera," *AARP Modern Maturity*, May/June, 2002, 10.
12. Irving Kolodin, "A Boston premiere for 'Moses and Aron,'" Music to My Ears, *The Saturday Review of Literature*, December 17, 1966, 41.
13. Osbourne McConathy, interview by the author, October 27, 2000.
14. Harold Schonberg, "Opera: 'Moses and Aron' Schoenberg's Opera Given US Premiere in Boston, Lack of Action a Drawback," *New York Times*, December 1, 1966, 56.
15. Irving Kolodin, "A Boston premiere for 'Moses and Aron.'"
16. Ibid.
17. Schonberg, "Opera," 56.
18. Michael Steinberg, "'Moses and Aron,' A Great Work Credibly Done," *Boston Globe*, December 1, 1966, 8.
19. "The Trickster of Seville," in *Spanish Drama*, ed. Angel Flores (New York: Bantam Books, 1962).
20. Harold Rogers, "Boston," *Opera News*, May 1967.

7

TOURING
AND THE ANOC

With Sarah, it was always that her reach exceeded her grasp. Estimates for the funding needed to sustain the full burden of operations for the American National Opera Company in its premiere season ranged as high as $1.3 million, far more than ticket sales would allow. The balance would have to be made up by private contributions and possible federal matching grants. The first year of the National Endowment for the Arts (1966) saw Sarah's company as the largest beneficiary of grant money ($50,000 for *Moses*). With Roger Stevens at the helm goading her on, it seemed there was no possibility of turning back.

Always willing to take risks with new talent, Sarah would now give American artists a better choice than going off to Europe or clerking and waiting for the next church job. Those artists who took their budding careers to Europe for finishing were absorbed into a foreign style. Sarah nourished the idea of another homegrown Rosa Ponselle or Lawrence Tibbett who could succeed without the imprimatur of a European success behind them.

She had already experienced touring and probably did it as well as anyone in her time. But Sarah was often too preoccupied with her muse to pay much attention to mundane matters such as currying favor with railroad officials, station agents, baggage masters, or truck and bus drivers, as others had done. Under these circumstances, mishaps were inevitable. When her 1960 nationwide *Voyage to the Moon* tour hit Seattle, an angry truck driver pulled away from the dock after unloading sets, costumes, and lighting, purposely failing to leave behind music scores. The cast then had to improvise from memory with piano accompaniment.[1] When the errant truck was located, musicians were finally able to take their places in the pit after forty-five minutes had elapsed.

When word reached the local apple growers association that a key moment in the plot of *Voyage* involved a gift of an apple by Dr. Blastoff to Queen Popotte, they intended to shower company members with baskets of apples as they journeyed through Washington and Oregon. Unhappily, many of these gifts were waylaid by insolent and indifferent truck drivers, leaving cast members empty-handed.[2]

Undeterred, Sarah soldiered on, determined to make a success of touring. However, tours were long and arduous, with cast and musicians passing the time aboard buses and trains. In these situations, the atmosphere around Sarah was influenced not only by her musical genius but also by her lack of attention to more mundane hygiene. Extreme measures—ranging from anonymous gifts of soap and flowers to "bombing" with aerosol deodorant—failed to bring about the desired result. As if blithely unaware of the effect she was having on the company, Sarah laughed off these efforts and continued to offend.

Well into her second season, Sarah boldly embarked on a fourteen-week coast-to-coast tour with *Voyage* but had yet to give up her position (and salary) on the faculty of Boston University. She was still obliged to conduct classes and could not be absent for any extended period. Trouble appeared on the horizon when she became stranded in a snowstorm in Iowa and was unable to return to Boston. The idea of tape-recording her lectures occurred to Sarah. They would be played back in her absence while she continued her tour. But when an angry dean learned the extent of Sarah's absenteeism, he summoned her to his office, threatening to cut her salary by half. Sarah resigned. Now she was fully on her own.

Returning to her *Voyage* tour, the bus stopped in Nebraska for refueling. Sarah turned to one of her artists, baritone Mac Morgan. "Mac, come with me!" The two headed across the street to an apparel outlet Sarah had spotted. Once inside, Sarah immediately headed for the first rack of coats. Without noting either style or color, she selected a new coat and transferred wads of bills she had stashed into the pockets before donning the new garment and settling with the cashier. On the way out, Sarah dropped her smelly old coat into a nearby trash receptacle as the two reboarded the bus.[3]

From the very outset, the name "Boston Opera Group" proved problematic. It implied a touring enterprise. Some saw a similarity with the touring entity the English Opera Group, founded in 1947 by Benjamin Britten and Peter Pears in the United Kingdom. They utilized a small number of singers and players, showcasing baroque works plus the chamber works of Britten. Sarah favored unusual editions of standard fare mixed with modern works that required a sixty-piece orchestra. In addition, Sarah was stuck with the clumsy and off-putting acronym "BOG," hardly suitable for merchandising paraphernalia such as T-shirts or shopping bags.

Columbia Artists Management Inc. (CAMI) had difficulty selling "BOG" to its markets. The name denied Sarah the recognition she craved as an important opera-producing entity. The word "group" implied the mounting of small-scale works and not the grand opera demanded by audiences. It wasn't long before CAMI's advance publicity was heralding the arrival of "Boston Opera Company." However, when word reached Boston, legal action was taken by a rival entity, The Boston Opera Company. It sponsored the Met's annual visit and was legally entitled to that name. With obvious embarrassment, Sarah retreated and changed the name of the company, issuing the following press release: "Today of our own free will we have chosen a different name for ourselves, a name which, we believe, will indeed appropriately describe our activities and purpose as Boston's own opera producing company and have began legal proceedings to adopt the name, 'The Opera Company of Boston.'"[4]

Sarah's early tour venture with *Voyage* incurred a loss of $20,000 at a time when she could least afford debt. Even before the receipts were in, CAMI was urging another tour for an English-language *La Bohème*, taking out a full-page announcement in *Musical America*. Many of the tickets in subscribing cities were presold to holders of community concert memberships, while others were sold publicly by local sponsors. Some were little more than one-night stands and were not economical. With Lois Marshall and Phyllis Curtin alternating in the role of Mimi in *La Bohème*, the tour fared little better than *Voyage*. Some of the tour dates failed to materialize, such as Chicago and Dallas. Sarah and the company often arrived before their "advance" publicity, which did not help fill seats.

An extreme situation arose when Sarah found herself in Little Rock for a performance. The *Arkansas Gazette*'s caption beneath Sarah's picture read, "Conductor of Boston Group's *La Bohème* is Arkansan." Sarah's time in Arkansas was hardly more than her brief attendance at two colleges. With her native roots in Missouri's northwestern panhandle pushed aside, it would suit her publicity needs (and her demanding mother in Fayetteville) to be rechristened as a "native" Arkansan. And so it was!

But Sarah had more important fish to fry, including being drawn into the mystique of launching a real American National Opera, even if it was impossible. Sol Hurok told Sarah that touring worked for him and it would work for her. Sarah would now establish her own quality touring company, just as Boris Goldovsky had done with his New England Opera Theater. However, Sarah's new entity would be heralded under the banner "Sol Hurok Presents," giving it added cachet as operating under the aegis of the Sol Hurok organization. It was a name to envy in American arts presentation, Hurok being the greatest impresario of his time, with a long list of legendary performers. After further words of encouragement from local sponsors that certain grant monies would be accessible, Sarah went forward with the launching of her new endeavor. Her announcement defined her aim as follows: "To bring together the highest caliber of American singing and producing talent, in order to create a uniquely American style of ensemble performance. The company will include gifted young American singers, many of whom are now engaged by European opera houses."[5]

With private contributions of $49,870 in hand, plus $200,000 guaranteed by the Opera Company of Boston and other matching dollars (all pyramided), Sarah ultimately garnered NEA "treasury" grant monies of $449,740, which promptly doubled with private donations. It was the largest grant agglomeration achieved to date, and it was hoped that additional contributions would be raised among regional opera centers visited by the company.

Edgar Vincent, one of her closest advisors, cautioned her that the undertaking was a trap. However, Sarah would not be deterred and set about deciding which operas and casts would be suitable for the upcoming tour, which would include *Tosca*, *Falstaff*, and *Lulu* for the 1967 fall dates, *Die Meistersinger* and *Cavalleria Rusticana* and *I Pagliacci* for March and April 1968. The Hurok organization reported that many cities involved had expressed interest, if not great eagerness, to allow the vacant dates left by the vanished Met National Company to ANOC. Additionally, some Southern cities could offer presold subscription series that would guarantee the cost of the visit, while a swing through towns in upstate New York could access funds through the New York State Council of the Arts. With these positive signs, Sarah saw this as her benediction to step onto a national scene with a new opera company, further raising her profile. *Newsweek* proclaimed, "Sarah Caldwell was a person capable of moving musical mountains."

Sarah promptly left for Europe and held auditions. In London she signed on a stellar Tosca, the flamboyant Australian diva Marie Collier, and British baritone Peter Glossop, her Scarpia and Falstaff. Later in Cologne she found Patricia Cullen, her Lulu. South African baritone George Fourie and American baritone Edmund Hurschell, both possible covers, came to her via the Komische Oper in Berlin. While in Europe, Sarah spread the word of a newly formed company, whose virtues she extolled to booking agents and artists managers and just about anyone who would listen.

The weeks prior to the tour were hectic. Before the rehearsals for *Lulu* could begin, Sarah was at her perch in the orchestra of the Back Bay Theater assigning various tasks. At one point, she handed a prop list to one of her runners to forage for various items, including a pistol, an artist's easel, and brushes. At the bottom of the list was "cuff links." "Should they be gold plated or plain?" he asked. Sarah seemed at the end of her patience and shouted, "No, just plain cuff links." It was soon apparent that Lulu was to be led away by the police, and Sarah had meant "handcuffs." Again confronted by the assistant, who dared to ask if she had not intended handcuffs, Sarah abruptly shouted, "Yes, cuff links!"

On the second day of lighting rehearsals for *Lulu,* which began midmorning and extended well into the afternoon, Sarah seemed blissfully awash in detail to the extent that even she had forgotten to have one of her runners fetch her usual lunch of take-out cheeseburgers and Cokes. In a fit of hunger, Sarah was munching on cheese crackers she had squirreled away in her voluminous bag, hardly noticing that she had failed to fully unwrap them. While shouting out light cues, streamers of cellophane dangled from the corners of her mouth.

Sarah and her legions settled into a prep school in the Berkshires—Rockwood Academy, a handsome mansion and once the location of a Jesuit seminary. With rehearsal pianos in place in a large fieldhouse with marginal sets and tape marking the ground plan, rehearsals began in earnest.

Later that summer, seven trucks full of sets, costumes, wiring, control boards, and portable lighting headed out for the campus of Butler University in Indianapolis for three weeks of final rehearsals. The full complement included covers for all roles. If Marie Collier could not go on as Tosca, Beverly Bower would be dispatched in her place. James Billings, the Sacristan in *Tosca*, would also serve as chorusmaster.

As the company's director, Sarah would bring *Tosca*, *Falstaff*, and *Lulu* to such regional centers as Detroit, Buffalo, Rochester, Syracuse, Columbus, and Madison, plus a swing across the South from St. Louis, Chattanooga, Knoxville, Birmingham, and New Orleans. Further, Sarah had decided that her *Tosca* would be bold and contemporary in an effort to appeal not just to opera lovers, but also to potential new audiences. Sarah rejected Oliver Smith's set designs for *Tosca*. Instead she settled for photo blowups, a montage showing reproductions of various Rome locales pitched at tilted angles to suggest an oppressive, police-state environment. They were designed by Rudolf Heinrich, who had by this time defected from Walter Felsenstein and was working for Sarah. His drops for *Tosca* in particular were larger and heavier than most companies tour with, but Sarah was determined to provide imagery on a scale otherwise available only in dedicated opera houses in major cities.

Sarah was always aiming to be ahead of the curve with her productions, employing innovative lighting designs, for example. For both *Tosca* and *Falstaff*, she collaborated with Broadway lighting designer Jean Rosenthal. She also tried to lure new audiences by scheduling both English- and Italian-language versions of operas back-to-back in tour cities whenever possible. An exception was *Lulu*, which was only presented in English.

To avoid additional expense by traveling with a chorus, for *Tosca*, both in the Act I "Te Deum" and the offstage madrigal in Act II, an organ would substitute for choristers so that a small traveling chorus would suffice. In the same way, the voices of a chorus drifting in through a window in Act II of the Palazzo Farnese residence would be attenuated. Still, the reduced number of chorus members superseded that of the previous Met National Company. Whereas the Met cadet company had toured with a forty-piece orchestra using a reduced orchestration, Sarah would deliver the goods with an orchestra of more than sixty to preserve the depth and sweep of the music. Sarah boasted that many were retired former first-chair players of well-known symphony orchestras. Her first flutist was John Wummer, who occupied that position for twenty-five years with the New York Philharmonic. Her concertmaster was John Stopak, formerly of the NBC Symphony. Among her first violins was Arthur Schuller, father of the composer Gunther Schuller. The orchestral musicians ranged in age from twenty to seventy.

Sarah's company would differ from its predecessor in other respects. While the former Met Company had three weeks of rehearsal before touring, Sarah would have five weeks. Established singers would appear in key roles rather than young singers still not yet firmly grounded or polished in their careers.

One of Sarah's advisors had cautioned her in her choice of repertory for the tour, noting that *Lulu* was an opera that existed on the margins of the standard repertory. When questioned, Sarah was quick to claim that she knew many who would drive hundreds of miles to see *Lulu*, while others thought that was wishful thinking on her part. As to *Falstaff*, even Giuseppe Verdi commented pessimistically on the relative lack of its box-office success. In America, the opera had only recently been hailed as a revelation in Zeffirelli's Met production of 1964. Furthermore, Sarah did not have Leonard Bernstein to conduct or the Met's fine cast to draw in the crowds. However, she was determined to offer something unusual along with the familiar works for what she hoped would be new audiences.

Prior to the tour, Sarah went the extra mile with her new productions to put the best possible face on the new company. She dispatched a crew of stage technicians on a pretour visit to ensure compatibility with the mounting of the company's sets and lighting. Many cities boasted that their orchestra pits were sufficient. After the tour, Sarah told the *Boston Herald*, "Ha! Ninety midgets playing oboes, maybe, but more like twelve regular men."[6] In some cases, several rows of front seats had to be removed to accommodate the musicians.

As to conducting assignments, Verdi's *Falstaff* would be under Sarah's baton while Osbourne McConathy would be responsible for *Lulu*. *Tosca* would be in the charge of Romanian conductor Jonel Perlea, who had suffered a stroke in 1957 that paralyzed his right side, but the disability did not keep him from wielding a baton with the left hand.

Since Sarah was primarily occupied with artistic matters and fundraising, the new company needed a business manager. At the suggestion of Oliver Smith, Henry Guettel was recommended to Sarah by Roger Stevens. Henry had produced profitable touring companies of

Broadway shows such as *Camelot* and *The Sound of Music* and had worked with Smith before.

With a weekly payroll of $60,000, the salaries paid to leading vocalists, the company landed in Indianapolis in mid-August prior to the opening on September 15 for four more weeks of rehearsals. They set up shop at the 2,200-seat Clowes Hall of Butler University, the very theater where the ill-fated Met National Opera Company had begun its first season two years earlier. The planned visit was for two performances of each of the three operas.

During the Indianapolis rehearsals, it suddenly occurred to Sarah she was lacking the costumes of ecclesiastical vestments for the Te Deum scene at the end of Act I of *Tosca*. One of her assistants was quickly dispatched to a Chicago firm specializing in liturgical paraphernalia including garments, with the purchase made on credit (the bill never paid). The new vestments were later "darkened" with an aerosol spray paint in order to blend in with the *Tosca* production.

In the final *Tosca* rehearsal, the temperamental Australian diva, Marie Collier, at the point of her entrance in the opera, walked onstage and immediately held up her hand, bringing the rehearsal to an abrupt halt. Proceeding toward the lip of the stage, Ms. Collier rudely addressed Maestro Perlea, saying, "I'm having trouble following your beat! Are you some kind of fucking cripple?" The unfortunate incident brought an end to that day's rehearsal. It took all of Sarah's persuasive powers to keep Maestro Perlea from leaving the company.

While in rehearsal for *Falstaff*, Sarah and her designer, Oliver Smith, had decided that they needed a mill wheel for the set. One was built (expensively on overtime) and shipped to Indianapolis, where Sarah and Smith decided that they did not need it after all.

The opening *Falstaff* did not draw the national news media as had opening nights in Boston. Paul Hume of the *Washington Post* and a representative of *Opera News* attended. However, *Time*, *Life*, and *Newsweek* were conspicuous by their absence. Hume could always be counted on to heap encomiums on anything Sarah would do, and his review was a virtual thumbs up, with some minor reservations.

Peter Glossop was the Falstaff for an audience unfamiliar with the work. A reporter for the *Indianapolis Star* dubbed the company debut "brilliant." For *Lulu* the following night, Patricia Cullen succumbed to a virus and was replaced by soprano Louise Budd at the last minute. Ms.

Budd had all the notes but, according to *Opera News,* "didn't rivet the viewer as a good Lulu should."[7]

Midway through the Indianapolis run, seven thousand of a possible eight thousand seats were sold, with the two remaining performances filled to capacity. The fall tour of the American National Opera Company under the banner of "Sol Hurok Presents" was off to an impressive start. It was estimated that at least two years of touring were needed to build attendance to the point of engaging local sponsoring groups. Sarah kept the ticket prices low ($3.50 and $6.50), hoping to encourage attendance by students.

The tour worked its way through upstate New York, continuing to attract good houses, and then settled into a two-day stint at the Brooklyn Academy of Music, exposed to the New York critics, who were enthusiastic in their praise for the new enterprise. Later, in Columbus, Ohio, and Madison, Wisconsin, ANOC played to packed houses. Despite the strike of the resident opera that fall season, Chicago audiences were disappointing. By the time the tour reached St. Louis and Little Rock, as many as two-thirds of the seats were empty. A surge in attendance greeted their final swing through the South via Chattanooga, Knoxville, Birmingham, and Mobile, ending satisfactorily in New Orleans. On returning to Boston from its twenty-one-city tour, the exhausted company offered two performances of each opera at the Back Bay theater. While the set for *Tosca* was being put in place, Osbourne McConathy arrived at the theater drunk, demanding to go on. Sarah discovered him and went on in his place, with several of her faithful stagehands protecting her.

In spite of the obvious fatigue and pressing problems, Sarah was in a jubilant mood at the tour's conclusion, claiming it a great success. She even told the *Boston Globe* that the tour made money, a dubious claim at best.[8]

Several months later, the spring tour headed out in mid-March and fared less well. A mixed reception greeted it during a two-night stand in Albuquerque. Afterward, the tour continued on to Tempe, outside Phoenix. The company played the Grady Gammage Auditorium, an impressive structure designed by Frank Lloyd Wright but one ill-suited to the needs of opera presentation with its oddly curved proscenium.

On the occasion of the last *Carmen,* both the tenor and his cover for the role of Don José were indisposed, with no replacement in view.

Sarah urgently telephoned James Billings, her resident baritone for the smaller roles. He was enjoying the evening off in the company of a few martinis. When initially studying to be a dramatic tenor, the baritone had once sung Jose; with that experience, Billings was able to deliver the vocal goods in a tenor role and save the day. He sang from the pit, dressed in a dark suit, while Ray Arbizu and Thomas Rall (the indisposed tenors) walked through the part in alternating acts.

Sarah's powers were sufficient to turn a baritone into a tenor if for no more good intentions than a sold-out house. Her singers often fulfilled roles that seemed far from their home territory. In some cases, Sarah persuaded them that they could; in others, they had a longing to perform roles which only Sarah would mount for them; in others, the desire of the two sides merged.

At Tempe, Arizona, her touring group gave its first road presentation of Stravinsky's *Rake's Progress*. Unlike Sarah's last 1952 BU Opera Workshop production, she opted for an updated version of the Stravinsky classic, instead of the planned touring *Die Meistersinger*.

The period of the piece would be transferred from eighteenth-century London to the mod sixties contemporary world of London, with Tom Rakewell making his way about London in leather jacket and motorbike, wearing a sweatshirt with "Stravinsky" emblazoned on it. This *Rake* quickly became known by its Boston audience as the "all Harleys and leather *Rake*," referring to the motorbike made by American manufacturer Harley-Davidson. However, they were really English Triumphs since the opera is set in England.

In the first scene, Tom was seen working on his motorcycle in the backyard of a dreary Midlands row house. Later, Baba the Turk arrived in a Rolls Royce hearse with an entourage of transvestite groupies in leather riding motorbikes. Sarah had been loaned six black-and-white Triumphs that were quite stunning in appearance. She was so excited about the black-and-white decor of the set that she even had the red tail lights of the motorcycles taped over. However, for the Bedlam scene, Sarah decided she wanted a white bike, so one of her prop men spent all day covering one of the Triumphs in white athletic tape. In the second scene, it became "Venus's throne" for Anne Trulove. Some of the critics were blown away by the symbolism of the bandaged bike. In Boston, Baba had appeared as a huge fuzzy image on a screen in Act II in the auction scene. However, in Tempe, she appeared on a small video monitor—not nearly as effective.

Helen Pond and Herbert Senn, Sarah's design team, were praised for their striking black, white, and gray sets, which managed to achieve an unusual depth of clever perspective. Sarah was able to engage Robert Craft, Stravinsky's amanuensis, to conduct. Perhaps the biggest flaw was casting John Ferrante, a countertenor, as Baba the Turk. Ferrante's voice fell strangely on some ears. One critic described Ferrante's voice as "an eerie and loud voice that sounded more like a wild bird than either a man or a woman." In this production, Ferrante wore a costume that made him look like a woman when he faced one direction and a man when he faced the other. Sarah's decision to cast Ferrante as Baba was an idea ahead of its time given the relative absence of countertenors on the stages of opera houses in the sixties.

Although in frail health, Igor Stravinsky traveled to Tempe from Los Angeles and appeared at the stage loading entrance, escorted by his wife, Vera, and a female attendant. Afterward, in the green room, felicities were exchanged. Fearing that Stravinsky had not approved of the production, Sarah appeared ill at ease. Stravinsky remained mum.

More difficulties plagued the company on opening day at the Dorothy Chandler Pavilion in Los Angeles. Earlier that morning Sarah arranged for a last-minute rehearsal at the Pasadena Playhouse. But when her artists arrived that evening at the stage door, they found their entry blocked by squad cars and the local sheriff. A disgruntled creditor, not paid for providing bus transport and acting under an apparent "color of law," had obtained a warrant to seize the company's scenery and costumes in lieu of payment. The sheriff wanted to know of Sarah's whereabouts and was told that she had just left the building. She was actually onstage, hiding behind a drop, leaving manager Henry Guettel to deal with the sheriff. It was often the case that money promised from donors never arrived on time. In order to avoid having liens placed on props and equipment, Sarah had cleverly put everything under the ownership of her parent company, the Opera Company of Boston. The sheriff was unable to attach a lien and engaged Guettel in an exchange of angry words. As one cast member recalled, "The LAPD gave Henry a terrible time. He damned near went to jail to save the performance."[9]

Further problems developed when the intended Falstaff, Peter Glossop, was stuck at the Hamburg airport and unable to appear for what was intended to be a first-night glamour cast. Instead, Robert Petersen, his cover, would be Falstaff. Martin Bernheimer, writing in the *Los Angeles Times*, observed, "The effect was undeniably crippling. Mr. Petersen is an appreciative actor and a reasonably competent singer. That is all. A dominant Falstaff must be more." Bernheimer also complained that the orchestra was "undernourished," and the rest of the cast was deemed "bland."[10]

Through the company's two-week visit to L.A.'s Dorothy Chandler Pavilion, barely half the seats were sold—even for *Carmen* with Marilyn Horne. Horne was considered a native daughter. Although born and raised in Bradford, Pennsylvania, she had studied in Los Angeles, appearing in both student and professional productions. She had debuted in opera in Los Angeles. It was her springboard through film work as the "voice" for *Carmen Jones* that led eventually to her national triumph in *Semiramide* at Carnegie Hall.

A subsequent English-language *Falstaff* played to quarter-filled houses. The touring *Tosca*, with Beverly Bower again in the lead role and Thomas Rall her Cavaradossi, with George Fourie as Scarpia, was even more of a shambles, according to critics.

The unusual *Rake* did manage to spur considerable comment from the L.A. audiences, although it received a less-than-friendly reception. In the Act I scene, both Anne and Tom appeared to sing their lines from a book of poetry, "The woods are green and bird and beast at play." Later, the kinetic visuals of Jacquie Cassen and Rudi Stern had Baba disappearing into a wall at the breakfast scene, only to appear as a giant TV image at the close of the auction scene and summon Anne with the words, "Come here, my child, to Baba." More problematic was a Timothy Leary poster seen in Tom's London flat—"Turn on! Tune in! Drop out!" The production was Sarah's one-time incursion into *Weltanschauung*.

Stravinsky attended one of the performances and sat unnoticed in the second row of the orchestra section. After the Los Angeles performance, he issued the following statement that appeared aimed at throttling various critics who had condemned the updating as violating the composer's intentions: "The Caldwell production exposes a wholly new point of view and is inventive in many, many particulars. Some critics who saw it in the East have not liked it because they are now defending the work that only a short time ago they loathed. But I like it."

During the Los Angeles visit, a mysterious woman appeared at the stage door of the Dorothy Chandler Auditorium demanding to speak with Miss Caldwell. When Sarah appeared, the woman approached and said, "I bring you news of your father." Sarah braced herself. Assuming her Buddha-like mask, she replied: "Thank you for coming, but I think it is best that you not give me the news." With that rebuke, Sarah turned and reentered the theater. Edward Fletcher Caldwell would have been eighty-two years old, assuming he was still alive.

Prior to the company's departure for a one-day stand in San Diego, the Sunday matinee of *Carmen* starring Gloria Lane had to be cut short. Dorothy Chandler management had booked a Jascha Heifitz recital at 7:00 p.m., which obliged Sarah to excise one intermission, the children's chorus, and the third act prelude, reducing the playing time by more than one hour. A considerable burden fell on Gloria Lane and Thomas Rall, the replacement Don José, but the truncated performance went off smoothly. Martin Bernheimer of the *Los Angeles Times* reported, "No one could have blamed the company for contenting itself with a half-hearted run-through. But it did nothing of the kind. Again we saw an uncommonly spirited, intelligently motivated, carefully balanced *Carmen*."[11]

The company's brief appearance in San Diego was not under the Hurok banner. Instead, two performances of *The Rake's Progress* were presented under the auspices of the San Diego Opera Company as a part of its subscriptions series. On the day of the performance, local newspapers blared headlines of the assassination of Martin Luther King in faraway Memphis. In keeping with the solemnity of the occasion, the curtain rose with cast members seen onstage holding hands and launching into the hymn "Precious Lord, Take my Hand" before commencing the performance.

The audience was awed with the glittering Mylar-encrusted scenery, the kinetic lighting, and the psychedelic effects. Mirror Mylar was a fairly new material at the time and became trendy in the following decades. But Sarah was again ahead of the curve in its use. As in Tempe, the closed-circuit TV did not work, and the audience had to settle for a twenty-inch TV screen, thereby losing the impact. There was a last-minute scramble in San Diego to find substitute equipment from local TV stations. Hoping to avoid further expense, Sarah dispatched one of her runners with the admonition, "The best equipment is the one you can get for free."[12]

Back in Los Angeles, two final performances of *Falstaff* and *Carmen* ended the West Coast tour, the company's resources exhausted, its artists and musicians running to cash their checks with many left stranded at the Los Angeles airport. As the protective deity charged with the welfare of musicians in the Roman pantheon, Minerva's failure to assist would surely have brought on the wrath of the gods. Instead, it would be left to her manager, Henry Guettel, son-in-law to the composer Richard Rodgers and a person of substantial means in his own right, to step forward with his credit card, generously funding the return tickets (the sum unreimbursed).

Addressing the dire situation, Sarah announced that there were no further plans until the company's finances could be resolved and immediately instructed her New York attorneys, Levin and Weintraub, to file a petition in bankruptcy on May 8, 1968, in the Southern District, State of New York, the state where the corporation had its charter. The petition under the Bankruptcy Act showed liabilities of the American National Opera Company of over $700,000 and assets of approximately $150,000. Those involved in providing goods and services to the company found payment sporadic or nonexistent.

When Sarah launched her national enterprise, she did so with the encouragement of Roger Stevens, Sol Hurok, and others. Sarah was the beneficiary of the largest federal grant money yet given by the recently established National Endowment for the Arts. She even claimed it as a sign or "benediction" validating her enterprise. Her love of touring had allowed her to escape from the pressures she faced in Boston. In each tour location, she was feted and indulged in her own self-promotion, which exceeded anything any press agent or manager could accomplish in her name.

The 1967 fall tour had demonstrated ample evidence that ANOC filled a void, as did the previous spade work by the Met National Company. It was a mission gladly undertaken, even if lacking in effective publicity generated by the Hurok organization. Had Sarah simply squandered many of her opportunities as was her wont? There were those who argued that some of the advance press generated by Lilian Libman of the Hurok office was not particularly creative or arresting.

For all their efforts, the Hurok organization may not have been selling to its usual performing arts markets either geographically or culturally. Another problem was the failure of the reviews (mostly negative) in Los Angeles to pull in the crowds. Still, there were instances of sold-out houses in the Midwest tour and evidence of high levels of audience enthusiasm. There was even the expectation that in a matter of time, Sarah's seriously undercapitalized enterprise might eventually galvanize sufficient local or regional support to allow it to survive.

That she was willing to invest countless hours and energies to pursue this goal was ultimately to her credit. If the National Endowment for the Arts and state-funded arts councils were only good at offering initial financial incentives and words of encouragement, much more would be needed to sustain such an ambitious enterprise. Lacking that, ANOC proved less able to survive than the Met National Company. In the practical world of 1968, the U.S. Congress had yet to fund more than token seed money.

Neither ready for a requiem nor willing to concede fallibility, this latter-day Minerva faced her disappointments with her usual equanimity. Some weeks after the debacle of the spring tour, Sarah returned to her "home roots" to accept an honorary Doctorate of Law degree from the University of Arkansas on June 4. The irony of the honors bestowed on her while being hounded by creditors must have underlined the instability of her calling. Bloodied but unbowed, Sarah accepted her parchment while showing no outward sign of unease over her most recent misadventures that spent her accumulated capital and goodwill as far back as her BU Opera Workshop days and the first years of her Opera Group.

With inadequate preparation, an overly ambitious and ill-supported tour, and a hopelessly optimistic and unrealizable financial base, Sarah had made the prospect of a national company more remote. Even her image as a miracle worker, fostered by her New York publicist, Edgar Vincent, had been tarnished. One demonstration of human weakness is enough to show Minerva's feet of clay—and the clay had clung to far more than her feet after the debacle of the year just past.

Back in Boston, Sarah's tenth season had ended on a tremolo of uncertainty. The Back Bay Theater was to be demolished by its new owners, leaving her company to resume its nomadic existence. Faced with the loss of a substantial number of her subscribers, this challenge required her to work her theatrical magic in such unlikely venues as basketball arenas, fieldhouses, and flower markets.

NOTES

1. Conversations with Mac Morgan, November 3, 2000, and James Billings, October 10, 2001. Their impressions from being on the tour were that the truck drivers were spiteful.

CHAPTER 7

2. Conversations with Mac Morgan and James Billings.

3. Mac Morgan, interview by the author, November 3, 2000.

4. Press release, Boston Opera Group, November 14, 1965.

5. Press release, American National Opera Company, April 20, 1967.

6. McLaren Harris, "Opera Tour Shows Profit," Notes on Music, *Boston Herald*, November 19, 1967, 11.

7. *Opera News*, September 1967, 21.

8. McLaren Harris, "Opera Tour Shows Profit."

9. James Billings, interview by the author, October 10, 2001.

10. Martin Bernheimer, "American National Presents 'Falstaff,'" *Los Angeles Times*, March 26, 1968.

11. Martin Bernheimer, "Truncated 'Carmen' at Music Center," *Los Angeles Times*, April 2, 1968, 17.

12. James Billings, interview by the author, October 10, 2001.

8

THE NOMADIC YEARS

The vagaries of running a company with only temporary homes here and there would severely tax Sarah's resilience. Nevertheless, she remained defiant and vigorous. Not deterred in the slightest, she made creative use of such diverse buildings as gymnasiums, hockey rinks, and flower markets while finding innovative ways to produce operas for subscribers. The net result was to bring her closer to her audiences than ever before.

With ANOC going through its death throes, a search was already under way for a new Boston venue. In the end, Boston's Shubert Theater, with half the capacity of the Back Bay theater, would serve as its temporary home for the 1969 season. Added performances were needed to satisfy the existing subscriber base, a costly situation. Sarah also tried other venues, some not yet approved by the fire marshall for that kind of use, which also resulted in delays and cancellations. In each location, Sarah did her best to make her Boston audience aware of the need for a performing arts complex. Igor Stravinsky's *Fanfare for a New Theater* was heard as a precurtain anthem.

The Eero Saarinen–designed Kresge Auditorium at the Massachusetts Institute of Technology might have impressed some as an unsuitable venue for opera with its narrow stage and shallow, curved orchestra pit, which posed considerable difficulties. But Sarah offered a compelling performance of Wagner's *Der Fliegende Holländer* for her 1970 season. By mistake, costumes loaned from London's Royal Opera House at Covent Garden went to Chicago, arriving a few days before performance. A crash effort ensued to alter them in time for opening night. As if that were not enough, an obdurate municipal fire inspector condemned the wooden structure that served as the Dutchman's ship as a possible fire hazard. To prove him wrong, Sarah lit a match on the spot to demonstrate that it was not overly flammable.

Just days before the premiere, Sarah discovered she had no spinning wheels for Act II, when the Spinning Chorus underlies "Senta's Song." A phone call to the Met found theirs currently in use. At the eleventh hour, word came of several women at the Massachusetts Historical Society of the Merrimack Museum who occasionally met to spin wool. Sarah coaxed them to bring along their spinning wheels. As the Act II curtain rose, they were seen among the chorus on the Kresge stage. The Pond/Senn design team was barely able to maneuver the scenery in place in time for the premiere, with the paint still drying. The Dutchman's ship, an imposing structure, was a haunting presence in the auditorium. Right up to the last rehearsal, Sarah continued her habit of making changes.

On this occasion, Sarah assembled three singers worthy of their roles. Thomas Stewart was a compelling Dutchman; Giorgio Tozzi was Daland. While Phyllis Curtin did not possess an opulent voice, she fulfilled Senta's dramatic requirements. Prior to the finale, Sarah had supers entering the auditorium to hoist a huge mast with large double red sails dead center in the aisle, allowing Thomas Stewart to sing his final lines from the middle of the audience. Ms. Curtin did not jump into the orchestra pit. Instead, a stunt double was used, which robbed the denouement of its impact. The Pond/Senn sets were atmospheric and as highlighted by Carol Hoover's inspired lighting effects, heightened the drama. Sarah conducted the original ending, without the orchestral and scenic redemption of Senta and the Dutchman. The postlude ended in tonic flourishes.

During rehearsals Sarah exchanged a few harsh words with the crew executing lighting cues, and in retaliation, during her solo bow, an angry electrician plunged the auditorium into darkness. But the mishap did not mar what was received as an excellent production, which made up for the company's poor showing in the preceding season.

It was an open question as to whether *La Fille du Regiment* would follow on February 21. The company's treasury was nearly empty. At the last minute, an unexpected contribution saved the performance. Previously, a check handed to Beverly Sills for her Lucia bounced. An $800 cashier's check per performance would have to be tendered to her dressing room before she would consent to go onstage. It was her first performance in the role of Marie in *Fille* before it became one of her calling cards in other houses, including one taped and shown on a nationwide telecast and later made available commercially.

Donizetti's opera was sung in French with spoken dialogue in English. At Sills's insistence, Sarah relinquished her baton to Roland Gagnon, who had prepared her vocal embellishments, variants, and cadenzas. He had conducted a prior concert opera performance at Carnegie Hall with a cast substantially the same as Sarah's. The performance at the Cousens Gymnasium of Tufts College began at the odd hour of 5:00 p.m. in order to avoid conflict with the regularly scheduled 8:00 p.m. basketball game.

Sarah arranged to borrow the Royal Opera Covent Garden's handsome costumes by Sandro Sequi. In turn, the Pond/Senn team coped ingeniously with the gym setting, coming up with sets that stretched alongside a wall, with stairs down to the basketball floor, giving the impression that this fieldhouse was built for comedy, or at least a place where the ensuing high spirits would logically unfold. Muriel Greenspon, as the Marchioness of Berkenfeld, arrived via horse-drawn carriage up the center aisle, with its sawdust floor. The Tufts University ROTC drill team provided the smartly maneuvered military cadre for the Tyrolean setting. A large poster of Napoleon glowered the recruiting strategy, "Napoleon a besoin de VOUS."

The waif that the twenty-first regiment of Napoleon's army had adopted some years ago was none other than one who had grown into the ebullient Marie of Beverly Sills, perhaps more Jewish mother than regiment foundling. During the Sulpice-Marie duet, Sarah used supers dressed as "little Beverlies," with each of them staging vignettes of Marie progressing from baby, child, adolescent to *vivandière*. Although there were barbs in the press about the performance, the staging was enormously clever and inventive. It was hard to resist the charms of this Marie, who was in rare vocal form, with Ms. Sills's brilliant, easy caressing of the lilting Donizetti arias. The relaxed and unusual setting of the fieldhouse allowed an infectious air of spontaneity to take hold. The parrying between performers, such as the spoken English dialogue invented for Donald Gramm's Sulpice and Muriel Greenspon's Marchioness, were moments of high camp. Greenspon intoned in French-accented English, "Do you speak the Engleesh?" with Gramm replying, "A leetel."

Grayson Hirst's white-timbered tenor approached "Pour mon âme quel destin" cautiously but delivered the many high C's. One of the imaginative props was a metronome with a cuckoo that, unfortunately, got stuck and continued its "cuckoo, cuckoo," until Gramm managed to reach up and wring its neck, at which time pandemonium reigned in the audience. Sills's portrayal of Marie as a fun-loving, feminine young woman could hardly have been topped. The evening ended with a stunning show of audience participation; those in bleachers on either side of the court had been enlisted to hold up red, white, and blue cards with a handout that read, "Please hold up this card to chest level when Ms. Sills passes down the aisle." These became the colors of the French flag while Sills as Marie and her beloved Tonio exited through the audience in an atmosphere heightened by general merriment. These two *Fille* performances are still remembered by many as high points of Sarah's inventiveness and unusual use of venue.

Sarah's choice for her next opera could not have been more inspired or timely. The prior weekend had seen a nationwide demonstration against the Vietnam War. Tailor-made for the occasion was an antiwar piece by American composer Robert Kurka, titled *The Good Soldier Schweik*. The message was the absurdity of conflict. In musical terms, it was neither a difficult piece nor one set in twelve-tone idiom. It was closer to operetta, comedy, or even a revue, than to an opera, but this antiwar satire did resonate with the American public of 1970. The work was mounted in Boston College's indoor hockey rink and also at the MIT Rockwell Cage with Sarah again using college students and even members of the Boston College baseball team as participants.

Schweik consisted of fourteen scenes, crisp and witty in style, playing over two hours. It had a thrust that was both sardonic and satirical, being scored for only sixteen wind and percussion instruments. Strings were omitted by the composer, who feared they would convey sentiment. Of Czech parentage, Robert Kurka was born in Illinois in 1921. Though he studied briefly with Darius Milhaud, Kurka was considered self-taught. Tragically, he died of leukemia in 1957, just six months prior to the New York City Opera world premiere of *Schweik*. There is an aura of Stravinsky's neoclassical period that hovers over *Schweik*, along with hints of Czech flavor, bits of Kurt Weill, and a dash of the music hall period of Milhaud thrown in for good measure. The opera's libretto was taken from the famous Jaroslav Hašek novel.

Two days before the April 11 opening, Sarah gave a preview performance of *The Good Soldier Schweik* for students at the McHugh Forum of Boston College, although the work was seen to better advantage when it opened at the MIT Rockwell Cage. Sarah had a platform erected, with audience members seated on all sides of the structure. Taped projections on large TV screens allowed spectators to follow the action should it range outside a viewer's immediate field of vision. Trenches were dug into the dirt floor of the arena, heightening the sense of a world gone mad with war. As a beginning touch, Sarah was driven to her podium in a golf cart disguised as a tank.

The raison d'etre of the production was to showcase Norman Kelley, who made a strong impression when he created the role of Schweik for the NYC Opera in 1958. The piece was oddly written in the vocal demands it placed on the tenor role of Schweik. Kurka's inexperience as an opera composer led him to write high notes (B below high C) for the tenor if he was in an ebullient mood, and low notes if he was depressed (G below middle C). Tenor Kelley later admitted that his G's were hardly more than "grunts." Unfortunately, Kurka's early death did not permit changes. Kelley repeated his signature portrait of a gentle nonentity who managed to survive harrowing circumstances. The kaleidoscopic range of minor characters were played by Andrew Foldi, Frank Hoffmeister, and Chapin Davis. However, there were complaints that the acoustics of the track arena distorted the orchestral balance. Harry Neville reported for *Opera News*, "Norman Kelley's Chaplinesque *Schweik* was visually a brilliant creation, and so was nearly everything else in a long list of characterizations and vignettes which extended all the way to the walk-ons and supers."[1] *Schweik* played to packed houses.

At the NYC Opera world premiere in 1958, *Schweik* fared poorly at the box office, playing to houses only 45 percent full. It could be argued that it did not have Caldwell's ingenuity, luck, and timing (the antiwar moratorium) that helped catapult *Schweik* into the much discussed and admired *pièce d'occasion* of her twelfth season.

On May 7 the Opera Company of Boston presented the world premiere of Gunther Schuller's *Fisherman and His Wife*, a project underwritten by the Junior League of Boston as its sixtieth-anniversary gift to the children of Boston. The League approached Sarah about whom to commission. She was thinking of a different composer but missed the meeting when the decision was made and found herself saddled with Schuller.

The opera was based on a Brothers Grimm fairy tale, with a text by John Updike. Despite its source, this was no children's opera full of cutesy Disneyesque touches. Instead, it was a parable with deeper meanings involving a fisherman and his shrewish wife. The fisherman catches a magic fish and then sets it free. His discontented wife wants the magic fish to grant her ever-increasing wishes for material possessions and power, which the fish obliges. When she demands to change places with the creator of the universe, the fisherman and his wife are returned to their humble origins.

The henpecked husband and his difficult wife did not make an inviting pair, and Schuller's score was monotonous. The couple's reuniting at the conclusion had a false ring. As with many of Schuller's compositions, there was sensory overload—jazz and rock elements mixed with electronic amplifiers, electric guitar, organ, and taped and live singers.

Sarah staged the work with sets from her Pond/Senn team assisted by Patton Campbell. David Lloyd was the fisherman, Muriel Greenspon his wife, Louisa Budd their cat, and Donald Gramm the fish. Schuller conducted, but was apparently so unsatisfied with his composition that he kept composing and rearranging the music through rehearsals up to the hour of the world-premiere performance, much to the vexation of the performers and musicians. At the final dress rehearsal, an assistant was seen distributing sheet music to the astonished principals, above the barely heard moans of cast members. "What's this?" was answered by the assistant, sotto voce: "New music!"[2] Schuller's last-minute dabbling with his score irritated the musicians, who walked out of the final rehearsal before the piece could be played to conclusion. Only at the premiere was the entire piece played to the end. As a result, the future relations between the composer and Sarah were clouded by a sense of wariness.

The 1970 season ended with Verdi's *Rigoletto*, seen at MIT's Kresge Auditorium, the site of her *Dutchman* triumph. Michael Steinberg of the *Globe* recalled the Pond/Senn production: "[They] once again delivered as though working in a non theater were no handicap at all. . . . [With] Benita Valente a touching Gilda, . . . Donald Gramm gave a superb performance as Sparafucile, suave, wittily observed with relish for the telling detail, musically, verbally, and vocally splendid." As the

Duke, John Alexander held his own. The biggest hand of the evening went to Michael Devlin's Monterone and not Vern Schinall as Rigoletto, who was thought to be lacking in experience for the role. Eunice Alberts departed from her matronly roles and was a fine Maddalena.

Michael Steinberg continued,

> Miss Caldwell also conducted. That is always a dubious venture. She knows what she wants and her musical ideas are persuasive; however, she is not a strong conductor technically, and her performances have sometimes made me wonder if she is not excessively preoccupied by her other function as director and thus insufficiently attentive to musical detail. On occasion it has worked—I still remember *Don Giovanni* and *Boris Godunov* with pleasure—but Wednesday's *Rigoletto* was singularly ragged in execution, uncertain, and flaccid.[3]

Others saw the 1970 season as one that roused Sarah Caldwell to her best levels with her innovative wizardry, even with the Schuller opera as a marginal success. The season had allowed her company to bask fleetingly in a positive light.

By any measure of ill fortune, the following 1971 season of the Opera Company of Boston was one of its most unlucky. The opening of Charpentier's opera *Louise* was delayed several weeks until February 24. The unlikely venue was Boston's Cyclorama Hall, known by some as the Center for the Arts and by others as simply the Flower Market, a 120-foot skylight dome located in a neighborhood that had seen better days. Like so much of Boston at that time, it seemed to be waiting for the next surge of urban renewal. It turned out that the Flower Market had not received the approval of the fire department for this kind of use. By the time the project was approved, all preparations had to be reworked. Some artists were not available for the later dates, notably Benita Valente, who was to have sung the title part. The recast opera opened with Carol Neblett as Louise.

Again, overcoming hurdles with her stage magic, Sarah and her designers strove to make something positive out of mounting an opera in such an unlikely venue. They created handsome, realistic sets in a rather limited area. Molly Friedl's impressive light show played across the dome of the rotunda. Outside the rotunda, audience members were greeted with kleig lights as if at a Hollywood premiere. Local residents came out of their inner-city dwellings to stare at well-heeled patrons arriving for the opera. The lights sweeping the night sky also had a planned counterpart in Sarah's clever staging at the conclusion of the opera, when Louise is seen dashing out into the Parisian night, as if most smitten by the city and its attractions.

Louise had long dwelt on the margins of the repertory, appealing to some for its atmosphere and its music, rejected by many as dramatically tedious and ill-focused. Exploiting the odd venue, Sarah's production and its imaginative staging explored the work in new ways, increasing its appeal to its admirers while making it accessible to those who had not regarded it highly. Some found the hall less than acoustically friendly, depending on the seat location.

"Neblett sang the title role with affecting intensity; visually she did not begin to suggest the heroine's surging, 'conflicting emotions,'" reported Harry Neville for *Opera News*.[4] Eunice Alberts played Louise's mother. Donald Gramm seemed strangely miscast as Louise's father, as did John Alexander as Louise's beau, Julien. While Sarah's occasional lack of skill in casting major roles was evident, she showed a more adroit hand with assigning the many *comprimario* roles for which the opera *Louise* is unique. Osbourne McConathy conducted.

The constant change of venue caused the level of the company's subscriptions to plummet precipitously to barely a third of what they had been previously. Soaring costs brought on by delays put Sarah's company in such desperate financial straits that the promised production of Verdi's *Aida*, featuring Elinor Ross and James McCracken, had to be canceled for lack of funds. In order to fill the void, Sarah turned to the Eastern Opera Consortium she had cofounded the previous year. That group had recently prepared and toured a successful college workshop production of Mozart's *La Finta Giardiniera*, given in English under the name *Down the Garden Path*. Now it was presented again in another unlikely venue, the Tufts University Cousens Gymnasium.

Caldwell was certainly no stranger to this early Mozart opera, going back to her Tanglewood days when she was suddenly thrust into directing the work after Boris Goldovsky fell ill. Later, she cobbled together her own translation of the work (again for Goldovsky) when he toured it under the title *The Merry Masquerade*. Afterward, she went on to produce it for her BU opera workshop to critical acclaim in November 1957, just before organizing her Opera Group. But for this revival, she used the dialogue provided by Eugene Haun, with added lyrics by Marvin Schofer and Gemi Beni.

La Finta Gardiniera introduces characters who bear a striking resemblance to those found in later works. The vengeful Sandrina bears resemblance to Donna Elvira in *Don Giovanni*, while the young poet Ramiro could very well be an early study of Cherubino in *Figaro*. But none of this was of interest to her subscribers. They were promised *Aida*, the grandest of grand operas. Hard feelings surfaced. Changes made without offering refunds to compensate for the canceled *Aida* put management in a bad light, a practice Caldwell would repeat, much to the dismay of her subscribers. *Finta* garnered a favorable notice from the *Christian Science Monitor*, but Michael Steinberg of the *Globe* was less enthusiastic. "Much was cut, including all the secco recitatives, but on the whole I would say that the performance was best whenever it most directly spoke to the music. . . . In other respects, though, the performance seemed to be involved in too effortful a hard sell of the idea that opera can be fun."[5]

As if to apologize to her audiences for the cancellation of preseason-announced *Aida*, the following appeared in the program of the last opera offered that season:

-No Place-
Louise was not
where it was supposed to be
or when.
Aida never was.
La Finta Giardiniera
most of us
had never heard of
until it was.
And Norma
is here and now.
You know where and
when that is because
you're here.
We didn't
when we went to press
so we can't tell you
in print.
It may sound silly

to be so confused
but if you had
no place to rest your head
tonight
you'd be hard put to it
to tell me where and when
you'd lay it down.
The thing is
the Opera Company of Boston
has no place to call its own
and so despite
its best made plans
it hasn't known
from production to production
where or when
it would produce
its scheduled operas.
Yet it has persevered
and we have had
some great productions—
the Boston Company's
own special Louise
in the cyclorama,
the charming La Finta
in the Tufts gym
and now Sills'
first Norma.
But shouldn't Boston
the Hub of the Universe
the seat of culture
and all that—
and shouldn't you and I
do better by Boston and us
than all this?
Once we had an opera house—
honest, we did—
Can't we have one again?

With this apology, Caldwell hoped to ameliorate the damage done to her subscriber base—the ever-changing venues, the dropped offerings that left her audiences demoralized and disaffected. Now, with the availability of yet another vaudeville house in the downtown district, previously called the Orpheum, now known as the Aquarius, Sarah was challenged to come up with something extraordinary. And true to her talent, she did.

NOTES

1. Harry Neville, "Boston," *Opera News*, June 13, 1970, 24.
2. Michael Kaye, interview by the author, February 1, 2000.
3. Michael Steinberg, "Sarah's 'Rigoletto,'" *Boston Globe*, June 4, 1970, 17.
4. Harry Neville, "Boston," *Opera News*, May 15, 1971, 25.
5. Michael Steinberg, "Hub Opera Stages Lively 'La Finta,'" *Boston Globe*, April 2, 1971, 17.

9

MORE FEATS OF
DERRING-DO

Sarah's drive for a suitable theater had become an all-consuming goal. For the moment, her dream for a three-theaters-in-one complex was on hold. Her reach had again exceeded her grasp. Beyond opera's value as spectacle, it should be relevant to people's daily lives, or so she reasoned, as shown in her fieldhouse production of *The Good Soldier Schweik*, with its strong antiwar message. But she had demoralized her subscribers by not giving them the grandest of operas, *Aida*.

Having failed that, she had a plan. It would be a gesture worthy of media attention and serve to galvanize her disaffected supporters. Knowing her audience's appetite for spectacle and pageantry, Sarah would present the first complete U.S. performance of Hector Berlioz's *Les Troyens*. Other U.S. companies were tilting toward the idea of a production of the Berlioz masterpiece, with the San Francisco Opera offering an abridged version for its 1968 season. Ever since she had worked with Boris Goldovsky on his abridged version back in 1955, she had longed to mount the complete work. This time, she would produce the work in a way that would trump her mentor's prior effort.

But the problem, again, was money.

After canvassing a number of foundations and institutional donors, the need to get her financial house in order became apparent. All of her persuasive powers would have to be brought into play to coax several of her well-heeled patrons to lead by writing personal checks for as much as $40,000 each, bringing her enterprise into semisolvency. Having done that, the remaining job of soliciting matching funds would not be easy. Just when things started to look bleak, word came from the Ford Foundation. They proposed a matching grant of $275,000. With that trump card in hand; Sarah sought an additional grant for $50,000 from the National Endowment for the Arts. She was further emboldened to approach the Gramma Fisher Foundation of Marshaltown, Iowa. They would provide an additional $75,000. In return, Sarah promised them the full five-and-a-half-hour epic with a fifty-six-piece orchestra.

The Back Bay Theater, the scene of many of her past triumphs, was no longer available; the Christian Science Group planned to demolish it. Upon learning that its actual demolition was under way, Caldwell dispatched volunteer members of the company's opera guild, costumed and in full makeup as operatic characters, then alerted the local media. Their images appeared on the evening TV newscasts and in newspapers. Demolition crews were startled when what appeared to be a theatrical troupe descended upon them while their bulldozers and wrecking ball were busy razing the structure. The photo op made good copy. But more importantly, it highlighted Sarah's point: the need for a permanent home for her company. Soon after, even the Boston Redevelopment Authority was obliged to pick up the cry against the senseless razing of theaters, saying, "Boston can ill afford to continue to lose another resource of such rare value and quality."

Since the 1957 demolition of the old opera house, there had been talk of a new performing arts complex. Once, plans for the new Prudential Center had included a possible theater. All of this had come to nothing. Now Sarah was obliged to take up residence in yet another fading vaudeville house, the Aquarius, sometimes referred to as the Orpheum. It had a twenty-six-foot-deep stage and no pit at all; the orchestra had to sit on the main floor and wait for Sarah to appear via a side door with the house lights dimmed while she made her way to a canvas director's chair that served as a podium.

Berlioz had his champions: Hamilton Hardy, Thomas Beecham, Colin Davis, and Raphael Kubelik, among others. *Les Troyens* needed heroic voices, an enormous cast, an extra chorus, stage bands, and ballet. The complexity of mounting it would tax the resources of a major opera company, let alone a small company such as Sarah's meager band, only recently tested by a prolonged nomadic existence.

Moreover, the five-act *Troyens* was considered a risky venture. It had never taken hold in standard repertory houses. Berlioz had divided the piece in two parts, perhaps with the idea that it would spur interest with other opera companies following suit, but only the second part was performed in his lifetime. Likewise, Sir Thomas Beecham had conducted the work in two parts, with "La Prise de Troie" and "Les Troyens à Carthage" performed separately. Likewise, Sir Thomas Beecham had conducted the work in two parts, with "La Prise de Troie" and "Les Troyens à Carthage" performed separately. Still, the idea of offering the Virgil/Berlioz epic in one evening was beginning to take hold. In its full-length version, it would be no longer than, say, Wagner's *Meistersinger* or *Tristan und Isolde*. Sarah opted for a separated version that would play over two evenings, garnering more income, rather than offering the full score at one sitting.

The scheduling of major, glamorous artists for a company noted for its hand-to-mouth existence seemed unlikely. Sarah's first choice for the role of Cassandra was soprano Grace Bumbry. She was unavailable. Instead, Régine Crespin, who had been Dido for San Francisco, would accept the assignment on relatively short notice. British tenor Ronald Dowd, who had sung the role in the previous season's revival at Covent Garden, agreed to be Sarah's Aeneas. Dowd arrived for rehearsals believing that it was to be given in English, only to have to relearn the role in French in a very short time.

The Orpheum/Aquarius had no dressing rooms. How to accommodate the large chorus, ballet, and supers? Across a narrow alley was a school for beauticians and cosmetologists. The logical choice was to lease the school for use as dressing rooms.

On opening night, February 3, 1972, freezing winds were whipping around the corner of that small service street with a major blizzard in play. Half-clothed chorus and ballet members rushed back and forth in full makeup across a narrow walkway with no roof over their heads. But inside the theater, the immediate challenge to Sarah's design team, Pond/Senn, was an extremely shallow stage (twenty-three feet from the orchestra pit to the fire wall.) The solution was found, as was nearly always the case with Sarah, by erecting additional gangways and bridging to connect nearby balconies and allow for more stage action.

Not hobbled by the debility, a Trojan horse was seen behind scrims, disgorging at least a few Greek soldiers. As they were only dimly perceived through the scrim, Sarah achieved heightened realism by using children in full costume as soldiers (plus one adult to keep order). Given the scale and distance from the spectators, the effect was surprisingly vivid. The Orpheum lacked backstage storage space of any kind. When not in use, the Trojan horse waited outside in the alley. Even more dramatic was the destruction of Troy, a special effect created by Esquire Joachem, which led to a riveting climax.

An unusual feature of Sarah's production was Gemi Beni dressed as Virgil. He appeared before the curtain prior to each act, narrating the action. But even more compelling was an offstage voice quoting actual Latin verses of the Roman poet.

Maralin Niska's voice seemed suited to Cassandra. Unfortunately, Sarah's blocking had Niska flailing herself across the center stage and side ramps. French Canadian baritone Louis Quilico proved an ample and vocally stylish Chorebus, whose French diction was admired. Above all, it was the French soprano Régine Crespin who remained the only truly international star in the cast, although she was unnerved by the hectic ambience and cramped working conditions of the vaudeville house and was seen pacing back and forth before her entrances, uttering "Sheet" (and not speaking of bedclothes). None of this unease was ever evident, though, in her totally committed and professional performance. John Freeman reported for *Opera News*, "Régine Crespin poured forth an evident love for the music and embodied the old-fashioned grandeur with which the composer imbued his Dido. Hers was no easy triumph, and its magnitude lifted the whole production from a level of provincial aspiration to one of high striving."[1] While Ronald Dowd's French was arguably not up to the standard of others in the cast, according to Freeman, "[He] basically had the right tenor voice for the role—neither too light nor too hefty—and rose to the occasion in his scene of deciding finally to embark on the quest for Italy."

Les Troyens was a significant triumph for Sarah and her company. As with her American premiere of Schoenberg's *Moses und Aron*, she had drawn both national and international press. With *Les Troyens*, Sarah's accomplishment catapulted her to the realm of myth. She had been counted down but not out. She barely managed to confound her detractors. It was one of her finest hours to date, but one that drove her to the edge of exhaustion. Afterward, she came down with the flu. It was the first time she had been ill since a childhood bout with the chicken pox.

With Sarah's efforts sapped by *Les Troyens*, the rest of that 1972 season's efforts sagged into routine with the *Tosca* and *Traviata* that followed, even though the former boasted Nicolai Gedda's only career appearance as Cavaradossi and the latter showcased Beverly Sills as

Violetta. It wasn't until her next season (1975) that Sarah regained her footing in injecting new life into old works, as she would have it.

"Wouldn't it be wonderful if they found him at the opera?" Sarah's mirth-provoking comment hit the local news media during the Boston Strangler scare. But taken in context with her worldview, the Boston Strangler was fair game, along with politics and even current events, her special "meat." In 1969, she thought she had introduced contemporary relevance into Mozart's *Le Nozze di Figaro*, going out of her way to engage black singers and chorus members to fulfill certain household roles. Correspondingly, whites were cast in roles as empowered figures, such as the Count and Countess, with the rest of the cast being victimized. The intended effect was never fully realized. Grace de la Cruz, the Countess in question, was of African-American heritage. Sarah had caught one of her performances in a provincial German opera house but failed to take note of her ethnicity. The curiosity of several African-American cast members was aroused. Baritone Simon Estes, who sang the role of Figaro, kept asking, "What exactly is Sarah up to?" As for Sarah, she was mum!

But her 1973 production of Bedřich Smetena's *Bartered Bride* suggested that Sarah had come up with an unexplored subtext that would infuse new life and give the piece contemporary relevance. In so doing, she would impose her own focus, illuminating past events as seen through her own prism.

During a visit to Prague to do background research, Sarah discovered that the librettist, Karel Sabina, was a satirist. Instead of being viewed as a delightful folk comedy depicting simple peasant life, as often assumed by foreigners, Sarah would show it otherwise by illuminating various aspects of the history of the Czech people.

With the aid of her set designer, Lester Polakov, convention was stripped away, such as the traditional cliché-ridden village square and tavern settings so often associated with this work. During the overture, a brief slideshow appeared on large screens. A panoply of Czech history unfolded before the spectators' eyes, including oblique references from a historical context, showing Austrian and, later, German suppression of the Czech people. Images focused on such matters as forced marriages and greedy parents looking for a lucrative match. The slides in question suggested the reality of shady dealings that lay behind Smetena's sunny tunes.

The casting was such that each singer was capable of not only being heard over the large orchestra but would convey the requisite sense of the comic style inherent in the piece. Sarah launched into the overture, maintaining a certain verve and buoyancy. Then, out of sequence, she borrowed the "Dance of the Comedians" from Act III. While it played, Mařenka and a circus clown gave a pantomime involving a balloon, a white dove, and a pistol. From aloft, projected slides flashed images of bucolic Czech villages. Suddenly, the balloon burst, releasing an onslaught of more ominous images, those of Hitler, Heydrik, German tanks on the streets of Prague, and the massacre at Lidice. Other slides followed: women in a dance sequence being roughly handled by men, a peasant's girl's parents leering menacingly behind straw masks.

By the time of the last rehearsal, the two male Czech imports began to realize Sarah's production was a piece of political theater and began to worry their participation might cause problems when they returned to Communist Prague. As a result, Sarah was obliged to tone down the slide show, eliminating two of the five screens. Now, several images would be projected simultaneously, creating a blurred collage effect. When her set designer complained about the erosion of his concept, she merely replied, "We can't endanger our Czech friends."[2]

For the last act, Sarah hired a dog act, tightrope walkers, and Emmett Kelly, Sr., of Ringling Bros., America's most eminent circus clown. He appeared briefly with the balloons in the first scene and later would introduce performing dogs, jugglers, acrobats, and other circus acts, followed by a ballet replaying the Dance of the Comedians. The supernumerary in a bear costume was meant to convey added significance as the standardbearer of the Prussian capital, Berlin.

There had never been any doubt that soprano Mary Costa would cast an aura of glamour to the role of Mařenka, but she surprised many who had thought she was in a vocal decline since the 1960s. What they now heard was a kind of vocal purity few could recall. Sarah's two Czech imports, Jaroslav Horáček as Kečal and Miroslav Svejda as Jenik, were unintelligible in the English translation but otherwise filled out their roles. James Atherton was the stunning Vašek, Mařenka's disappointed suitor.

Despite the blurring of Sarah's original concept, enough remained that was entertaining and visually arresting, leaving most audience members with the impression that they had witnessed a minor masterpiece that Sarah had somehow elevated to the front rank. In a gesture that nearly brought down the house, Sarah handed her baton to Emmett Kelley, Sr., who accelerated the performance to a rousing conclusion.

With this success behind her, Sarah was busily engaged with her design team, Pond/Senn, in preparation for her staging debut at the New York City Opera, the U.S. premiere of Hans Werner Henze's *Der Junge Lord* (The Young Lord), which opened on March 28, 1973. The work had its world premiere in Cologne in 1967 at a time when the composer's musical idiom had returned to tonality, a fact that probably troubled Sarah and may have put her at odds with the piece. The underlying dark and bitter satire took it far from the opera buffa it purported to be. Furthermore, its mocking tone was off-putting, if not confusing. Characters were more types than individuals. Its few musical jokes a la Stravinsky, Mozart, and Verdi did not register with the New York audience. Sarah's muse seemed out of sorts as to what to do with the piece.

Much interest (and publicity) centered around the appearance of Sir Rudolf Bing, no longer the Metropolitan Opera's general manager, but still an *éminence grise* in his own right—a celebrity in a cameo role of a mute Sir Edgar. In spite of Sarah's best effort, or because of it, Bing had little or no stage presence. The emperor had no clothes! The opera had failed to gain a substantial foothold in the European repertory. Sarah's staging talents, whether inspired or otherwise, could not alter that outcome.

Back in her customary Boston environs, her 1973 season saw an inspired production of Bertolt Brecht and Kurt Weill's *Aufstieg und Fall der Stadt Mahagonny*. From the very first scene, Sarah's designing team of Pond/Senn delighted the audience with an old truck that brought the founders of Mahagonny onstage. Patricia Zipprodt's costumes for the girls of *Mahagonny* had the right look and were perhaps even more stylish than those seen a few blocks away from the Orpheum in the city's nearby Combat Zone. Sarah's production found its metaphor in the sheer grittiness and grossness of the characters, such as having the smoke of cheap cigars wafted into the auditorium or hoisting a pair of women's panties as the flag for the newly founded city of Mahagonny.

Sarah had wisely engaged singers of sufficient vocal heft and breadth, even if they lacked the overpowering glamour of the Met cast later in that decade. Otherwise, Sarah's artists benefited from the smaller, more intimate confines of the Orpheum as opposed to the vast expanses of the Met. Sarah's production focused on the small stage; the side loges were not used. The second act was probably the most brilliant in its feel for action and pulse. Michael Steinberg reported in the *Globe*, "Caldwell was in charge of the music, too, and conducted a stylish, well-paced performance."[3]

With Sarah's worst financial crisis behind her, the subscription base had shrunk to one-third of its previous level. But with increased demand from 1974 onward, Sarah and her board decided to expand the season from three to four operas. The annual operating budget ballooned to an unforeseen $1.3 million. There was every affirmation that the previously announced Ford Foundation matching grant was within reach. A newly established audience-development department was redoubling its efforts to reach out to private donors, corporations, foundations, and wealthy individuals.

Prior to the start of her 1974 season, Sarah had accepted the Houston Grand Opera's invitation to stage and conduct Verdi's *La Traviata* with Beverly Sills as Violetta. Veriano Luchetti was scheduled to sing Alfredo but canceled. At the last minute he was replaced by Kenneth Riegel. However, it was Sills's Violetta and Louis Quilico's Germont père that dominated the performance. Sarah restored Germont's cabaletta in Act II and reinstated other cuts usually taken in performance. Carl Cunningham, writing for the *Houston Post*, noted, "Miss Sills took some unusually marked ritards that tended to brake the natural progress of the music, but her voice rang true, brilliantly clear and often unusually sweet in tone." Although Sarah was thought to be supportive of her singers, Cunningham observed that "the true Verdian surge of the music was somewhat muted."[4]

Sarah's design duo, Pond/Senn, created lavish sets that fitted the demi-monde world of the French Second Empire. In the first-act party scene, Sarah had champagne corks popping almost in time with the music. Simultaneous bonfires erupted when a pair of supernumeraries performed one of Sarah's time-honored gags, flaming cherries jubilee. Unfortunately, the exuberance of one caused the singing of his eyebrows. Subsequent performances found him wearing tinted glasses. In Act II, Scene II, Flora posed for a nude portrait as the curtain went up. Act III's party revelers were seen as in a dreamlike vision while an impoverished Violetta languished in a cold rooftop garret.

Several singers in minor roles were outstanding, and one in particular caught Sarah's attention. She had her eye on Joseph (Joey) Evans, a schoolteacher, whom Sarah pulled aside and told, "You can have a career in opera if you want it!"[5] He followed Sarah to Boston, appearing almost immediately in several *comprimario* roles, abandoning his former calling. Evans was to sing over thirty roles with the company.

After returning to Boston, Sarah launched her 1974 season on February 20 with an unusual production of Jules Massenet's *Don Quichotte*. Noel Tyl, a tall bass, took on the title role, Mignon Dunn was Dulcinée, and Donald Gramm a sympathetic Sancho. The Pond/Senn team provided a modest but atmospheric set. To research the locales, Sarah and her designers flew to Paris and combed about Montmartre, relishing the chance for travel, combining business with pleasure.

Sarah prided herself on background and research, starting with Henri Cain's libretto, derived from the Jacques Le Lorrain play, *Le Chevalier de la Longue Figure*. It occurred to Sarah that Le Lorrain was so absorbed in his fantasies as to allow himself the fiction that he was Don Quixote reincarnated, a man enobled by a vision while rejecting a world that did not live up to his lofty ideals. The incidents of the stolen jewelry and the bandits did not appear in anything Cervantes ever wrote, but it did not stop Le Lorrain from incorporating them into his play (or Sarah from giving her audiences a quite different take on the piece).

The area we know as Montmartre was rural at the time (with many windmills) and not yet absorbed into greater Paris. Reversible 180-degree panels on the Orpheum stage alternated reality with illusion—a cabaret *intime* instantly morphed into a fog-bound streetscape where the episodes of the stolen jewelry, the windmills, and the bandits would likely unfold.

As Don Quixote catapulted aloft on a windmill turning blade, audience members gasped, thinking it a real person, not realizing it was a life-sized dummy. Of the impressive props, two were an enormous horse and donkey fabricated in East Berlin by a freelance artist skilled in making realistic animal costumes. Sarah's musical pacing was deemed first-rate, as was the choreography by Ciro.

The approach had strong audience appeal even though Noel Tyl, thought to be six feet ten inches or thereabouts, lacked both physical and vocal charisma, so essential for the title role. Still, the evening was greatly enhanced by Donald Gramm's Sancho Panza and mezzo-soprano Mignon Dunn's blowsy Dulcinée, no longer an aged courtesan but a young singer-actress in a cabaret.

That Sarah had Don Quixote die by suicide instead of heartache gave pause. But Sarah would no doubt argue that her concept was more in sync with the Le Lorrain fixations and delusions as taken from Henri Cain's libretto, rather than being based solely on Cervantes.

Sarah's foray into "lesser Massenet" made for a very vibrant and unusual evening of musical theater, one that again demonstrated her uncanny sense in getting the atmospherics right, to the point of showing Massenet's *Don Quichotte* as a work superior to the sum of its parts.

May 8, 1974, saw another one of Sarah Caldwell's triumphs unfold—the American stage premiere of Sergei Prokofiev's *War and Peace*. Previously, only an abridged 1957 version of the work was seen on NBC-TV Opera. Sarah used the Edward Downes English translation first heard at Sadler's Welles Opera/London/Coliseum in October 1972. The long evening with its single intermission passed quickly before a rapt audience. Sarah's magic was again in evidence, fitting a sprawling historical epic onto the narrow Orpheum stage. Side boxes were made to hold not only the augmented percussion section, but "instruments" such as the cannon firing blanks straight into the audience, bringing frightening realism to such scenes as the reenactment of the battle of Borodino, the burning of Moscow, and the final scene in the snow. Patricia Collins's lighting helped burn these images into memory.

Michael Steinberg of the *Globe* noted, "The performance of the evening—no, of many a season—was Donald Gramm's as Kotuzov. . . . He had played the dashing Lt. Dolokov in the first part act, now he reappeared sagging, bagging, crumpled, with a Krushchev nose, and beer-belly, masterful in the economy and rightness of gesture, simple and magnificent in song, completely believable as a vulnerable, tired, wise hero. This was real Tolstoy."[6]

Donald Gramm's Kotuzov and William Neil's Pierre were among other elements that helped override some misgivings one could have about the score. Additional music Sarah claimed was suppressed during the Soviet time added little to the performance. As Steinberg observed, "Some of the Andrei-Natasha music is lovely and warm, but in a short-winded way, and it gets plugged relentlessly. Later, Marshal Kotuzov's aria, a fine and luminously scored piece, gets plugged in the same way."[7]

One of the marvels of professionalism was soprano Arlene Saunders as Natasha. While in rehearsal, she learned her father had passed away. She had held back tears as she sang Natasha's line to the effect, "Oh, God, if he were only here!" Cast members knew she was grieving and would have preferred to cancel the performance. The likely result would have been cancellation of all performances, arguably one of the triumphs of the company.

The Pond/Senn team provided simple but flexible sets that added to the flow of the drama. The strength of the company showed in the many fine cameo portraits ranging from Lenus Carlson's Andrei down to James Billings as Napoleon. The choreography of Ben Stevenson brought a certain elegance to the ballet sequences. "As conductor, Miss Caldwell led a firm, large-scale performance with her first-rate chorus and orchestra," observed Robert Jacobson of *Opera News*.[8]

For the final opera of that 1974 Boston season, Beverly Sills sang her first Rosina in Rossini's *Il Barbiere di Siviglia* in Italian. With the help of musicologist Dr. Phillip Gossett; Dr. Stephan Stampor, dramaturg of the Komische Oper Berlin; and other European library sources, a new musical text, based on the Alberto Zedda version, was realized. Rosina's second-act aria, "Ah, se 'il ver," was restored, with a cabaletta incorporating parts of "Non piu mesta" from another Rossini opera, *La Cenerentola*, appearing just before the storm. The instrumentation for the aria was reconstructed by Osbourne McConathy. Ms. Sills also sang the Adolphe Adam variations, "Ah, vous dirai-je, maman," with her own embellishments after the traditional lesson scene aria. It all added up to a long but brilliant vocal display from Sills, who was in excellent form.

Donald Gramm, as a befuddled Dr. Bartolo, played off Ms. Sills to the delight of the audience. It was a rare display of two of Sarah's finest singers at the height of their powers. Unfortunately, Sarah's touches of humor in some cases were over the top, such as having the colors of Figaro's costume resemble a barber's pole. Almaviva wore a jacket studded with leather bookbindings and a hat that looked like an open book to tell us he was Lindoro, a student. Sills appeared on a second-level balcony costumed with plumes to suggest a bird trapped in a cage. The balcony even had a swing. Alan Titus as Figaro surprised the audience with his skill at guitar accompaniment for Almaviva's serenade. Another timeworn gag that did not seem to have exhausted its Boston audience appeal was having a glass held by Donald Gramm shatter when Beverly Sills hit an especially high note.

While the two-tiered set was eye-catching, Sarah's conducting remained decidedly earthbound. Jacobson summed up the performance as follows: "Bruce Brewer's Almaviva lacked masculine tone, though he negotiated the notes effectively. Alan Titus's Figaro was dashed off with superb Italianate style and charming lightness."[9] In another odd touch, Sarah had chorus members appearing as house movers who happened to be serenading and singing some of the famous arias of *Il Barbiere*. It proved something of an embarrassment when Frank Hoffmeister demonstrated that he was capable of singing "Ecco ridente il cielo" far better than Bruce Brewer, the Almaviva of the evening.

The 1975 season began with a lackluster *Falstaff* followed by *Così fan tutte*. It could be said that Sarah more than compensated with her very fine production of Hector Berlioz's problematic and seldom performed *Benvenuto Cellini*. It was an American premiere (May 3) and featured Jon Vickers in the title part. Sarah and Osbourne McConathy cobbled together a workable score. Many thought Sarah's conducting ragged and unfocused as if lacking in rehearsal. Jon Vickers did much to rescue *Cellini*, not necessarily from Caldwell's staging, but from Berlioz's uneven work, which seemed to teeter between comedy and tragedy. Sarah had difficulty in convincing Vickers to undertake the role. After looking through the score, with its high A's and B-flats, he was reluctant to sing the part. Sarah told him that if he had any qualms, she would have Joey Evans backstage to cover the difficult notes and the audience would not be the wiser. When it came to the actual performances, Vickers's voice warmed up and attained the notes with relative ease.

The most memorable touch was the casting of the statue of Perseus by Cellini when the opera reaches its climax. Here set designers Pond/Senn built a likeness of the statue of Perseus standing over a fallen Medusa that they then concealed inside a giant, onstage mold with a furnace underneath. Cellini's task was to melt and pour bronze into the brick structure through ducts. Caldwell's theatrical magic was able to override any shortcomings. She had Jon Vickers racing up and down a ladder next to what appeared to be a large conical furnace, from which flames and smoke spewed. Vickers smote this mold with a mighty blow, initiating an explosion that appeared to knock him to the ground with a flash of light. When the lights again came up to reveal the gleaming and resplendent gold statue that had been cast in the furnace, the audience broke into cheers and applause. It was one of Sarah's most exciting *coups de théâtre*. Her magic had again worked to marvelous effect.

One feat of derring-do that season that did not work out was the much-awaited (and much postponed) U.S. premiere of Roger Sessions's *Montezuma*. Back in 1964, Sarah, with her mother in tow, traveled to Berlin to witness the world premiere. It was an occasion to honor the special bond she had forged with the composer in her Tanglewood days.

Afterward, Sarah told him, "There were too many processions, . . . too many girls carrying jars on their shoulders."[10]

Presenting the opera in Boston became one of Sarah's goals. She would right the wrongs visited on the piece and assailed the project with a sense of messianic zeal, traveling to Mexico with her Pond/Senn team. Whether it was the sour acoustics of the Orpheum or Sarah's failure to rein in the brass or, possibly, the libretto itself that preempted success, one cannot say.

Richard Dyer of the *Globe* noted, "The decision to amplify so much of the singing didn't do what it was supposed to—attain a balance between singers and orchestra and clarify the text—while taking away the physical presence of the voices which is a basic component of the real operatic thrill."[11] Hardly acknowledging the misfire, Sarah was adamant. In a postperformance symposium with the composer in attendance, Sarah was unfazed: "I am grateful for the privilege of doing 'Montezuma'; it will have a long and active life. The work is not difficult—just complex."[12]

Sarah's notion of "complexity," combined with her apparent fascination with contemporary cultural values (the hippie generation), may have led her to British composer Michael Tippett's opera *The Ice Break*, offering the American premiere in her 1979 season. Music critic Andrew Porter, having witnessed the Covent Garden world premiere two seasons earlier, declared it to be "one of Miss Caldwell's highest achievements."[13]

If Tippett addressed America's prevailing subculture, its undercurrents, and alienation from the mainstream, that suited Sarah fine. With the spare sets of her Pond/Senn design team buttressed by an excellent cast, her production of *The Ice Break* was brought to a fine realization. Once more Sarah proved herself adept in managing the crowd scenes, with the ritual dances in Act III enhanced by Talley Beatty's choreography. Other observers were less positive. Robert Jacobson, writing for *Opera News*, complained of awkward lines that struck the ear with "unwelcome topicality," such as "Burn, baby burn!" and "What's bugging you, man?"[14]

As to Tippett's other works for the stage, Sarah remained wistful and boldly spoke of a "Boston Tippett Festival," reprising not only the aforementioned *Ice Break*, but his *King Priam*, *Midsummer Marriage*, and *The Knot Garden*. Meanwhile, Tippett's operas slipped from the scene in the United Kingdom, while performances of his works in America were fitful, notwithstanding the 1983 San Francisco U.S. premiere of his *Midsummer Marriage*, and ten years on, the cause of the same work was advanced with the East Coast premiere at the New York City Opera, and later in the 2006–2007 Chicago Lyric Opera season.

With *LIFE* magazine still extolling the virtues of her company as "the most exciting new venture of its kind in the country," there was hardly any need to make apologies for misfires or Sarah's penchant for mounting problematical pieces. Her short Boston season continued to maintain its hold, drawing critics and opera buffs alike from as far afield as San Francisco, Chicago, and New York.

Some years on, in an interview with Lynn Gilbert, who was profiling a gallery of contemporary American women of note, in a rare moment of epiphany, Minerva approached the ineffable with regard to the daily workings of her creative muse:

> With every opera production I do, I enter a new world. It's kind of a time machine. . . . One comes in touch with real people who really lived, who really sat in a particular kind of chair and wore particular kinds of clothes and had a particular set of problems. . . . It's like being in another world for a little while, and that's interesting, that's fun, that's really being alive.[15]

Now more focused than before, Sarah had not abandoned the idea of setting up yet another company, one that would provide more robust employment for fledgling artists as well as nurture new talent. Several surrounding New England communities expressed interest in such an enterprise. To meet that challenge, her next endeavor would be something called "Opera New England."

NOTES

1. John Freeman, "Boston," *Opera News*, March 18, 1972, 31.
2. Herbert Senn, interview by the author, August 18, 2001.
3. Michael Steinberg, "'Mahagonny' Angry, Simple, Direct—and Superb," *Boston Globe*, April 16, 1973, 23.
4. Carl Cunningham, "Sarah Caldwell Shows Genius," *Houston Post*, January 22, 1974, 4C.
5. Joseph Evans, interview by the author, November 3, 2001.

6. Michael Steinberg, "Caldwell Comes Up with Exciting 'War and Peace,'" *Boston Globe*, May 9, 1974, 17.

7. Ibid.

8. Robert Jacobson, "Boston," *Opera News*, July 1974, 54.

9. Robert Jacobson, "Boston," *Opera News*, September 1974, 54.

10. Richard Dyer, "Sessions Happy with Caldwell 'Montezuma,'" *Boston Globe*, March 28, 1978, A9.

11. Richard Dyer, "Caldwell Gives Hub Another Musical First," *Boston Globe*, April 1, 1976, 40.

12. Richard Dyer, "Caldwell and Sessions on 'Montezuma,'" *Boston Globe*, April 2, 1976, 23.

13. Andrew Porter, "Musical Events," *New Yorker*, June 11, 1979, 133.

14. Robert Jacobson, "Boston," *Opera News*, September 1979, 65.

15. Lynn Gilbert, *Particular Passions* (New York: Crown Press, 1981), 239.

10

SEIZING THE MOMENT: OPERA NEW ENGLAND

By 1970, bearing in mind her 1968 ANOC debacle, Sarah would craft a different approach to opera touring, one that would tap into funds available from the newly established state councils of the arts. With the aid of a cosponsor (the identity of whom was not noted in any of Sarah's press releases), plus a $35,000 Rockefeller Foundation grant, Sarah launched her new Opera Consortium enterprise. The stated purpose was to share talent, finances, and facilities of seven New England colleges, fostering the development of gifted singers, designers, and technicians. It was a resource Sarah both nurtured and tapped occasionally for her own productions, for example, the touring *La Finta Giardiniera*, which promptly replaced the canceled *Aida*.

Unable to expand her regular Opera Company of Boston (OCB) January–June season and emboldened by the limited success of her Opera Consortium, Sarah seized the opportunity in 1974 to found her own cadet company and approached several interested groups in nearby New England cities that would host the new enterprise, communities such as Worcester, Massachusetts; Manchester, New Hampshire; Portland, Maine; and Pomfret, Connecticut. All expressed their willingness to fund what were essentially one-night stands on the stages of local high school and college auditoriums.

Opera New England would provide additional off-season employment for her artists and crews, as well as serve as a training ground to hone new talent. Sarah promised that her new enterprise would include a separate educational outreach targeting children with pieces such as Lukas Foss's *The Jumping Frog of Calavaras County*.

Lessons had been learned! Sponsoring groups that booked performances would financially guarantee the underpinnings, with Opera New England acting more or less as a shell company. It occurred to Sarah that a new financial setup would allow for double and even triple dipping. For instance, at the top of the pyramid sat OCB, Sarah's parent company. It could well join in the fray by providing services directly to either Opera New England or, say, Opera Worcester, a satellite entity. It seemed as if Sarah's wizardry, one capable of figuring all the odds, was again at play in a scheme that was a perfectly legal as well as clever approach to getting opera out to more rural locales.

To avoid legal entanglements, Sarah guarded her language in defining Opera New England, describing it as "a regional arm" of the Opera Company of Boston. In effect, Opera New England would serve as a franchising entity, selling twice-yearly visits to localities. Its first season would offer Puccini's *Madama Butterfly* under the banner of Opera Worcester, although produced and toured by Opera New England. Each locality would petition funds through its respective state arts council as well as the National Endowment for the Arts, whereas Sarah's OCB could apply for federal funding, if the production originated with them. Opera New England promised to provide interested cities along the New England circuit with full-scale, highly professional performances sung by talented singers and with artfully designed sets and costumes.

With few exceptions, Opera New England performances were one-night stands, toured once in the spring and fall. A parallel program aimed at youngsters was often performed as a matinee on the same day, sometimes with school participation. On one occasion, Sarah even sent established artists along the Opera New England circuit. Otherwise, lesser-known artists came up through the ranks of Opera New England and then graduated to other assignments, including Maureen O'Flynn, Suzanne Marsee, Nancy Williams, Joseph Evans, David Evitts, and Neil Rosenshein.

The productions were initially budgeted between $8,000 and $13,000. Sarah had scouted several possible venues, such as the Worcester State College Auditorium, with a seating capacity of 1,200 and fairly decent acoustics. When Opera New England achieved full force in eight different venues, the potential audience reach was approximately eight thousand. Ticket prices initially ranged from $3.50 to $6.00. Costs not covered by box office receipts would be borne by local sponsors. Memberships were $50 each, with the aim of aggregating up to two hundred individuals to meet additional costs. Opera touring as Caldwell had known it had become untenable. More grassroots support was needed to cover escalating costs; additional fund-raising could be realized by holding annual opera balls, flea markets, or fiestas offering light entertainment. In this way, opera would become a reality to smaller communities across New England. Once established, more distant localities came on board, such as Bangor, Maine, and Burlington, Vermont.

Sarah made the rounds of various New England cities, organizing local sponsorship for her new enterprise, which she happily referred to as "my baby." At a reception held at the Worcester Art Museum, she cautioned, "Opera New England is not a touring company. Rather it will be a shared company with a number of homes. We want to make it part of the Worcester musical community."

Opera Worcester had been formed the previous month and was in the throes of a membership drive. It had already completed its membership goal of $350 each. Other regional committees were organizing and applying for grants from state councils of the arts. Opera New England and its satellite entities were off to a brilliant start.

In the fall of 1974, Giacomo Puccini's *Madama Butterfly* arrived in Woodstock, Connecticut, a neighboring village of Pomfret, where a suitable auditorium had been located, the first production to make the rounds of the Opera New England circuit. The Ming Cho Lee production, newly freshened up, had a proven track record and could be counted on to draw in the crowds.

Prior to each performance, Sarah dispatched her artists with a piano accompanist to perform at the home of a local sponsor. They provided a brief analysis of the opera, with the soloists singing various arias. Locals eagerly opened their homes to host these affairs.

Buoyed by the success of her new venture, it wasn't long before Sarah offered more ambitious fare for her new audiences. In an unusual departure, her production of Puccini's *Girl of the Golden West* featured well-established artists, such as Arlene Saunders as Minnie, William Lewis as Dick Johnson, and Giorgio Tozzi as Sheriff Rance. It was a unique melding of Opera New England with her main company.

While Opera New England productions were rehearsed in Boston and sent out on the road, Puccini's *Girl of the Golden West* would

accomplish something different. To avoid the higher cost of renting rehearsal space in Boston, Sarah gladly accepted an offer from one of the
founding cities, Pomfret, Connecticut, to provide rehearsal space at a
fraction of the cost.

The relaxed rural environment of Pomfret seemed to bring Sarah
closer to her muse. Richard Dyer of the *Boston Globe* wrote, "Her staging was infused with cunning detail. . . . Things like the fights in the
first act, Minnie hiding her drying linen before her gentleman-bandit
caller arrives, . . . all of this, together with the principals throwing themselves into their roles, helped bring the evening alive."[1]

An English translation by Ruth and Thomas Martin was used. The
Martins, husband and wife, had been responsible for a number of well-
known translations. However, this particular Puccini opera pits us
against our myth of the golden West as seen in countless Western films.
The fact that we have ceased to take the improbabilities of the libretto
seriously becomes evident in any production of the opera given.

Arlene Saunders's voice brought sheen to the vocally demanding
role of Minnie, while tenor William Lewis was taxed to sing the lines of
Dick Johnson and was seen casting frightening glances toward Sarah in
the pit. It was the first time that major artists toured the Opera New
England circuit. Sarah planned to open up a traditional cut involving
the Act II love duet. But after consultation with both Arlene Saunders
and William Lewis, a decision was made not to restore it. Giorgio Tozzi
was less at ease with Rance, a role that, for the most part, lay above his
basso cantante range.

The shallow stages of the various high school auditoriums were a
challenge to the Pond/Senn design team in its attempt to provide a realistic environment to complement Janet Papanek's costumes.

When Opera New England's *Girl of the Golden West* premiered at the
Mertens Theater at the University of Bridgeport, Sarah spoke at a special symposium titled "The Art of Making Opera," expressing the need
for verisimilitude. As an example, Sarah arranged horses to appear in
the final scene of *Fanciulla*. This entailed the use of a portable ramp to
allow access to various auditoriums along the New England circuit. In
one venue, the horses arrived in advance via the school's main entrance
and were held in one of the dressing rooms an hour before the performance, awaiting their stage cues. It was a bit of "Caldwell magic" that
made a world of difference. Prior to performance, Sarah was seen

schmoozing with the two geldings, speaking in low, deep tones to put them at ease.

As Opera New England was getting off the ground, fame finally caught up with Sarah in a variety of ways. Her image appeared on the cover of *Time* magazine. New England colleges and universities were bestowing their honorary parchments on Sarah at graduation time. Moreover, before the year was out, her upcoming January debut was announced at the Metropolitan Opera as the first female conductor in that house. Not only had Caldwell promised each of the Opera New England venues the brightest young stars of the Boston/New York circuit, but she also pledged to conduct two performances each season. Naturally, many audience members began to feel they should also bask in Sarah's new celebrity glow at these performances and were dismayed when she sent surrogates to conduct. Still, Caldwell would occasionally monitor performances, showing up briefly with car and driver prior to curtain, only to disappear shortly thereafter.

Robert Z. Nemeth, writing in the *Worcester Telegram* on the Opera New England *Tosca*, summed up Sarah's occasional absence from the podium: "The orchestra tended to be too loud, frequently drowning the voices. . . . Without Miss Caldwell in charge, the magic is just not there."[2] It was said at the time that Opera New England audiences wanted three things, in the following order: Puccini, Verdi, and Sarah.

With the passing of each season, costs escalated to maintain the venture, nearly doubling within a span of a few seasons, making funding more problematic. When it came to fund-raising, Darien, Connecticut, proved its citizens to be the most tightfisted of Yankees. Adding insult to injury, Darien police insisted on "fees" (tantamount to bribes) before they would provide security for any events at the local high school. Eventually, Darien withdrew, replaced by a new venue Sarah found at the University of Bridgeport. Just when she thought the matter settled, Reverend Moon of the Unification Church and his "moonies" took control of the university, barring further use.

By 1981, Brockton, Massachusetts, discontinued its participation. In each case, Sarah was obliged to find other New England cities where Opera New England would be welcome. In so doing, she had to cast a wider net to rope in Burlington, Vermont; Bangor, Maine; and the town of Sandwich, on Cape Cod, the latter becoming a stalwart. In the meantime, Sarah thought it necessary to curtail or possibly discontinue the children's program upon learning that some unruly schoolboys threw coins down inside the tuba player's instrument.

Despite these and other difficulties, Sarah did not completely abandon her idea of introducing children to opera. Her David Sharir production of Humperdinck's *Hansel and Gretel* was so elaborate as to require transport of five truckloads of scenery, the equivalent of the three operas she had toured with the ANOC. Instead of the usual ballet of angels that had become a banality seen with many *Hansel* productions, Sarah had fourteen puppet angels descending from the flies. Children were equally enthralled with the ingenious sets that showed a gingerbread house that looked candylike and innocuous from the outside but then turned evil-looking when each of the individual panels rotated 180 degrees. At the conclusion of the performance, costumed children skipped through the aisles of the theater throwing candies while local volunteers sold gingerbread cookies in the lobby.

Sarah also brought unusual operatic fare to her far-flung audiences, such as Heinrich August Marschner's *Vampire*, which toured during Halloween in the 1979 season. Marschner's *Vampire* played to half-filled houses and failed to take hold, perhaps due to confusing cuts in the story and score. More important, local sponsors railed that Sarah was fobbing off operas *she* wanted to do, rather than operas *they* wanted to see.

Still, Sarah continued to tinker with her productions to make them as authentic as possible. Lukas Foss's *Jumping Frog of Calavaras County* featured an old-fashioned hand pump that actually worked. It was all a part of Sarah's determination to bring theatrical magic to her regional audiences. However, a production of Aaron Copland's *Second Hurricane* proved problematic. It required an extensive chorus, and to cut costs to the bone, the chorus for each venue would need to be found locally—not always an easy task. Another ploy that helped draw in the crowds was the use of celebrities. Onetime MGM film star Kathryn Grayson appeared as Miss Public Opinion in a touring *Orpheus in the Underworld*. By this time, her memory had faded. To overcome, Sarah had a plan: Jan Curtis appeared as her assistant, a certain Miss Poll, and fed the missing lines in a comic way to the "forgetful" Ms. Grayson—making a moment of humor out of it. Sadly, Ms. Grayson's appearance in *Orpheus* failed to stir public interest along the Opera New England road show.

In its 1988 spring season, Opera New England featured a large cast in a Marc Blitzstein English translation of Kurt Weill and Bertolt

Brecht's *Threepenny Opera*. Sarah's AIDS-inspired *La Traviata* showed her determination to stretch her audiences, even in a semirural milieu, as well as offering through her children's program the rarely seen 1927 Ernst Toch piece *Die Prinzessin auf der Erbse* (The Princess and the Pea). Finally, Sarah began to realize her Opera New England audiences were not as adventurous or welcoming as their Boston counterparts when it came to unusual rep. Similarly, Sarah's idea of presenting Leila, the Ceylon priestess of the *Pearl Fishers*, as a Catholic nun left many scratching their heads.

In the end, Opera New England remained a troubled venture, geared more to community tours. Because Opera New England was an outreach program, it was hoped that philanthropic dollars would flow more readily with it in place than was the case with her home company. Sarah kept it in operation, in the process robbing Peter (Opera New England) to pay Paul (Opera Company of Boston).

In developing her dreams for a major resident company and a stronger regional presence, Sarah found herself both nurturing new artists and conforming established ones to her approach. However, in spite of her zeal to spawn great talent, no artist of any sizeable vocal endowment rose through the ranks of either Opera New England or the Opera Company of Boston.

By 1988, the Opera Company of Boston was in serious financial turmoil, causing Opera New England to split from the parent company and continue on its way. With it passed the organization that Sarah had once hoped would prove to be her retirement annuity. Afterward, it still played various New England communities but on a far reduced scale, its vision stunted, its aim shortened.

NOTES

1. Richard Dyer, "Laughing with Puccini's 'West,'" *Boston Globe*, May 14, 1976, 15.
2. Robert E. Nemeth, "Opera New England, 'Tosca,'" *Worcester Telegram*, April 3, 1978.

11

WORKING
WITH SARAH

Despite the difficulties of circumstances that attended many of her productions, Donizetti's *Don Pasquale* in her 1978 season was an example of Sarah showing herself capable of investing an old piece with new interest where the components of her unique slant came together, as she often managed. It featured Beverly Sills and Donald Gramm, who had already demonstrated their unusual stage chemistry, sense of timing, and knack for pacing a performance. Now it would be up to her design team, Helen Pond and Herbert Senn, to provide a suitable setting that revolved around an old man's last desperate fling.

With Caldwell, it was often the case that she would throw in a visual element or add a scene that was not necessarily implied in the libretto. Each was capable of spiking interest to make a point. Often it was tied to a current event that might spark a collective frisson. If she divined that a scene lacked human interest, or had characters not readily definable, that was her special challenge, her special "meat." Sarah told the *Christian Science Monitor*, "Opera cannot continue to exist unless it comes out of our world."[1]

Donizetti's *Don Pasquale* was possibly the best example of what Caldwell could accomplish in terms of an innovative approach. The production was also seen as a repertory item with her cadet company, Opera New England, and was played in high school and college auditoriums in no fewer than eight New England cities as well as the stage of the Houston Grand Opera. Unfortunately, no video of the Boston production or its reincarnations is known to exist. Caldwell went on to conduct the work for the EMI recording with the London Symphony Orchestra, featuring two artists long associated with her company, Sills and Gramm.

Before meeting with her design team, Caldwell would research an opera to the maximum, diligently consulting photocopies and microfilms of composers' manuscripts, libretti, original production manuals, and any significant source material before finalizing her concept.

In working with designers, she would often ask them to present their ideas first and then try to pick and choose what she wanted, which made her difficult to work with, according to both Robert O'Hearn and Ming Cho Lee. But with her regular design team of Helen Pond and Herbert Senn, she found the right creative match to which she became yoked in many of her productions, to the point that the result was a seamless flow. You could never tell who did what or where, although the "Caldwell touch" was never in question.

For *Pasquale* her designers initially contemplated two interiors plus a terrace garden. But Caldwell's response to their first blush of ideas was, "No, no, no!" At this stage, she was nearly always capable of many insights and inspirations, offering a spirited tossing up of suggestions out of which would usually come a better idea. Several days later, the telephone rang at the company's scene shop in Jamaica Plains. It was Caldwell on the line eager to talk to her designers, asking, "Just how far along are you?"

Her normal practice was not to impose a concept on a work. Instead, she sought to come up with a credible, discernable approach, to lead the audience along her creative path. She collaborated intimately with designers, and no suggestion was ever dismissed out of hand. She sought to create scenes that were readily identifiable to her audiences, constructing "moments of magic," as she called them. Those ineffable moments surfaced on occasion, usually when Caldwell felt something special was happening that she alone recognized. Her associates didn't always know what the magic might be. Still, there was no mistaking her reaction, as she uttered in a low, soft voice, "It's magic time."

While keeping the Rome setting for *Pasquale*, Caldwell allowed a modest updating to the time of the opera's composition, circa 1838–1840. If Donizetti was content with stock characters in his operas, some almost weak to the point of being unvarnished, Caldwell would have none of that. Her inclination was to morph them into figures her audience might recognize or understand. Sarah was determined that her *Pasquale* would not be a stillborn production of the kind so often encountered, one mired in irrelevant and vulgar gags, implying that the title character was merely the brunt of a cruel joke. To accomplish this, she would dislodge the characters from their generic *commedia dell'arte* roots and airbrush them into fuller portraits.

Her first task was to soften the harsher aspects of the plot. Each character would be illuminated from within, infused with individuality. For example, Don Pasquale traditionally bears a resemblance to the classic Pantalone figure, the oft-mocked elderly lawyer or merchant, whereas, in Caldwell's production, he became less a buffoon and more a figure of Mozartean warmth and poignancy. While Norina typically is an ill-defined soubrette, a Colombine, or a coquette who plays cruel tricks on would-be suitors, she now emerged as a strong, self-assured professional: a successful milliner with a shop of her own. With Beverly Sills in the part, Sarah saw her as ironic and high-spirited, qualities that often seemed to spring naturally from the "Bubbles" persona.

Dr. Malatesta, originally played by Alan Titus, became more than just Don Pasquale's wily, untrustworthy friend. He was an actual physician whom Pasquale consulted for a medical checkup. If Pasquale was seized with sudden dreams of a young wife and family, it was only logical, Sarah reasoned, that he would want to know his true state of health before embarking on such an enterprise. Her design team assigned themselves the task of researching the appropriate medical paraphernalia for a medical office of the 1830s, including a vintage examining table and weight scale.

Sarah had specific ideas about Ernesto, Don Pasquale's nephew, (played by tenor Joseph Evans). The assumption of the time was that Ernesto, who showed no visible means of employment, might be recognizable to Boston audiences as a hippie type, or so she conjectured. A guitar would be slung over his shoulder to suggest a prodigal wastrel on the verge of family estrangement, presaging Alfredo of *La Traviata*. Ernesto would be seen making his rounds about Rome on a bicycle, that is, before it was brought to Caldwell's attention that the bicycle had not been invented until the 1860s. "So, how about a velocipede?" Sarah wondered.

Within a short time, the number of scenic transformations blossomed from three to twelve. The designer used a nineteenth-century "toy theater" concept, a diorama with easily movable props and scenery, to accommodate the rapid changes to a number of well-known

Roman locales; a snapshot tour of Rome that would add visual humor and color.

Act I, Scene 1: Dr. Malatesta's office with a period weight scale and surrounding shelves of apothecary jars. Don Pasquale is at the office for a checkup. He disrobes to his long underwear while awaiting his physician, Dr. Malatesta. He furtively checks his weight on the scale before the doctor arrives. In the meantime, a nurse walks through intermittently, each time causing Pasquale to cover himself with embarrassment.

Act I, Scene 2: A waiting buggy as Pasquale exits Malatesta's office. After climbing into the stationary carriage, Don Pasquale breaks into the boisterous cabaletta "Ah! Un foco insolito." The carriage wheels turn while a scenic panorama of Roman monuments whizzes by, including views of the Fontana di Trevi, the Colosseum, and other landmarks.

Act I, Scene 3: The kitchen of Pasquale's home. After being quickly undressed by attending servants, Don Pasquale steps into a large wooden tub filled with soap bubbles to bathe before meeting his prospective bride. Ernesto appears, a quarrel ensues, and the old cook brings a bowl of pasta to calm Pasquale. The invented scene shows Pasquale as a happy bachelor surrounded by adoring servants. When Pasquale informs his nephew of his forthcoming marriage, Ernesto realizes that his inheritance will be cut off, thus thwarting his plans to marry Norina. In a more somber mood, Ernesto launches into his aria, "Sogno soave e casto" (Fond dream of love, no more).

Act I, Scene 4: Norina's hat shop. The set replaces what was originally meant to be a chic drawing room, but Sarah thought she had a better idea. She made Norina a milliner, a forerunner of a modern career woman, thereby reinforcing the irony of "Quel guardo il cavaliere" (Glances so soft and bright). During her subsequent cabaletta, "So anch'io la virtù magica," several well-dressed gentlemen are seen through a large picture window passing by the shop, casting admiring glances at Norina as she adorns hats with silk flowers and stuffed birds.

Act II, Scene 1: A small cafe instead of the usual setting of Don Pasquale's house. Caldwell showed Ernesto disconsolate, seated alone in a small cafe. A trumpet solo is heard offstage, with Ernesto writing a farewell note to Norina, singing his famous aria with trumpet obbligato, "Cercherò lontana terra." Ernesto's suitcase and guitar are strapped to a baggage rack on the velocipede. Shortly, a stationary platform with unseen wheels rolls in with a set showing a travel agency, "Agencia Viaggio," symbolic of Ernesto's thoughts about leaving the city.

Act II, Scene 2: Pasquale's living room. As Ernesto exits on his velocipede, an offstage wagon ushers in the next set, an "old-fashioned" rococo interior in dusky pink. The action proceeds along traditional lines with the mock marriage.

Act III, Scene 1: Pasquale's drawing room. Norina is supervising a complete redecoration in colors more flattering to Ms. Sills's red hair. Three sets of blue-and-green Empire-style wings slide in covering the pink wings as new borders descend from the flies to cover old ones. Shutters cover all windows but the one window in the back wall. The sofa and deck are replaced by new neoclassic ones, concluding the interior makeover. Caldwell has Norina discharge the former servants, who are now seen departing in tears; new servants enter in elegant black-and-white livery.

Act III, Scene 2: Garden terrace. The garden gate unit upstage is now revealed with the rear shutters drawn off and the remaining wings and borders covered by a number of "cut" garden drops that fly in. A coach and cut-out horses arrive via stage left to transport Norina to the opera, with coachmen and footmen disappearing offstage as the kitchen wagons close in.

Act III, Scene 3: Pasquale's kitchen. Don Pasquale observes as the new servants set up for a banquet with wine bottles and an impressive cake from the oven. The chorus intones "Che interminabile andirvieni," while Pasquale assumes that the spread is meant for him but is horrified when the servants sit down at the table themselves.

Act III, Scene 4: Pasquale's drawing room. The blue-green decor is restored as the kitchen set slides away. Pasquale confronts Dr. Malatesta with the letter that Norina had deliberately dropped from her coach. Pasquale and Malatesta, standing in opposite proscenium boxes, sing one of the most famous duets, "Cheti, cheti immantinente."

Sarah asked her design team for something visual to heighten the effect of the rollicking show-stopping duo. In a burst of inspiration, they obliged by providing two side boxes adorned with canopies, each fitted with its own pull-down shade, thus allowing Pasquale and Malatesta to conclude their "argument" with a theatrical coup, the abrupt and synchronized slamming down of the shades. The effect sent paroxysms of laughter through the audience.

Act III, Scene 5: Pasquale's garden terrace. The main stage design with the house framed by the garden portals with lighted translucent windows creates an incandescent atmosphere for Ernesto's serenade, "Com'è gentil."

Act III, Scene 6: A kitchen wagon rolls in, providing a setting for the happy finale with Pasquale and former servants welcomed home, with all served plates of pasta. During the concluding moralizing strophes, the members advance downstage to convey the message, "When you are old, act your age."

With the additional scenic transitions smoothed by the Roman diorama and "wagons," Sarah was able to offer her spectators a colorful eyeful implicit in the Eternal City setting. While the fleshed-out characters heightened audience involvement, the opera gained a new sense of forward momentum, as one scene flowed into the next.

In the rehearsal phase of producing an opera (typically a period of three weeks), Sarah's first task was to create an environment conducive to exploring the musical text. With the aid of a rehearsal pianist, each participant was honed in his or her respective role. Afterward, Caldwell, seated at the lip of the stage, would informally discuss the work with her principals. From these sessions, attempts were made to plant ideas for each to enlarge upon. Sometimes, she would ask artists to stay after hours to work on staging details. Once they had left the theater, many crew members observed that Caldwell seemed closer to her muse on these occasions than during normal daytime rehearsals. The following morning would find her in the theater, vaguely punchy, as if she had spent the night there (quite often she did), but ready to go to work.

Now secure in their roles, with the cast achieving total familiarity with the score, each individual performer was encouraged to find his or her own way to the character in question, with stage movement and synchronization naturally falling into place. Subsequent revivals would require that new artists set off on their own voyage of discovery, thereby averting blind adherence to conventional blocking and allowing for new subtleties and nuances.

As a part of the total immersion with the score, Caldwell preferred her artists sing out in rehearsal rather than mark. In this way, any nervousness would be minimized or eliminated, with the artists gaining the requisite self-assurance needed to bring their respective roles to life. Most artists found her methods helpful, but it is only fair to add that a minority found them alienating.

In one of the final rehearsals on the shallow stage of the old vaudeville house, when sets with their intricate panels, drops, and wagons were in place, one of the stage managers raised his hand to halt the proceedings to say there was not enough room to accommodate the set. Each flat was designed to be pushed individually, which caused a minor traffic problem. Not deterred in the least by the challenge, Caldwell, seated at her director's table in the darkened auditorium, headed for the stage. Once there, she immediately began to work with the stagehands for what seemed an interminable time so that all of the borders and wagons fell into place; she dogged every aspect like a general, to the exhaustion of nearly all involved. One of her designers recalled, "In our many years in the business, we had never seen anything like it."[2] The exact timings devised for the set relied on a great degree of precision and accuracy in their execution and proved to be some of the most demanding in the thirty-two year history of the company.

In the end, it was Sarah's passion for the medium that often goaded her artists and set a high bar for what she demanded of herself in pursuit of her ineffable "moments of magic." Tenor Jon Vickers, who appeared in two roles with the company, first as Florestan and later as Benvenuto Cellini, once turned to a male colleague in their shared dressing room and mused, "I wonder why we keep coming back here." The answer was clear: many felt that they learned more about themselves and their potential than they had experienced with any other director at the time. For them, working with Sarah Caldwell would remain one of the greatest experiences in a lifetime of performing. As Mr. Vickers himself acknowledged, "Her love of the medium was enough to bring out the best in you."[3]

NOTES

1. Joanne Leedom, "Consortium Ensures Opera for New England," *Christian Science Monitor,* June 5, 1970, 21.
2. Herbert Senn, interview by the author, August 25, 2001.
3. Jon Vickers, interview by the author, January 23, 2004.

12

OTHER ARTISTIC WORLDS TO CONQUER

Sarah started to realize that other worlds could be hers for the conquering. From being a significant fish in a small pond to a notable figure in a still localized but wider arena, now she was on her way to becoming a colossus of national dimensions. As far back as 1974, she had already raised her baton over the symphonies of San Antonio and Detroit. She told *New York Magazine*, "It's nice once in a while to spend a few days not worrying about staging and scenery. That's very relaxing. For the past few years I've had to concentrate on one way of life, one set [of priorities], and that can be very exciting." By the end of the year (December 22), Sarah made her Carnegie Hall debut, conducting an abridged version of Prokofiev's *War and Peace* given in concert. On that occasion, John Rockwell of the *New York Times* wrote, "One can only hope that she will appear again here soon as conductor, and often."

These engagements indicated that there was not only the opera world, but also the concert world for Sarah to conquer, with her mother egging her on. "You're nothing until you've conducted the Beethoven Ninth." When conducting she often wore long black dresses, frequently hiding tennis shoes or comfortable moccasins. At the time the guest-conductor invitations began pouring in, Sarah's weight was nearly three hundred pounds—distributed over a five-foot-three-inch frame. The excess did not permit her to stand for any extended length of time, and so in her appearances with various orchestras, Sarah usually elected to sit high at the podium, behind a stockadelike enclosure. This device prevented the audience from focusing on Sarah's large rump instead of concentrating on the performance itself. However, the enclosure was of no value to the orchestral players, who were not spared a most unfortunate view—Sarah tended not to wear underpants.

Public attention provokes private advice. Those close to her insisted she must do something to look more presentable. Realizing she would have no peace to concentrate on her work until her well-wishers had no more reason to prod, Sarah good-naturedly gave in. One bright chilly morning, her hair stringy and matted, Sarah exited a cab on Fifth Avenue in midtown Manhattan and headed for the entrance of the Elizabeth Arden beauty salon to fulfill an appointment made by her manager. Under her arm was a score of *Fidelio*. Immersed in Beethoven's work, Sarah hardly noticed that she'd been sitting unattended for almost an hour, but even she began to think the length of time odd and asked to speak to the salon's manager. It seemed the hairdresser assigned to her, unnamed here but identified as Harlequin, had called in sick. A quick telephone call managed to summon Truffaldino (also a pseudonym), who had been enjoying his day off but who obligingly agreed to rush to the shop. When Truffaldino arrived at the salon, he found a large woman at his station engrossed in what looked like a music score and seemingly unaware of his presence. After circumnavigating Ms. Caldwell, Truffaldino broke the silence. "Are you some kind of bandleader?" Without even looking up, Sarah replied, "I am the band."[1]

Truffaldino managed to work wonders as he darted about Sarah with his combs, scissors, and hair dryer, eventually creating soft curls. Now ready for prime time, she exited the shop for her next appointment, the studio of a photographer who would capture her now-kempt image for the cover of *Time* magazine later that fall.

On November 10, 1975, Sarah made more headlines when she conducted the New York Philharmonic's pension fund concert, sponsored by *Ms.* magazine and dedicated to compositions of female composers. The occasion was in observance of the United Nations International Women's Year. From then on, it seemed that Sarah's name was on everyone's lips. People who never cared for or attended opera spoke of her with admiration.

Sarah had never been particularly identified with the women's movement, but it was a card she was willing to play, telling a reporter from the Cleveland *Plain Dealer*, "I never felt disadvantaged as a woman. . . . I was happy doing what I was doing, and I was never terribly conscious of any obstacles."[2] Perhaps the lack of consciousness was a blessing to her, but it was also a hinderance when she failed to realize how vulnerable she was in certain ways that would later hobble her in pursuit of a concert career.

As was her custom, she consulted various composers and experts on the upcoming New York Philharmonic pension fund program. Gunther Schuller had suggested a short piece called *Sands* by Peruvian-born Pozzi Escot, who had studied composition at the New England Conservatory.

During the first rehearsal, she severely exposed her limitations to the point of personal embarrassment with the orchestra, showing herself to be totally at sea with the Escot composition. Feeling defeated, and un-used to the sensation, Sarah retired to a nearby Lincoln Center hotel in the company of two assistants and tried to figure out what to do next. The three worked through the night, devising a plan. The score had never been published and was a great sheaf of paper, more closely re-sembling an architectural drawing than a musical composition. The timings for the Varèse-like blocks of sound in the middle section were particularly baffling since the composer meant it to be of undeter-mined duration. After breaking down the piece mathematically, the three were able to apply certain metric notations.

When she returned to the podium for the next rehearsal, she un-folded the large score with her habitual fanfare. For her eyes only, a crib sheet was placed atop the elaborate score to guide her through the shoals of the difficult piece. The result was inconclusive: the critics praised Sarah for her efforts but thought the program overly ambitious.

Sarah drew more headlines when it was announced that she would become the first female conductor at the Metropolitan Opera on Janu-ary 13, 1976. In the media, this was seen as a groundbreaking (and gen-derbreaking) event. Back in the 1930s, the Met had once considered inviting a female conductor, Antonia Brico, but when word of the plan leaked, Met baritone John Charles Thomas threatened to go to the newspapers to declare that he would never perform under the baton of a woman, and the matter was dropped. Times had changed. Although several women had served on the musical staff at the Met as coaches, assistant conductors, prompters, and rehearsal pianists beginning with Max Rudolf's musical administration, Sarah was the first woman to con-duct a public performance. In reality, her debut had little to do with Met management's vision but was owed to the insistence of Beverly Sills, who would be singing Violetta in *La Traviata* for the first time in that house.

Sills had been promised James Levine as conductor, and Sherrill Milnes would be her Germont père. Neither was to be found as rehearsal time approached, and the diva threatened to cancel—unless Sarah could be persuaded to preside in the pit. In that case, Ms. Sills would reconsider, and for the Met, anxious at the time to mollify a soprano with considerable draw, that was that!

At 8:05 p.m. sharp, Sarah Caldwell, wearing a black sequined dress, walked out of her dressing room on a lower level of the Metropolitan Opera House and into the pit of the orchestra. She turned to face a standing ovation.

Bill Zakariasen of the *New York Daily News* reported, "The focus of attention was squarely on the orchestra pit, from which Sarah Caldwell rose, Erda-like, to be the first woman conductor ever in the ninety-three-year history of that organization."[3]

"It is easy to see why Miss Sills rooted for her at the Met," reported Harriet Johnson in the *New York Post*, covering Sarah's debut at the time.[4] Sills was somewhat guarded about working with John Dexter, who was slated to restage *La Traviata*. She had sung the role with Sarah four years earlier. With Dexter, she might have to relearn parts of it in the midst of a busy season. She preferred working with Sarah, a known quantity, thinking the blocking would be similar to what they had worked out previously. Also, Sills wanted to wear her own costumes.

Zakariasen reported, "Sarah received a standing ovation even before she gave the downbeat . . . [to] the performance which orchestrally, at least, more than lived up to our hopes." Harold Schonberg, writing for the *New York Times*, said, "When the conductor made her appearance, many in the audience rose to greet her. It may have been more than coincidence that the greatest number of risers were women. There is a nice cartoon idea here: all the women in the audience standing to cheer Sarah Caldwell, all the men sitting glowering."[5]

Prior to the performance, Sarah had the Met music librarian send her the orchestra parts for study, and then systematically had an assistant erase all of the dynamic markings. This must have infuriated the Met when they subsequently discovered what had happened to their archival score. Sarah later said that she wanted the Met musicians to think of the piece more freshly.

Consequently, Sills held on to a few notes for longer than was notated in the score, which was probably done with Sarah's approval. Supporting Sills were Stuart Burrows as Alfredo and William Walker as Germont. Though Walker was a substitute for an indisposed Ingvar Wixell, the consensus was that his outstanding portrayal compensated for Burrows's limitations.

Sarah had hoped to present Verdi's score note complete, as she had done in Boston four years earlier, but it was not to be. The restoration of cuts would probably have not added more than fifteen minutes playing time and would not have jeopardized the budget in terms of musicians' overtime. Unfortunately, however, Ms. Sills sprained her back a few days before the first night, and her stanzas were cut out of consideration to her. In addition, William Walker would not have had the time to learn the extra music. Nonetheless, tenor Burrows did sing the cabeletta after "De' miei bollenti spiriti" because he had sung it with Caldwell four years earlier in Boston.

In any event, it was Sarah's evening, a triumph perceived as being not only for her personally but for women and for the women's movement. She had shown what a woman could be—or, more important, that her achievements were an example of—what had been denied them. Given the chance, John Charles Thomas might never have adjusted, but now Sarah Caldwell was appearing in the finest concert halls and opera houses.

Nearly two hundred of her supporters came to New York to celebrate her Met debut. Afterward, she was feted by a gala party in the Met's Eleanor Belmont Room in honor of her debut. The next day, Sarah appeared on NBC-TV's *Today* show before a nationally televised audience.

A few weeks later, Sarah was occupying a suite at New York's Americana Hotel, having just been flown in via private jet from Washington where she had been rehearsing the National Symphony for an upcoming concert. Forty-eight floors below in the Americana's grand ballroom, Sarah was to be honored before four hundred concert managers assembled for the annual banquet of the trade publication *Musical America*. Her agent was determined that she look her very best before these particular flesh peddlers, who could be very influential to her future bookings. She put herself back in the skilled hands of Harlequin and Truffaldino of Elizabeth Arden's salon. Above the whoosh of the hair dryer, Sarah mused with Alan Rich, writing for *Boston Magazine*, about her newly found fame as a concert maestra. "I know, for example, that when I arrive in some city for an engagement, the manager is looking at me and wondering if I'm going to sleep in the aisle of his concert hall. . . . I do have to be extra careful, however, to make Boston realize that I'm taking good care of things back home."[6]

As with any rising star, the more commitments she made, the more the invitations began pouring in from far and wide. One offer she could not resist earned her a $10,000 fee endorsing the American Express Company in a nationally televised ad campaign, with Sarah uttering the campaign's catchphrase, "You know me!" Sarah was seldom recognized in public, and it is doubtful that any viewers had the vaguest idea as to who she was. Afterward with friends, Sarah seemed to take a childlike mischievous delight in the absurdity.

Between dates at the Met, her Boston company, and Washington's National Symphony, Sarah had also agreed to stage and conduct the world premiere of John La Montaine's patriotic oratorio, "Be Glad Then, America," for Pennsylvania State University on February 6, 1976. Four days later, she also led the Pittsburgh Symphony. Her increasingly tight schedule in the coming weeks nearly drove her to exhaustion, so much so that when she arrived at the airport, she asked to be met by an ambulance, rather than a limousine. The attendants who loaded her into the ambulance were stunned that even the wail of its siren didn't keep her from dropping into a deep sleep. They were even more stunned when, upon arrival at the concert hall, Sarah immediately awoke and alighted from the ambulance on her own. She then regally strode into the concert hall, leaving the ambulance staff wondering if they had been participants in some kind of scam.

On February 21 Boston had its opportunity to honor Sarah, a $100-per-person banquet/dinner dance, a black-tie affair at the Boston Sheraton attended by three hundred of her friends and admirers. Allison Arnold of the *Globe* reported, "Although a Missourian by birth, Sarah's heart belongs to Boston. . . . A beach ball of a woman, . . . because of her weight, she directs sitting down."[7]

Sarah was busy with her repeat performances at the Met and had just concluded her three-performance run of *Fidelio* with her own Boston company. Together with her numerous guest appearances with orchestras, Sarah had difficulty sandwiching in the event and was late arriving for the 8:30 dinner. Truffaldino and Harlequin were at the hotel to ensure the correctness of Sarah's coiffure, after which she got into a two-piece, teal-blue crepe dress. "Sarah is more concerned about her looks than seems apparent. . . . Like most geniuses, Sarah is absent-minded except about her work. She is always leaving her purse in odd places, and if a button pops off, she often replaces it with a brooch.

Sometimes several dangle from her dress. But no buttons popped on Saturday night," Alison Arnold added.

Sarah was accompanied by her seventy-three-year-old mother, now wheelchair bound. Gratification turned to annoyance at the evening's postprandial entertainment, Anna Russell with her calling-card spoof of Wagnerian opera, which turned Sarah's pleased expression to a glower directed at the comedienne.

Sarah went on to make her belated conducting debut at the New York City Opera in the fall of the next year but seemed more occupied in sweeping the concert world. Her hectic summer schedule found her conducting the Chicago Symphony at Ravinia and the Philadelphia Symphony at Ambler (Temple University) as well as directing orchestras at Syracuse, Atlanta, and Indianapolis. And finally, in January 1977, she came home to make her conducting debut with the Boston Symphony Orchestra at Boston's hallowed Symphony Hall.

Sarah conducted the performance behind her traveling enclosure. With the BSO, Sarah was up against the numbing power of past performances associated with its legendary conductors. It was a daunting list, and Sarah would have known that whatever selections she chose for her debut program, comparisons both favorable and unfavorable would be drawn by the Boston concertgoing public and critics alike. In this regard, she was probably wise to start off with a minor Haydn Symphony (No. 8, "Le Soir"), which she managed quite well. Next came Elliott Carter's Symphony No. 1, which, Richard Dyer, writing for the *Globe*, reported, "was a spacious performance."

But it was probably ill-advised for Sarah to conclude her program with Stravinsky's *Petrouchka*, an extremely difficult work often associated with Serge Koussevitsky and before him, Pierre Monteux, who led the BSO for a number of years. Her deep admiration for the composer probably led to the decision, not to mention the personal affection she'd developed for Stravinsky since he'd accepted her invitation to conduct his *Rake's Progress* in her Boston University workshop days. During the last rehearsal, Sarah had difficulty with the piece, to the extent that the concertmaster pulled her aside and tried to explain certain things. Dyer judged her performance of the Stravinsky to be "not in the same league" as that given by her illustrious predecessors with the orchestra. Again, Sarah had failed to come to grips with her own limitations, even knowing full well the past associations of the piece for the Boston public, and set forth to make her own statement out of hubris.

Perhaps Boston was being unfairly harsh, or perhaps conducting Stravinsky really was beyond her. In any case, her take on his piece had failed to win approval. Furthermore, in taking her bows, Sarah apparently forgot to single out at least one BSO player deserving of separate applause that evening—a serious breach of podium etiquette.

Following her performances at Symphony Hall was a date in Baltimore to conduct its symphony. Afterward, Missouri-born Sarah Caldwell was off to St. Louis to fulfill an engagement with its orchestra, where the mayor proclaimed April 20 as "Sarah Caldwell Day" in her honor. On this occasion, accompanied by Carrie Margaret, Sarah conducted a special St. Louis Symphony concert played in her honor at the campus of Northwest Missouri State University at Maryville. Sarah and her mother were feted and heralded around Nodaway County but did not venture as far as Burlington Junction. In any event, her father had passed away, and the Caldwell property had been sold. By this time, Carrie Margaret was toothless and had to wear dentures. Worse still, there were many occasions when she was unable to recall where she had left them, so that considerable time in Maryville was spent trying to find them.

Later that summer of 1977, Sarah was back in Tanglewood to conduct the Boston Symphony, then went to the Saratoga Festival and the New York Philharmonic before going on to Mexico City to lead the Mexico National Symphony. After a stint with the Cleveland Orchestra at the Blossom Festival, Sarah had further reason to kick up her heels, flying to London where she made her one and only complete commercial opera recording, Donizetti's *Don Pasquale*, which reunited her with her own Boston cast, except for Alfredo Kraus as the tenor lead. She spent the rest of the year concluding her sweep of major U.S. orchestras. Her public image received further burnishing with the decision by *Harper's Bazaar* to include her on its list of Top Ten Women in the United States.

Sarah maintained her tight schedule, balancing concerts, opera rehearsals, and performances in Boston. On March 5, 1978, she made her conducting debut with the Brooklyn Philharmonic at the Brooklyn Academy of Music. It was her first New York venture into standard symphonic literature, featuring an all-Berlioz program. Joseph Horowitz of the *New York Times* reported, "a stirring success . . . in particular, the composer's *Symphonie Fantastique* . . . there were a couple of novelties. In the second movement (the ball), she employed a delightful trumpet obbligato this listener had never heard before. During the opening pages of the third movement (the scene in the country), she had the oboist play offstage so that his part would echo the English horn solos from afar. It worked beautifully."[8]

Concurrent with the Brooklyn engagement, Donizetti's *L'elisir d'amore*, with Judith Blegen and José Carreras, would serve as Sarah's final Met assignment. Later, when Luciano Pavarotti joined the cast as Nemorino, the two did not have a good rapport. In fact, Pavarotti complained to management. And the critics piled on. It was said that she failed to energize things from the pit, and, according to Donal Henahan of the *New York Times*, "Miss Caldwell has had better evenings. Just why she did not make a stronger impression, one cannot say." He added, "There were instances of nontogetherness between singers and orchestra, and the lack of precision was matched in a way by a somewhat lackluster reading of the score."[9]

Sarah also managed to rankle many of the Met musicians. During the *Elisir* rehearsals, she requested the orchestra be reconfigured so that the contrabasses were placed along the back wall of the orchestra pit. This placement is known to make the "bass line" much more prominent in most theater acoustics. However, it would make changeovers between rehearsals and performances difficult in that house. Sarah was never again invited to conduct at the Met. For years after her Met engagements, her photo was hung on a filing cabinet in the Met's rehearsal department with an unflattering caption.

In the summer of 1978, Sarah went to Wolf Trap to conduct the National Symphony Orchestra with Van Cliburn as soloist for Tchaikovsky's Piano Concerto No. 1 in B-flat Minor, which drew an enormous crowd. The Tchaikovsky concerto had become Van Cliburn's calling card and was the work with which he had won the Tchaikovsky competition in Moscow twenty years earlier. The program commenced with Rossini's Overture to *Il Barbiere di Siviglia* and concluded with Berlioz's *Symphonie Fantastique*. Wendell Margrave, reporting for the *Washington Post*, noted, "Caldwell, with her years of success in opera, was predictably an excellent accompanist."[10] With the Berlioz, she was at her best, but the Rossini overture sounded under-rehearsed. In August, she conducted the New York Philharmonic in one of its annual Central Park concerts and then directed it at the Saratoga Arts complex.

With her upcoming opera season a scant five months away, Sarah held a press conference to announce the schedule. This was contrary to her promise to subscribers of a three-year plan as her model for advance casting to engage big-name artists. Questions were raised as to who had her highest priority, the Opera Company of Boston or far-flung concert appearances. Doubts and discontent began to make themselves felt while Sarah was gallivanting across the country, building her well-deserved fame and glory on the concert circuit while the company had failed to obtain a $200,000 private matching grant, a lapse the cash-strapped company could ill afford.

By the summer of 1979, Sarah had become a regular at Wolf Trap. She conducted the National Symphony Orchestra on August 22 with pianist Ivan Davis as soloist. Though the facility had managed to survive its eighth season, it was still big on dreams and short of funds. Catherine Filene Shouse, heiress to the Boston-based Filene's Basement department stores, had occupied a summer place there for a number of years before donating the land for the cultural park. Being from Boston, she knew Sarah and admired her. She had witnessed the Boston company's production of Prokofiev's *War and Peace* at Wolf Trap. It was the first venture beyond greater Boston for the parent company in a number of years. Wolf Trap's open space swallowed much of what came from the stage and pit; therefore, sound enhancement was used. Paul Hume of the *Washington Post* reported, "Never before, in its four years, have Wolf Trap's fullest stage resources been seen and obviously never before have they been so impressively employed as in Prokofiev's and Tolstoy's spectacular drama." Hume was carried away by the spectacle, as were certain audience members who even applauded stage snow and a horse. At the podium, Sarah was seated but often rose to her feet to give a clear, precise beat, according to Hume. Of Sarah, he added, "She is a special treasure in the world of opera, one of the geniuses."[11]

It was not surprising then, on October 27, 1979, when Wolf Trap announced Sarah as its new music director, a gesture offered and accepted enthusiastically. The new assignment promised to further burnish Sarah's image as a concert maestra.

Speculation surfaced in the Washington press as to how these two formidable ladies, Catherine Filene Shouse and Sarah Caldwell, would get along. Beverly Sills, an artist who had performed at Wolf Trap from its inception, stated, "Mrs. Shouse is a very strong woman with very positive ideas. She and Sarah, both being strong people, will probably have a few goes at it, but I think what will emerge will be very positive."[12]

After ten years of existence, the local press had begun to complain that the programming at the facility had become too conservative, and possibly Sarah's appointment was meant to shake things up a bit. It was said that the Shouse-Caldwell partnership was to herald a more daring approach to the range of events offered, in the hopes of drawing new audiences. But Mrs. Shouse was quick to add, "She [Caldwell] will be music adviser and director. We'll call on her for advice. I'm very happy to have her suggestions, though I still hold responsibility for programming."[13]

No sooner was Sarah established as Wolf Trap's new music director than she began pushing her long-cherished dream of a smaller, extra venue specifically built to showcase baroque or chamber operas, a dream Mrs. Shouse and her Washington entourage did not share. Not only were they alarmed by Sarah's all-too-grand vision, but they were extremely skeptical about the monetary wisdom of throwing a sizeable amount of change at baroque opera, of which most people were barely cognizant at the time.

Wolf Trap's management decided to launch a trial balloon. Area residents of rural Vienna, Virginia, were invited to a reception to assess their views of a possible expansion of the facility. Sarah attempted to seduce, persuade, convince, and enthuse Shouse and company and those assembled of the brilliance of her baroque idea, but all of Sarah's blandishments and wiles over cookies and soft drinks fell flat. Instead, area residents expressed their concerns about increased traffic and congestion. Afterward, the architect that Sarah had brought to Wolf Trap from Boston, Mary Otis Stevens, was sent on quite a different errand. Her new charge would be to locate two "performance barns" dating back to the time of the American Revolution that were found in upstate New York. These rustic barns would be dismantled and transported to the farm park. They would eventually serve as modest venues for performances for both chamber music and jazz concerts. The barns were a great solution but came in after Sarah's watch.

Back at Wolf Trap for the summer of 1980, Sarah conducted concerts with the National Symphony Orchestra with André Watts her piano soloist. The program paired Bizet's Symphony in C and Ravel's *Daphnis and Chloé* Suite between two concerti: Saint-Saëns's G Minor and Liszt's A Major. Paul Hume's account in the *Post* glowed with praise: "Caldwell took the measure of the Ravel with a keen ear and delivered it to her listeners in a way that gave much pleasure."[14]

When Sarah returned to Wolf Trap in 1981, she conducted a hastily assembled concert on July 14, prior to her departure for China. As late as press time, public announcements failed to list the program to be performed. It was symptomatic of the problem that always seemed to plague Sarah. She seldom knew what she wanted to conduct. Frustrated concert managers, booking agents, and musicians were often dismayed. Part of the problem lay in her determination to present an entirely new program to each and every audience, rather than prepare a limited repertory that she could present with some authority, as many others had done. Sarah once told *Time* magazine, "I'm not one to take the money and run by playing the same works all over the country."[15] While the sentiment was admirable, the tack worked against her.

The spring of 1982 found Sarah embroiled in a union dispute in Boston. It was at this time that she learned that a sudden fire had destroyed the Filene Center at Wolf Trap. By this point, Sarah's take-charge attitude with Farm Park staff, whom she treated like servants, was at a point of rupture. The fire also seemed to foretell the end of that relationship. It came at a time when her concert career, once so brilliantly launched and promoted by her publicist, Edgar Vincent, began to wane. Her role as gender breaker no longer seemed to stir public interest or even engage the minds of concert managers and agents. There were those who felt her conducting style lacked the refinement and the fine-tuning discipline that would ultimately yield consistent results with orchestral ensembles.

Sarah was fine for Richard Strauss's *Till Eulenspiegel* or any composition that had a certain theatrical appeal or a concerto accompanying a soloist. However, the big symphonic pieces baffled her; she had trouble balancing the various sections of the orchestra, and how to shape that kind of music simply eluded her. Generally speaking, she maintained a busy little beat, very close in, and rather foursquare. Originally, back in her Boston University days, Sarah conducted without a baton but was later cautioned that she would not be taken seriously unless she mastered the technique of using one. Her weight compelled her to be seated for performances, and this may have had a limiting effect on orchestra members' view of her direction. Furthermore, it was speculated that musicians had difficulty in reading her beat to discern her intentions. When Sarah was on her home turf, the results could oftentimes be good. There were occasions when, as she became more involved in what was happening onstage, her beat could be rather vague or even flag. The musicians she had assembled in Boston, some freelance and some from the BSO, knew her signals better or could gain some idea of communication just from observing her very telling facial expressions. At times she failed to live up to the praise heaped on her by music critics such as Andrew Porter of the *New Yorker* or Paul Hume of the *Washington Post*, but it would be wrong to dismiss her conducting talents, as some did. Sarah was known for throwing herself into a piece, researching it fully, and even speaking in advance with noted musicological experts. She was enormously talented and prodigious, often displaying an intuitive sense of what was needed.

Other than her foray into the symphonic and concert world, it must have seemed to her that nothing was outside her ability to conjure magic, or perhaps she simply wanted to express her love of theater in a venue beyond music. While it may have felt inevitable to her, in retrospect, her next undertaking was a reckless invitation for the gods to bring her down for hubris.

Late in 1978, the Vivian Beaumont Theater, which had been dark since the previous summer, would reopen under a new six-person directorate. Sarah Caldwell's name headed the list of directors, which included Edward Albee, Robin Phillips, Ellis Rabb, Liviu Ciulei, and Woody Allen. Sarah had mastered juggling the roles of opera régisseur and orchestral conductor, and now she would add to her Indian clubs theater director in a new field she had never tried.

Richmond Crinkley, the executive director of the Beaumont, had seen one of Sarah's opera productions and admired her stagecraft so much that he had been in conversation with Sarah for well over a year on the proposed directorate. In view of the comments she had often made to associates that her interest in theater had waned since the days of attendance at the Brattle, the acceptance of the Crinkley offer struck some as insincere.

Sarah told the *New York Times* that she would concentrate on "classic plays," raising more than a few hackles in theater circles. Sarah had never directed or produced plays professionally; predictions were that her reach would exceed her grasp. But Sarah's directorship wasn't the only aspect of the project to raise skepticism. Joseph Papp, who had been the last theater director and tenant at the Beaumont, lashed out at the concept of a directorate, predicting that it would fail, as had many previous enterprises in that theater.

Ever since the Beaumont had opened, it had been beset with problems. It had a thrust stage and very uncomfortable seats. Already several repertory theater company efforts had failed there. Significant financial losses had been incurred under various artistic directors. Now, into this breach was flung an "artistic directorate." Although no financial commitment was required of Sarah, many speculated that her involvement was a mistake for various reasons, one of which was that the directorship could only drain her energies from her pressing responsibilities of her stewardship of the Opera Company of Boston.

Perhaps to defy the Cassandras, Sarah chose to produce that most problematic and accident-prone of plays, Shakespeare's *Macbeth*, whose name many distinguished actors refused to utter out of superstition, referring to it as "the Scottish play." *Macbeth* is mounted with fair regularity but almost never wins success with either the critics or the public. It was definitely a reckless choice, but Sarah's boldness may have been bolstered by her success with Verdi's operatic version. She was to learn the hard way that directing a play demanded different disciplines than those required for staging of an opera. The casting of voices with enough amplitude and compatible timbres in the lyric theater is quite a different thing from that of the legitimate stage, where a theater director must ensure the cast is speaking their lines with inflection and a uniformity of acting style within the pace the director determines, while communicating a certain vision of the work. Sarah's ear was attuned to hearing these roles sung, with the composer providing the meter; the fine points of "orchestrating" pure speech may have eluded her.

Still, Sarah made every effort to heighten the drama, even commissioning prerecorded fanfares and flourishes as provided by American composer Edward Barnes. But her Pond/Senn design team failed her, concocting an obstacle course of a set capped by an elevated bridgeway near the proscenium and way above the stage, reached by side staircases. The actors found it difficult at best, nerve-wracking at worst. Sarah trustingly accepted Crinkley's suggestion of Philip Anglim for the title role. Anglim had just been lauded in the Crinkley-directed *Elephant Man*, which had a highly successful run on Broadway. He was an intelligent, handsome, and manly actor but had nowhere near the experience or weight of presence to carry off a role like Macbeth. His Lady, Maureen Anderman, was similarly lacking.

In the end, Sarah's efforts were attacked by a hostile press and ignored by a disinterested theater public. Though such reactions are usual and predictable with the "Scottish play," she had not only learned for herself but shown publicly that her magic had its limits. As a result, her career at the Beaumont was over, and she was never again to direct plays in the commercial theater.

Richard Dyer, the music critic of the *Boston Globe*, once observed that Sarah held and played many cards in her time; the women's movement was one of them. Another important card was the implied threat that if she did not get her three-theaters-in-one arts complex, she might leave Boston. With her company installed in another old vaudeville house, her dream for a combined theater complex remained an ever-receding mirage. However, an opportunity was now at hand to permanently occupy another theater that had a deeper stage (thirty-three feet versus the twenty-three feet of the Orpheum), called the Savoy. There was a further possibility of expanding the stage depth. A wealthy donor would provide the capital. Her board thought it the right move when there were few other options. But the question was how easily Sarah, who was loathe to compromise, would relinquish her long-standing dream of a three-theater-in-one performing arts complex.

NOTES

1. Louis Scalmagi, interview by the author, September 18, 2003.
2. Wilma Salisbury, "Miss Caldwell Comes Bearing Gifts," *Cleveland Plain Dealer*, August 14, 1978, 8C.
3. Bill Zakariasen, "First Lady of Opera: Sarah," *New York Daily News*, January 15, 1976, 64.
4. Harriet Johnson, "Met's Dynamo Duo: Sills and Caldwell," *New York Post*, January 14, 1976, 52.
5. Harold Schonberg, "Opera: Caldwell at the Met," *New York Times*, January 15, 1976, 21.
6. Alan Rich, "A Hazard of New Fortunes," *Boston Magazine*, February 1976, 62.
7. Allison Arnold, "Boston's 'Divine Sarah,'" *Boston Globe*, February 21, 1976, 14.
8. Joseph Horowitz, "Miss Caldwell, Philharmonia in all Berlioz," *New York Times*, March 5, 1978, 21.
9. Donal Henahan, "L'Elisir d'Amore," *New York Times*, March 4, 1978, 52.
10. Wendell Margrave, "Crowd Pleasing Van Cliburn," Washington Post, June 19, 1978, B6.

11. Paul Hume, "Caldwell's 'War and Peace,'" *Washington Post*, August 31, 1974, C4.

12. Joanne Sheehy Hoover, "Wolf Trap at Age 10," *Washington Post*, May 25, 1980, G1.

13. Ibid.

14. Paul Hume, "Performing Arts—National Symphony," *Washington Post*, August 30, 1977, C4.

15. "Music's Wonder Woman," *Time* magazine, November 10, 1975, 52–65.

13

A HOME AT LAST

Sensing that her long-cherished dream of a three-theaters-in-one complex had reached a tipping point, Sarah hired one-time general manager of the Metropolitan Opera, Schulyer Chapin. He made twice-weekly rounds among Boston's elite in the belief that his sterling Eastern establishment credentials might be better engaged in pursuing her cause. Upon learning of Chapin's involvement, Governor Michael Dukakis summoned Chapin into his office for a brief meeting. Dukakis' parting words to Chapin: "Do whatever you can to keep Sarah in Boston."[1]

By early 1977, a number of articles appeared in the Boston press spearheading the search for a seven-acre site. But how to pay for it? Construction estimates ranged from 20 million to 40 million. A possible site under discussion was Columbia Point, where the JFK Presidential Library was under construction, but at the time it was thought to be too remote and inconvenient to public transportation.

In the meantime, the wanton destruction of Boston's old vaudeville palaces continued unabated but was starting to resonate publicly. The Boston Redevelopment Authority (BRA) favored retrofitting the four-thousand-seat Music Hall (also known as the Metropolitan), a fading grand dame of Boston's movie palaces, which later morphed into what became known as the Wang Center.

On the other hand, the largest theater on Sarah's three-theaters-in-one wish list was pegged at two thousand seats, as opposed to the Music Hall's four thousand. The Metropolitan was still suitable for the Met's annual visits, so, the logic went, why was it not suitable for Sarah?

But Sarah's vision included a school for opera, two other theaters, more rehearsal space, and an opera library as a part of the package. Advocates claimed that the all-purpose Metropolitan offered the best possibility, at an estimated cost of $6.5 million. Sarah scoffed at the notion, declaring, "An all-purpose theater is a no-purpose theater."

Still, at both the municipal and state levels, Sarah's three-theaters-in-one concept was being taken seriously. However, those who opposed her grand design continued to question whether or not the project was capable of attracting sustained government funding. Without action by the state legislature, nothing would get off the ground. In a press release, Sarah announced that she and her board stood willing to meet with the BRA to discuss the proposed site at Columbia Point, with Sarah playing the card, "If I do not get what I want, I might leave Boston."

Another rumor at the time was that Sarah was engaged in raising money to buy the Orpheum from Boston realtor Burt Drucker. Drucker denied the claim, saying that the Orpheum was not for sale but that he would be happy to continue to lease it, as he did to rock groups and other presenters. Standing in the way of a possible purchase was an estimated $2 million in renovations thought to be needed to make it suitable for long-term use. If Sarah could raise that kind of capital, she might have better use for it than as a long-term investment in an old physical plant. Before that rumor could be laid to rest, another one surfaced. It was said that Mr. Drucker had been approached by a group of investors willing to buy the Orpheum, demolish it, and erect a shopping mall on the site.

By 1978, an economic recovery in the Northeast facilitated a boost in ticket sales, but resistance continued to hamper further fund-raising. Sarah's two-day spring "Opera-thon" only mustered one-third of its stated aim of $100,000, a troubling sign.

More scuttlebutt erupted over the possible sale of the Savoy, another fading vaudeville house on Washington Street. There was talk that one of Sarah's wealthiest backers, Susan Timken, of the Timken roller bearing fortune, stood ready to donate a very substantial sum toward the purchase of a suitable theater, if one could be found.

Sensing that the Massachusetts state legislature would never act, members of Sarah's board grew alarmed: a golden opportunity to buy the Savoy was being shunted aside. Sarah was not only cool to the idea, but outright refused to discuss it. Weeks passed before members dared raise the subject out of fear of getting Sarah's cold shoulder. When the company was homeless, the Savoy had served as a onetime venue for the world premiere of Gunther Schuller's *Fisherman and His Wife.*

With the state legislature continuing to dither, Sarah's board members were able to win her over. Now the purchase could go forward. On October 19, 1978, it was announced that a down payment of $285,000 (total sale price of $885,000) allowed the purchase of the 2,850-seat Savoy. Other pledged notes totaling $600,000 closed the sale. The Savoy would be named the Opera House and serve as the company's new home. The theater configuration was typical of the vaudeville houses of the twenties. The bulk of the structure and its commodious lobby occupied more the rear of the block than the front, connected by a long and narrow gallerylike entryway to shabby Washington Street, which had seen better days. Bundled into the sale came another parcel a short black away on Tremont Street, overlooking the Boston Common, connected by a "walk-through" across Mason Street. But the Boston Common suggested a more respectable location, one more ideal for a box office than the narrow Washington Street store frontage.

Built in 1928, in the heyday of vaudeville, it had opened with some fanfare as the B. F. Keith Memorial Theater. Unlike the Orpheum, it did have an orchestra pit designed to contain a small pit band. Fortunately, it was capable of enlargement. The backstage area of the theater was equipped with spacious quarters—now converted into twenty-one rental studio apartments with inside access walled off and reached via an outside alleyway entrance. With alterations, they would be converted to dressing rooms. However, the immediate need was to repair the roof and commit the expenditures to make the theater operational.

Upon the closing of the sale, Sarah and her minions were poised to take charge, with only ten days to convert the stage for use as a proper theater suitable for opera. On October 20, demolition crews began an around-the-clock effort to knock down and remove a concrete wall blocking the proscenium. Another wall erected by the former owners carved out a smaller cinema from a cavernous section of the side stage and wings. It, too, would be removed. While leading a press tour through the auditorium and adjoining public areas, Sarah laughed and said, "We summoned our volunteers who vacuumed the theater, cleaned the elegant chandeliers, and removed tons of chewing gum."[2]

In a pre–Great Depression world where vaudeville still thrived, Edward Franklin Albee and his new partner, ambassador-to-be Joseph Kennedy, conceived of a palace, originally known as the Keith Memorial Theater. The name memorialized Benjamin Franklin Keith (1846–1914), Albee's late business partner, who had earned the dubious sobriquet "the father of vaudeville." But when the theater opened on October 19, 1928, it simply became known as the B. F. Keith Memorial Theater. Joseph Lamb, a prestigious architect of the day, designed a sumptuous setting, one that would attempt to convince patrons that vaudeville was something more than a seedy art form consisting of troupes of jugglers, trained seals, and circus acts. But within a very few years, the theater was given over exclusively to the exhibition of motion pictures. With the Al Jolsons and the George M. Cohans who once trod the boards fading into memory, people began to recall the films they had seen there. By 1965, the theater was purchased by Ben Sack and given the name "Savoy," later changing its name to the "Sack Savoy."

But in those golden days of vaudeville, no expense was spared to make it the most dazzling showcase for the touring vaudeville acts that were seen up and down the entire East Coast. Crystal chandeliers, walnut paneling, and columns of imported Italian marble finished in Vermont gave one a feeling of opulence and splendor. The grand staircase in the foyer was vaguely suggestive of the Paris Opera. The public rooms had a sumptuous tone, such as the men's smoking room and the ladies' lounge, all complete with vanity tables and marble fireplaces; lounges suitable for smoking, reading, and even writing were deemed to be some of the finest of architect Thomas Lamb's achievements. The theater ceiling was muraled, and each seat commanded a fine view of the stage. Sarah was saddened to learn that the furnishings of the public rooms had been moved to the basement then appropriated by the former owners and could not be reclaimed.

Noticing a faint echo at some seat locations, Sarah urgently summoned Mary Otis Stevens, as she had for Wolf Trap. Stevens brought along a noted acoustical consultant. After tests, the two huddled. They told Sarah the theater's acoustics were only so-so—clearly not the news Sarah was hoping to hear. Fearing for the worst, Sarah was again on hand late one night, but this time it was in pursuit of a covert mission worthy of the CIA. Throwing the latch on the stage door, Sarah admitted crews with sound equipment and technicians whose task it was to install a sound enhancement system.

But its installation was no secret to the Boston critics. While Sarah openly boasted to the *Boston Globe* about the theater's fine acoustics, "as perfect a sound as one could experience in a house designed for vaudeville in which a whisper can be heard in the last row of the balcony," they kept mum.[3]

On opening night, Sarah appeared before her audience and with a voice heavy with emotion said, "Welcome to our new home." It was a signal moment for a company, one that she had fought so hard to keep on the boards, even if the venue was not the complex she wanted. But now the various components of her company could be brought under one roof. Other than the venue for performances, the company occupied four locations scattered around the Boston area: a business office on Boylston Street, a set shop out in Jamaica Plains, and a costume shop on the fourth floor of a warehouse in the North End, plus a rehearsal hall on St. Botolph Street.

The thirty-three-foot stage of the Savoy made the purchase seem out of the question, but there was talk the BRA, the same entity Sarah had hoped to win over for her three-theaters-in-one concept, might consider the extension of the Savoy stage back to Mason Street, a cul-de-sac. It had become the redoubt of the homeless, with Sarah's performing artists referring to it as "Piss Alley," so strong was the stench of urine. The proposed extension would allow the enlargement of the stage to a depth of seventy-five feet. It was that argument that several of her board used to overcome Sarah's resistance, and the purchase went forward.

For Tosca, the seats of the first three rows of the orchestra section were removed to accommodate the full Puccini orchestration in the shallow pit, including the second violins, the brasses, percussion, and the composer's "wind band." The basses and percussion were moved aside so that the harpist could tilt her harp forward, thus allowing the stage curtain to open and close. The show could now go on.

Prior to all the excitement and hubbub surrounding the move into the Savoy, it was learned that Magda Olivero, the Tosca for the occasion, preferred an escort. She spoke little English. Sarah deputized assistant conductor William Fred Scott to fly to Milan and bring the ageless Magda to Boston, hoping the two would establish a good rapport.

Magda Olivero arrived on Scott's arm, looking a bit tired but apparently still capable of delivering one of her signature roles. Since the new dressing rooms were still being built out of former apartments, Ms.

Olivero showed herself to be a good sport and willingly occupied, without complaint, what was a former stagehand's latrine.

Although her performance was studied at best, it pleased the Boston audience, who felt themselves fortunate to witness this charismatic diva in one of her signature roles. As to the other cast members, tenor William Johns, her Cavaradossi, did not rise to the level of vocal glamour to match his inamorata's appeal, and even if Giorgio Tozzi's Scarpia was a bit of a reach, it was still a noteworthy evening.

When Tosca leaped from the Castel San Angelo at the opera's conclusion, Magda landed safely in the arms of waiting stagehands. Although Sarah was listed as staging the production, Magda's idiosyncratic style did not bow to Sarah's approach. Richard Dyer in the *Globe* noted, "She had engaged a soprano whose style of acting, in the decadent form in which you see it in other singers, is one Caldwell has spent a career trying to eradicate."[4] Still, the evening was an auspicious one for the Opera Company of Boston. It now had its very own theater.

Once established in a new home, Sarah had hoped to start off her 1979 season on February 9 with a rarity, Tchaikovsky's *Mazeppa*, but it was not to be. British designer Leslie Hurry, whom she had engaged for the production, died suddenly, leaving incomplete his designs. Not only did the required stage rigging need to be installed at the Savoy, Hurry's production had been designed to fit the stage of the Orpheum. Under such circumstances, Sarah felt she had no alternative but to postpone the premiere of *Mazeppa* to the following season (never performed).

Soon after the aborted *Mazeppa*, Sarah departed for Moscow, leaving it to others to solve the many problems related to the ongoing renovation work of the theater. Some took it as a sign of Sarah's lingering annoyance with being stuck with the Savoy, which took her farther away from her three-theaters-in-one project. In fact, she failed to make any decision as to what should be done to the shallow orchestra pit, tailored to the needs of a vaudeville house. In her absence, assistant conductor Scott took it on his own to enlarge the pit, with the work completed by the time of Sarah's return.

While in Moscow, Sarah was a guest of the Ministry of Culture. She was introduced to Soviet composer Rodion Shchedrin. There was talk of Shchedrin's opera, *Dead Souls*, which was taken from the Gogol play and premiered at the Kirov in 1977. At the time, Sarah had seen the work but was not particularly impressed, judging its musical idiom as not advanced. Still, when introduced to the composer and his wife, the

Soviet ballerina Maya Plisetskaya, Sarah glossed over her prior misgivings and spoke glowingly about *Dead Souls*. From this brief camaraderie came the commitment that Sarah would mount Shchedrin's opera at a future date, a promise that came to fruition with Boston's "Making Music Together" festival.

Sarah next headed for Spain, anticipating her Manuel de Falla double bill planned for April. Her last stop was London, for a working session with British composer Sir Michael Tibbett, whose opera *The Ice Break* would receive its U.S. premiere. Those who accompanied Sarah on these jaunts often found very little got done. Mostly, it was left to Sarah to busy herself, renewing old contacts while forging new ones.

Upon returning to Boston, with the theater-refurbishing work nearly completed, Sarah led members of the press on a special tour, pointing out the enlarged orchestra pit, the repairs to the heating plant, the mending of the roof, and the installation of a new lighting grid. Backstage rigging would now allow for the hanging of sets. The twenty-one rental studio apartments, formerly leased almost exclusively to prostitutes, were now the company's new dressing rooms, with access provided from inside the theater. Accumulated mounds of rubbish awaited removal from the basement, where a new costume shop would be set up. An area adjacent to the dressing rooms would provide for an on-premises office for the opera company. Also, small microphones feeding speakers offstage were installed to aid singers waiting for their stage cues.

Sarah showed sensitivity to the plight of the homeless in the rear of the theater and occasionally fed them. Sometimes, usually during a very cold night, they gained entry to a trunk room high up on stage left that once had access to the stage via a long-gone hoist used to lift up trunks for storage. Sarah left them alone. Only occasionally did they become quarrelsome and noisy.

Not all was going according to plan. The theater experienced occasional electrical outages, and peeling paint and plaster fell throughout the theater. An additional $120,000 had to be spent to bring the theater up to reasonable standards, deferring the question of fund-raising that would be needed to put the structure in first-class condition.

In the meantime, the company became embroiled in a squabble with the former owners of the Sack Savoy concerning a clause in the contract of sale granting them the right to rent the theater when not in use. Caldwell's general manager, Thomas Smilie, pointed out that ongoing work was still too intensive to permit exercise of the clause.

It was estimated that the cost of expanding the theater back onto Mason Street would be in the range of $2 million, a sum that was beyond the means of the company. Lacking municipal support, the project was shelved for the time being.

With the company now firmly installed in its new home, word came that the Massachusetts legislature had failed to act on Sarah's three-theaters-in-one complex at Columbia Point, effectively killing the project. Absent that, Sarah had her eye on a nearby property in the downtown area, the Saxon Theatre. It could serve as a home for small works or for baroque operas, if the facility ever became available. Finally, the larger open space Sarah envisioned to mount experimental works would be the last to fall into place.

Sarah's nineteenth season offered an unusual pairing—Gluck's *Orfeo ed Euridice* alternated with Jacques Offenbach's spoof, *Orphée aux Enfers* (Orpheus in the Underworld). For the Gluck work, Sarah's design team, Pond/Senn, came up with an inspired baroque proscenium and a beguiling stage setting that flattered what promised to be a first-rate cast, led by Shirley Verrett as Orfeo, Benita Valente as her Euridice, and Marianna Christos as Amor. Of the several Gluck scores, Sarah opted for the French, although it was sung in Italian, a mixture of the Vienna and Paris versions.

Andrew Porter of the *New Yorker* found Ms. Verrett to be in poor voice. "The lower reaches were furry and unfocused when soft and harsh under pressure; above, the tone became strident and impure. . . . Miss Caldwell's reading lacked force, accent, and firmness . . . backed up by an undernourished chorus." Sarah had twenty-one choristers, while Porter was quick to point out that the original Vienna version had forty-seven. Had Sarah skimped on the chorus? Richard Dyer of the *Globe* noted, "There is no collision between chorus and dancers because the chorus sings from the pit."[5] Given that the Orpheum had no pit, they were arrayed behind the orchestral musicians; one would be hard pressed to find space that would accommodate forty-seven choristers (plus musicians).

Sarah managed to keep the dance elements in check (which is not often the case in productions of Gluck's masterpiece), even if she could not resist infusing additional bits of storytelling. Charon, Pluto, and Proserpine appeared as background figures, with Ixion shown turning on his wheel while Tantalus grasps in vain for the cooling drink.

Andrew Porter was more approving (with minor reservations) of Sarah's production of the Offenbach opus and his take on the Orpheus legend, while bemoaning Maralin Niska's strident tone as Eurydice: "Her trills were so hideous that the audience laughed at them, thinking she intended a Florence Foster-Jenkins-type joke. Maybe she did—but Offenbach didn't." Otherwise, he declared the evening "a triumph," displaying the "energy, vivacity, and imaginative force that were missing in *Orfeo*."[6]

With the Offenbach work showcasing the talents (popular name recognition) of Margaret Hamilton, the one-time "wicked witch of the East" in the MGM film *The Wizard of Oz*, as "Miss Public Opinion," plus the stage presence of TV luminary Fred Gwynn of the popular series *The Munsters* as John Styx, Sarah had a hit on her hands.

But even its limited success did little to bolster the company's meager resources. At the time of the opening of the twentieth season, the annual operating budget had ballooned to a hefty $2.3 million, a large sum at the time. Plans were under way for a new production of Donizetti's *La Fille du Regiment*, starring Beverly Sills and Donald Gramm. It, too, would be scrapped in favor of a revival of the much-traveled *Barbiere*, last seen at the New York City Opera.

For the Tippett *Ice Break*, Sarah accessed an $18,000 grant from the National Opera Institute, with the remaining funds sought from foundations and wealthy contributors. Unfortunately, the company's increased borrowing and debt service were siphoning off money needed to run the company.

When she could least afford it, an additional financial drain arose due to Sarah's insistence on showcasing three of her company's offerings at Wolf Trap while she was still music director. Her company's last visit to Wolf Trap saw the much acclaimed *War and Peace*. Plans were under way for a four-day engagement that included Sarah's time-honored production of Puccini's *Madama Butterfly*, her recent *Der Fliegende Holländer*, and two performances of her new production of Verdi's *Aida*, with Shirley Verrett in the title role, James McCracken as Radames, and Elizabeth Connell as Amneris for opening night.

In a preseason conference earlier that year, Sarah explained that her *Aida* was inspired by the original Cairo production, one fitted to a small stage. Sarah's regular design team, Pond/Senn, had become experts at making do with the limitation of the narrow stages of Boston's vaudeville houses—first the Orpheum and now the Savoy—through the use of flats and clever perspective. Richard Dyer recalled, "The first notes of the prelude, stealing out of the silence, were an indication that this was not going to be an ordinary performance. Sarah Caldwell gave the violins the space to inflect the theme with real tenderness. Throughout the evening her views of the music were unusual and revelatory, and the clarity of many details showed that slovenly traditions were being ignored. The numerous passages for solo cello and for solo winds were played with infinite nuance while the passionate passages of the Judgement scene surged ahead with wild desperation."[7]

Obviously, having struck a fine rapport with her own ensemble on her home turf, it was Sarah's desire that they accompany her to Wolf Trap, but her plan ran contrary to what the D.C. Federation of Musicians would allow. They defined her Boston ensemble as a pickup orchestra, which as such, lacked proper standing as one with customary union protection. After a standoff of several weeks of bickering back and forth, Sarah was finally obliged to capitulate and hire local musicians at a significantly higher cost, one that she could ill afford.

Even so, everything went well for the opening night *Aida*, which drew a capacity crowd. Paul Hume of the *Washington Post* said it was "the most impressive performance of Verdi's *Aida* seen or heard here in more than three decades."[8] On the last day of the short visit, however, with only a few hours to go before the final Sunday evening *Aida*, an electrical storm passed through northern Virginia, discharging a lightning bolt that struck and blew out Wolf Trap's electrical transformer, effectively cutting off power to the stage. In spite of urgent attempts to locate an emergency generator, none could be found. It was the company's worst nightmare. Up to 6,500 tickets had to be refunded to disappointed patrons, while an enormous traffic pileup frayed the nerves of angry motorists as they were waved away by the park police.

Losses incurred by visiting performing entities at Wolf Trap were not reimbursable, according to the contract, and Sarah's role as music director was of little help, functioning more or less as a traffic cop in the selection and scheduling of events. Furthermore, the Farm Park was short of funds, with few prospects to raise any. Eventually, reimbursement came by way of a court settlement, with the insurance company picking up the tab. Unfortunately, Sarah was put in the awkward position of having to sue her employer in order to access relief through Wolf Trap's multiperil insurance policy.

With debts mounting by the day, a new source of money came to light in an unusual announcement on St. Valentine's Day, 1982, from faraway Manila in the Philippines. A newspaper photo showed Sarah seated beside Imelda Marcos, the wife of that country's then-president, Ferdinand Marcos. It was reported that Sarah and her OCB personnel were in Manila to assist and advise the Manila-based Philippine Cultural Center (and Imelda Marcos) in establishing a new opera company. The announcement of this joint project played up the education and training of locals. No contractual arrangements were indicated, but the reported fee was $100,000 per year, to be paid on a five-year installment plan.

With this move, a very strange chapter began to unfold, one that would usher in events that would have far-reaching negative ramifications for both Sarah and her cash-starved company.

NOTES

1. Schuyler Chapin, interview by the author, October 11, 2001.
2. Richard Dyer, "Caldwell's new home," *Boston Globe Magazine*, December 10, 1978, 3.
3. Richard Dyer, interview by the author, November 18, 2000.
4. Richard Dyer, "'Tosca' Glitters with Stars," *Boston Globe*, November 2, 1978, 15.
5. Richard Dyer, "No nonsense 'Orfeo,'" *Boston Globe*, June 9, 1977, 13.
6. Andrew Porter, "Musical Events," *New Yorker*, June 27, 1977, 91.
7. Richard Dyer, "Verrett Dominates Memorable 'Aida,'" *Boston Globe*, May 31, 1980, C11.
8. Paul Hume, "Sarah Caldwell's Ideal Aida," *Washington Post*, June 14, 1980, D5.

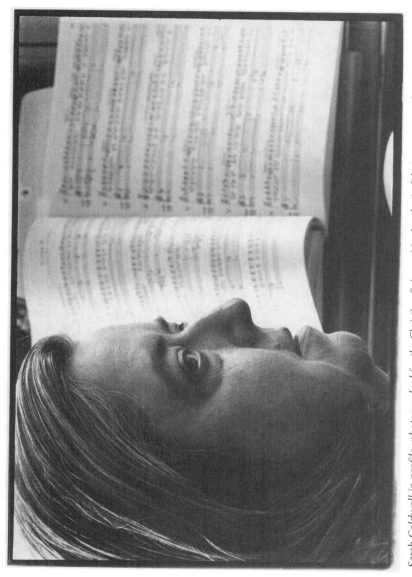

Sarah Caldwell in profile, photographed for the Christian Science Monitor by Judith Aronson. Used with permission.

"Operation Opera," Sarah Caldwell's 1959 kickoff subscription campaign for her Boston Opera Group. Cartoon by Francis W. Dahl. Reprinted with permission of the Boston Herald.

Sarah as a puppeteer? Cartoon by Gene Langley, February 1976. Reprinted with permission of the Christian Science Monitor.

Sarah Caldwell on the cover of Time *magazine, November 10, 1975. Time/Life, courtesy of Getty Images.*

Dorothy Ahle Illustration

Sarah Caldwell . . . 'disorganized autocrat.'

"Sarah Caldwell . . . 'disorganized autocrat.'" Cartoon by Dorothy Ahle that appeared in the Boston Globe in 1983 at the height of Sarah's "Imelda Marcos connection." Copyright Dorothy Ahle.

Don Pasquale (Donald Gramm), reacting to the slap in the face given by "Sofronia" (Beverly Sills) in Act 3, scene I, of the 1978 Boston production of Don Pasquale. *Photo by Herb Senn. Author's collection.*

From left to right: Dr. Malatesta (Alan Titus), Pasquale (Donald Gramm), Norina (Beverly Sills), and Ernesto (Joseph Evans) in the final scene of the 1978 Boston production of Don Pasquale. *Photo by Herb Senn. Author's collection.*

Sarah's home in Lincoln, Massachusetts, a Boston suburb, was often referred to as "the bunker." The Stevens/McNulty House. Time/Life, *courtesy of Getty Images.*

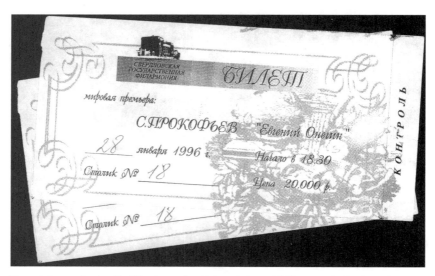

Two ticket stubs in Cyrillic from the Yekaterinburg Philharmonic Society Concert, January 28, 1996. Sarah Caldwell conducted the world premiere, Serge Prokofiev's Eugene Onegin, *with a narrative taken from Pushkin.*

14

SARAH AND THE IMELDA MARCOS CONNECTION

Following on the heels of the Chinese Cultural Revolution and the subsequent warming of relations brought about by the Nixon China visit, the U.S. State Department began to encourage exchange visits. Just about anyone who was anybody with a particular expertise found themselves in this program, including Sarah, who received an invitation in the spring of 1981. Her late-summer visit would follow in the wake of other American artists who had visited China.

Her plane arrived late at night in Beijing in the midst of a driving rain, a few days before she was to conduct seven performances of Verdi's *La Traviata* for the Central Opera Company. Given the time constraints, Sarah was asked the next morning over tea if she preferred to rehearse in the morning or afternoon. Without hesitation, Sarah replied, "Morning, afternoon, and evening."[1]

As was her wont, Sarah threw herself into the project with typical zeal, without regard to fatigue or jet lag. Her Chinese hosts marveled at her twenty-hour days, interrupted by visits with other members of the local opera company. Working with the aid of an interpreter, Sarah announced, "I just want you to remember that the wonderful thing about music is that there is no way of performing it the right way. If I ask you to do things differently from how you have done them before, it is not to be different, but because this is the way we do the piece in the West. Maybe you'll like it, maybe you won't. Let's find out."

Sarah was told by her Beijing hosts to be critical and not to spare her remarks. She obliged. Her Chinese colleagues in the pit had the tendency to run ahead, and Sarah admonished them, "You are like a machine that wants to run under its own power, but you must run under my power. Follow me closely! Music is flexible. It needs room to breathe, and I must be free to give it breath."

Each performance was miced, with an announcer giving a running account before each act, said to be a holdover from the bad old days of the Cultural Revolution when all music and speeches were heavily amplified. Audiences tended to talk during performances, with spectators drinking beverages and eating ice cream. In spite of these distractions, the performance was thought to go well, and the house was sold out. At a postperformance party, Verdi was toasted, with all participants expressing a sense of satisfaction.

During her brief stay, Sarah was able to forge useful contacts with her Beijing colleagues, in particular with Wang Linyou of the Central Opera Company and his design team. Later on, this led to the acquisition of the spectacular costumes and props for her upcoming *Turandot* production.

On the return leg to the United States, Sarah was invited to stop over in Manila to conduct master classes at the newly established Cultural Center of the Philippines. On that occasion, the American ambassador introduced her to Imelda Marcos, the flamboyant wife of Ferdinand Marcos, the president of the Philippines.

It is not clear that Sarah was aware that Imelda's interest was driven by the glamour and prestige that attends operatic events rather than the love of music. Imelda often took on the role of chanteuse at her elaborate parties. She also spoke glowingly of attending the opening of the new Met at Lincoln Center in 1966 as guests of then–California governor Ronald Reagan and his wife, Nancy. With the glitz of that gala New York opening dancing in her head, Imelda's vision for the Philippine Cultural Center would be another excuse to make her elaborate personal fashion statements, including ball gowns, jewels, and accessories (shoes), each of which were changed in time for display at every intermission. Unfortunately, Imelda's subsequent offer of a financial arrangement for the Opera Company of Boston would ultimately prove a Faustian bargain.

It was only a short time afterward that Sarah accepted an invitation by Mayor Shlomo Lahat of Tel Aviv and the Ministry of Education to travel to Israel that November. She would assess the potential for establishing what was later to become the New Israeli Opera Company. In effect, this meant that if Sarah accepted an offer to serve as its artistic director, she would be stretching herself across two different oceans plus the Mediterranean Sea.

At the end of her five-day stay, Sarah declared there was a great deal of talent and boundless enthusiasm. She told the Israeli press that, if asked, she would set up a new organization and that she planned to return to Tel Aviv the following March. She saw it as an opening not only to expand her own horizons with additional conducting and directing dates, but as the opportunity to tap the benefits of shared production costs among three companies (conjoined in her mind) with herself as the common driving force.

The following summer, Sarah returned to Manila to prepare for the first performances of Mozart's *Magic Flute*, as well as a children's opera double bill, *The Frog Who Became a Prince* and *Zetabet*, by Edward Barnes, as given by the Philippine Cultural Center. Among the OCB cast members who accompanied Sarah were Eunice Alberts, Rose Marie Freni, Robert Orth, and Philippine-born Noel Velasco.

Meanwhile, criticism was mounting from human-rights groups in Boston. Sarah's Philippine connection in particular had antagonized the local chapter of an organization calling itself the Friends of the Filipino People. Also heaping criticism on Sarah was a nun, Sister Claire O'Rourke, who had served in the Philippines. She circulated a petition, signed by about ninety of Caldwell's musical colleagues (admittedly, only one worked for the OCB), citing an Amnesty International report of human-rights abuses and asking that the Opera Company of Boston abandon any ties involving Manila.[2]

"There is a certain ludicrousness about this," Sarah intoned in a statement given to the press, speaking of herself in the third person. "Why, suddenly Sarah Caldwell and the Opera Company of Boston are singled out when what we're doing is such a nice, good thing to do." While expressing disgust over the human-rights violations reported by Amnesty International, Sarah added, "Obviously the Marcos government has been connected with many things in the Philippines, including a nutrition center. The only thing they don't seem to have developed is a very good public-relations campaign."[3]

Sarah agreed to appear before Boston's "Cambridge Forum" on July 21 and face down her critics. While maintaining her customary icy composure, she stated her case before the assembled throng. Hoping to regain the moral high ground, Sarah emphasized she had no kinship with dictators, noting her oft-repeated claim, "Operas such as *Fidelio* and *Intolleranza* are full of dangerous messages and therefore inimical to tyrannical regimes." She went on to highlight the educational and beneficial aspects of what she was undertaking, focusing on outreach programs in schools. "Poets and composers would be encouraged to write operas that would spring from their own culture and history." She further addressed her critics in a *Boston Globe* interview: "I cannot believe that training singers can be of any comfort to any political regime."[4]

One of Sarah's strongest detractors was former Philippine senator Benigno "Ninoy" Aquino, now settled in Boston and a fellow at MIT. Aquino was a descendent of a prominent old Philippine family. He was a Marcos rival. When Marcos had declared martial law in 1972, Aquino was immediately arrested and placed in solitary confinement, languishing there for seven years before pressure from the Carter administration forced his release. Aquino was not opposed to the Cultural Center, whose construction Imelda Marcos had spearheaded. It was the cost overruns related to the lavishness of the project that went against the grain of what a country like the Philippines could afford. Imelda scoffed at his complaints and proceeded with the project. Therefore, it was Aquino's attack on Imelda's extravagances that was the perceived threat to the Marcos regime.

Sarah's critics were not appeased. Instead, they tasted blood. While acknowledging Sarah's money situation, approximately eighty musicians in the Boston area circulated a petition demanding she sever any and all ties to that government. In response, Laszlo Bonis, president of the OCB, admitted that the company's finances were in a parlous state. The current season had left the company a further $375,000 in the red (although some placed the figure at nearly $1 million). At the time, one of Sarah's board members recalled, "The situation was so dire that the company's future existence was in question."

On February 18, 1983, Sarah Caldwell commenced her twenty-fifth-anniversary season, under siege as never before, with public opinion increasingly polarized. She experienced problems with the musicians' union, only then to be pressed to pay increases by the International Alliance of Theatrical Stage Employees, who also manned the picket line in pursuit of higher wages. Joining the fray was the Boston Committee on Human Rights and the Arts. As a result, attention focused on a growing sidewalk protest vigil.

The opera company had taken out a loan from BayBank (a local financial institution) the previous season, narrowly avoiding bankruptcy. In order to alleviate the situation, Sarah and her board decided that the time was propitious to sell off the adjoining parcel on Tremont Street. An upswing in real estate values realized a windfall, selling the building and the land for $600,000, of which $200,000 was reportedly passed on to Sarah, in lieu of sums due her. She claimed it was back salary. The remaining proceeds were used to pay back payroll taxes and other indebtedness of the company.

By March, Sarah was again off for a five-day trip to Tel Aviv, Israel, where it was announced she would be the artistic director of a newly formed opera company. There was no mention of fee arrangements, with Sarah promising to spend two months a year in Israel, stressing it would not pose any conflict with her Boston duties. Sarah went on to raise her baton over the Israel Philharmonic. With the need to please her Israeli hosts uppermost in her mind, she volunteered to conduct a number of free opera workshops that ran for eight weeks that summer. But her visit to Israel came hardly a year after Rolf Liebermann, formerly of the Hamburg and Paris operas, was invited on a similarly announced errand, and nothing had come of it. Mysteriously, her Israel connection soon withered. With little or nothing to show for her efforts, Sarah came to the realization that the Israelis were more adept than she in getting something done at little or no cost to themselves.

But later that summer, events in the Philippines took an ominous turn. On August 21, Aquino, the Philippine expatriate, was assassinated as he stepped onto the tarmac at the Manila Airport. The suspected assassins were henchmen in the employ of the Marcos regime. Aquino had resided in Boston. This news hit home. Sarah was under maximum storm and stress, dogged more than ever by protestors. Unkind notoriety and even mockery followed her wherever she went. At the end of October, Laszlo Bonis, president of the OCB, announced that the planned cooperation between the company and the Cultural Center of the Philippines had been abandoned. It had lasted eighteen months, and the way was now clear to put this unfortunate matter behind the company and allow it to move on.

While the many protestors had their own agenda and were not interested in supporting the opera company, the connection with the

Philippines had the unfortunate consequence of making Sarah (and her company) a lightning rod for criticism. Fund-raising was made even more difficult, with Sarah obliged to give her full attention to the very survival of the company. Her absences had taken their toll, with the local operatic calendar becoming less arresting and innovative. As a result, the premiere of Peter Maxwell Davies's opera *Taverner* was postponed.

With each of her prior seasons, Sarah had raised audience expectations. Now it was clear that her 1984 season lacked the needed excitement of a major premiere or unusual revival to draw in audiences. Consequently, her company seemed to slip off the radar screen, with the loss of out-of-town coverage. Even Boston's redoubtable *Christian Science Monitor* gave Sarah's productions scant notice. The season concluded on November 30 with a performance of Jacques Offenbach's *Les Contes d'Hoffmann*. Sarah's name was not listed as stage director or as conductor. Instead, she passed her baton onto Neville Dove with Bliss Hebert as director. This production was a far cry from the one Sarah had mounted in 1965, a slavish recreation of Felsenstein's production which had excited interest. Commenting on the 1984 production, Richard Dyer of the Globe lamented, "Before the evening was over everyone was missing Sarah and the Caldwell touch."[5]

As in previous years, the 1985 season was late in being defined. Finally, in October 1984, a *Globe* ad appeared announcing the lineup. It showed Sarah with baton in hand, imploring the reader with a more-than-usual tortured elocution of spin, "See Jon Vickers in *Samson* as my guest," referring to Handel's oratorio *Samson*. It also promised subscribers *The Makropulos Case*, a revival of Puccini's *Girl of the Golden West*, the delayed American premiere of Peter Maxwell Davies's *Taverner*, and *Lucia di Lammermoor*.

Sarah had not cut back on her many engagements and travel. When she attended the annual New Year's Eve party held in the commodious Savoy lobby, Sarah was seated next to Boston mayor Ray Flynn. Her appearance was more haggard than usual. Overwork had led to an aggravated bronchial condition, which brought on double pneumonia. On January 3, Sarah was admitted to Boston's Massachusetts General Hospital, her condition listed as serious. Her very survival hung in the balance.

Since Sarah's board was mainly in the habit of rubber-stamping her decisions, they were uncertain as to what to do, not knowing if they should go forward or cancel the upcoming season. Without Sarah, there seemed few viable options. Her involvement in each of the planned productions was so total, no one could be expected to pick up the pieces. More worrisome still was the effect of missing a season, a prospect that was thought to be disastrous. The burdensome debt had already put the company on the edge of bankruptcy. No assistant director that the board thought capable of carrying on in Sarah's absence was in place. After weighing the limited options, the board voted to cancel the season. Sarah's habit of "eating through" assistants left the company with only one person capable of carrying on: Sarah.

NOTES

1. Takashi Oka, "Peking Cheers Sarah Caldwell's Direction," *Christian Science Monitor*, July 17, 1981, 6.
2. Sharon Sexton, "The Road to Manila—Sarah Caldwell's Foreign-Aid Program," *Boston Phoenix* (Boston After Dark ARTS Entertainment), November 16, 1982, Section Three, 10.
3. Ibid.
4. Richard Dyer, "The Question of Caldwell's Link to Manila," *Boston Globe*, August 1, 1982, 12.
5. Richard Dyer, "'Hoffmann' Missing the Caldwell Touch," *Boston Globe*, December 3, 1984, 15.

15

UNDERSTANDING SARAH

During the last half of her career, Sarah's health had been a subject of intense speculation. As instances of blackouts became more frequent and noticeable, it was suggested Sarah was afflicted with narcolepsy. At a 1975 performance of *Falstaff*, she had to restart *da capo* to coordinate the orchestra and fell asleep during the final fugue. Her reputation was saved by first-rate players, an experienced cast, and a concertmaster desperately throwing signals to keep the performance going. Despite the final applause that awakened Sarah, not everyone was oblivious to anything amiss. Michael Steinberg, the *Boston Globe* critic at the time, commented, "The lusterless and muddy strings, raucous and out-of-tune woodwinds, never did come to sound really with it."[1] Subsequent performances of Bellini's *I Capuleti ed i Montecchi* were conducted by her assistant, William Fred Scott.

For some time, Sarah had been in the habit of closing her eyes, not only at board meetings, but also at opera conferences, where her appearance was referred to as that of "a benign Buddha" by some with bemusement. Those more sympathetic claimed that Sarah's mind was so full of ideas and possibilities that she had to "shut down the visual to accommodate them."[2] Sarah herself later explained it as a deliberate tactic on her part, adding, "How else am I going to know what they're saying about me when they think I'm not listening?"[3] At rehearsals, particularly the long and tedious ones to set up lighting cues, Sarah would indulge in catnaps. Just when the lighting technicians thought she had nodded off, her clarion voice would suddenly cut through the air of the dimly lit theater: "That one to your left, move it!"[4]

Her continuous drive to be the last word on all matters, large and small, had taken its toll. The use of amphetamines by those in the performing arts was then rife, and there was talk about a certain "physician to the stars" who prescribed a drug called "Miracle Max," the amphetamine du jour. As early as her fourth season, Sarah was using Benzedrine. With her lack of interests outside her work and her unwillingness to delegate decision, she welcomed anything that would keep her awake. She would slog on for days until she reached a satisfying stage in her current project (whatever it was), then crash. For years, she was known to occasionally recline in the aisles of the theater for brief intervals, or atop a pile of costumes backstage. Virtually everyone who performed with the company had a story of nearly stepping on Sarah's inert form, indistinguishable in the aisle of a darkened theater prior to opening night. But this pattern was observed as early as her Tanglewood student days, when she auditioned and became a part of the student orchestra program in the late 1940s and was occasionally found sleeping in the orchestra pit. By this time, Sarah's neglect of self had taken hold as she gained excessive weight, no longer feeling shame about her girth *or* hygiene.

When rehearsals for her 1962 production of Verdi's *Rigoletto* came along, Sarah's fatigue and exhaustion had finally gotten to her. What the opening night audience saw almost resembled the 1935 Marx Brothers film *A Night at the Opera* rather than the product of any gifted and serious director. Sarah failed to finish the staging of Act I when Gilda is abducted. She simply told the chorus to "wing it," leaving cast members in a quandary as to what to do.[5] Then, the orchestra got lost when Rigoletto re-entered, half of the players thinking that Sarah was conducting in two and the remainder that she was beating in four. Adding to the ignominy, the stage curtain could not lower—it was snagged on a projecting sconce, leaving part of it suspended.

To understand the apparent disintegration of the tower of strength Sarah seemed to be, it is necessary to step back to her beginnings. It was then that she learned to vehemently drive herself, at the cost of balance and her health. The need to succeed, despite formidable odds, was something instilled in Sarah at an early age by her mother, Carrie Margaret Baker. Carrie Margaret's determination to survive would later be transferred to Sarah with emphasis on economic security, wise counsel that had been given her by a well-respected author and music educator, Osbourne McConathy, Sr., then on the faculty of Northwestern in a sabbatical stint from Boston. Coincidentally, a generation later, his son Osbourne McConathy, Jr., would become a key and sometimes behind-the-scenes figure in Sarah's life in a semiromantic attachment.

Sarah's bond with "Ozzie," as McConathy was called, was to last all the years of her life, with many ups and downs. He pursued the path of a horn player, and for a time was part of the BSO ensemble. His appointment ended, it was said, due to a superseding commitment to alcohol and a brawl that left him with a busted lip. For a time, he served as assistant music librarian for the BSO until he got into an altercation with Erich Leinsdorf that precipitated a parting of the ways. He taught at Boston University in the late 1950s and found himself next door to Sarah Caldwell, who, while department head at BU, was then doing wildly creative things with her budding opera workshop and later with her newly founded Boston Opera Group.

In the midst of Sarah's second season, Ozzie joined the company to conduct *Tosca*, his first assignment. On the evening of his debut, he appeared at the Donnelly Memorial very much under the influence. He became unruly when told that he could *not* go on. Several cast members tried to restrain him, as did Sarah. In the struggle, McConathy suddenly broke free and decked Sarah. That she was able to go on in his place was, in itself, an amazing display of the total self-control and grim determination that she often exhibited in the face of trying circumstances. She conducted the performance as if nothing had happened. As for McConathy, it took three cast members to force him out the stage door.[6]

Two weeks later, he finally raised his baton in a performance of *Hansel and Gretel*. McConathy turned out to be one of Sarah's "causes," in which she could play the role of redeeming heroine, a la Senta or Brünnhilde, one who could save him from his personal addiction to alcohol. But Ozzie had a wife and family. Sarah would have to settle for living with certain facts that could not be changed, if she wanted him as a helpmate to sleuth through operatic dustbins and prepare scores for historically informed performances.

Sarah had heard mention of McConathy's father, the music educator and author from her mother's days at Northwestern. When Sarah later chanced upon Ozzie at BU, it must have registered that another generation had come full circle. Sarah must have felt preordained to feel an even deeper bond with him, owing to past associations, yet tempered with the deep sadness that his weakness for alcohol was the same affliction that had brought down Edwin Fletcher Caldwell and ended her parents' marriage. Even so, some went on to suggest a romantic bond, with various trysts rumored. In particular, it was said that Ozzie had a decided interest in "larger-form women," and Sarah was one of his dalliances.[7]

This predilection of Ozzie did not stop with Sarah. While in rehearsal for Verdi's *Otello*, Ozzie's attention was seized by the appearance of Dorothy Cole, a hefty mezzo-soprano in the lesser role of Emilia, Desdemona's lady attendant. During a break, witnesses recall Ozzie in hot pursuit of Ms. Cole around the set while Sarah's eyes filled with tears.

On more than one occasion, Sarah was seen weeping over McConathy's womanizing and drinking problems. In spite of the obvious difficulties, Sarah's fondness for him still shone through, both professionally and personally, and nothing was ever done to completely sever the bond. In fact, in many instances, Sarah went out of her way to praise McConathy's abilities to orchestral members. At the conclusion of the performance of the aforementioned *Hansel*, he received a standing ovation from the pit. Sarah reasoned that such displays would renew his faith in his abilities, allowing him to rise to a superior level and bring out the best in him as an artist. In spite of the lip debility that forced him to lay down his horn forever, Ozzie was still, in his own way, a perceptive musician, one who could also show an affinity for the text. Still, McConathy instinctively felt that Sarah would never tolerate a conductor, pet or not, who might eclipse her own star. Therefore, it was left to Sarah to suffer the pangs of unrequited love and follow in the footsteps of so many writers, poets, and others of a creative bent who had channeled their deepest longings and frustrations into their creative art.

In later years, the one person Sarah cared most for was her possessive and tyrannical mother. Whether this sprang from her need to continually seek parental approval or as a result of demands made on her by Carrie Margaret, one was never sure. But the relationship was double-edged. Years after Sarah's well-earned success, Carrie Margaret continued to make impromptu and out-of-context remarks addressed to virtual strangers. "I always told Sarah she should get her doctorate degree in music."

By 1969, Sarah's stepfather, Henry McMillan Alexander, suffered a heart attack and passed from the scene. Shortly thereafter, Carrie Margaret started to neglect herself. Former friends from Maryville who chanced to call on her while in the Fayetteville area were shocked at her condition. Midday found Carrie Margaret answering the door dressed in a soiled nightgown, her hair mussed, having misplaced her dentures. Her appearance was a far cry from the immaculate dresser they had known in former times. Shortly, Sarah would be obliged to take matters in hand and move Carrie Margaret to Boston.

From then on, she was a presence at both rehearsals and performances, social functions or any occasion honoring Sarah's latest triumph. Sarah never showed any embarrassment over the fact that Carrie Margaret was toothless, and there was speculation that Sarah had given up on replacing lost or misplaced dentures. But there were those who saw a darker or more sinister motive, suggesting the "disappearance" of her mother's dentures was not accidental. After all, it had the ameliorating effect of silencing her mother, whose comments sometimes made Sarah uncomfortable.

Although genuinely proud of her daughter, Carrie Margaret could still sound as if she were trumping Sarah's experiences or achievements. When Sarah was preparing Massenet's *Don Quichotte*, Carrie Margaret recalled earlier times when she had seen the work at the old Chicago Opera Company with Mary Garden and Vanni Marcoux, implying it was theatrically and/or vocally on a higher plain than Sarah's effort. Her claims of superior perceptions extended beyond her daughter. When Sarah traveled to Berlin in 1964 to witness the world premiere of Roger Sessions's opera *Montezuma*, Carrie Margaret was a part of Sarah's entourage. She did not take kindly to dissenting views and could oftentimes be spitefully querulous. When an angry demonstration erupted at the conclusion against the production and the work, Carrie Margaret came to the defense of the composer, managing to get into fisticuffs with a protestor.

Sarah continued to maintain a close watch over her mother, even taking her along on the annual visits to East Berlin, then reached by crossing a heavily fortified border in the middle of the divided city. While most visitors to the "East" made it a point to avoid more than one trip per day, Sarah or those traveling with her found themselves pushing her mother's wheelchair through "Checkpoint Charlie" twice daily in each direction to attend rehearsals and evening performances.

Carrie Margaret also accompanied Sarah to Washington for concerts at Wolf Trap, even while suffering bouts of incontinency, a condition that infuriated the housekeeping staff at the Mayflower Hotel. Sarah and her mother were reportedly barred from returning there. A similar situation arose on the Opera New England circuit, with Carrie Margaret soiling just about every bed in Pomfret, Connecticut, it was said. Back in Boston, Carrie Margaret's sudden appearance at rehearsals caused staff members to scurry about, placing a rubber sheet across a certain dedicated seat in the orchestra just before her arrival in the auditorium. The lengths to which Sarah would go to placate her mother's needs were sometimes painful to witness, according to staff members at the time. One had the impression that Carrie Margaret's willingness to put her daughter through such daily humiliations, combined with reports of her more than slighting remarks about Sarah to bystanders, may have sprung from a hidden envy of her daughter's success, or possible desire for her failure.

Partly through the intervention of generous patrons, Sarah and her invalid mother acquired a house with ample grounds in the Boston suburb of Lincoln; a house whose gloomy atmosphere inspired her associates to refer to it as "the bunker." Peter Sellars, whom Sarah was to invite to produce Handel's *Giulio Cesare* in her OCB 1987 season, once owned a house designed by Frank Lloyd Wright. Sarah also craved the cachet of residing in a modern house, as if to show the world she championed those who worked on the cutting edge. The bunker was designed and built by Mary Otis Stevens and her husband, Thomas McNally, who raised their three children there. Stevens had once worked in the office of Walter Gropius, which suited Sarah just fine.

Sarah's next-door neighbor and closest friend was Olga Monks Pertzoff, grandniece of John Lowell "Jack" Gardner (the husband of Isabella Stewart Gardner, benefactress of Boston's famous museum). Olga's husband, architect Constantine Pertzoff, had designed their home. Olga served as the first vice president of Sarah's Boston Opera Group and Opera Company of Boston. Also a talented costume designer, Olga created costumes for Sarah's 1961 production of *Otello*, as well as for a local theater group in Concord. Olga hosted chamber concerts in her home, which pleased Sarah.

When completed in the mid-1960s, *LIFE* magazine called the Stevens/McNulty house "a sculpture for living . . . a house without windows or doors." Its iconic image graced the pages of European architectural magazines. *Architectural Forum* paid homage by featuring the house on its cover. But in Lincoln, most regarded it as an aesthetic outcast.

A bird's-eye view would have shown the house as a narrow series of advancing concavities or elongated arcs that embraced the landscape. Inside, the interior round spaces displayed a discernible acoustical echo, making conversation awkward.

Sarah furnished the house with contemporary classic pieces—Ludwig Mies van der Rohe, Gropius, and Alvar Aalto. "Mostly uncomfortable" was the comment regarding Sarah's house furnishings from those who called. But in Sarah's view, they were "pure."

The structure itself was poured concrete, inside and out, topped by a flat roof. The oddly constructed two-story house largely consisted of a ground floor that, like a two-tiered wedding cake, was considerably longer than the second floor. By the curved exterior walls of the house stood several fruit trees that soon died upon Sarah taking occupancy, possibly out of neglect. The interior walls had no plaster topping, which made driving a nail to hang a picture a near impossibility. There was radiant heating that functioned unevenly. Cracked glass panes in the skylight let in outside air. The house was unheatable! Finally, out of desperation, Sarah installed a wood stove.

The interior had no doors, making it easily navigable for wheelchair-bound Carrie Margaret. There was not even a door to the master bedroom. In a bathroom, Sarah had a hose bib installed plus a drain in the tiled floor. When Carrie Margaret had an "accident," it would be easier for Sarah to simply wheel her mother to the bathroom and hose her down.

Still, no amount of money kept the roof from leaking. A former owner observed, "When it rained, the walls wept!" Water ran down the walls and large buckets around the house collected drips. Sarah soon summoned Mary Otis Stevens, and it was agreed that the ceiling and walls would be plastered.

Despite all the problems, Sarah adored the house. When the property was sold in 2001, the new owners simply tore it down. Its demolition caused architectural scholars and conservators much hand wringing. Sarah also suffered much anguish, even if the anguish was double-edged. She had every reason to suspect the new owners were intent on razing the house but went through with the deal in the hope of realizing sufficient proceeds from the sale to save her opera house.

Some years after, one of Sarah's associates recalled a particular Thanksgiving dinner at the house, described as a "Thanksgiving dinner from hell!" As was often the case, Sarah and her mother were in a tug-of-war. Sarah was busy in the kitchen basting a turkey in the oven under Carrie Margaret's watchful eye. Suddenly, another, less attractive, aroma signaled that Carrie Margaret had suffered an accident. Hardly showing any annoyance with the interruption, Sarah immediately attended to matters by wheeling her mother into a bathroom, and on this occasion, deliberately or otherwise, Sarah did not properly adjust the water temperature. From a far-off corner of the house, screams erupted. It was Carrie Margaret upbraiding Sarah, "You're killing me!"

Sarah also showed considerable compassion for her half-brother, George Baker Alexander, despite the gap in their ages. Not long after George was born, family friends noted a decided shift in Carrie Margaret's attention away from Sarah, in favor of George. As a young man, George was sturdy and athletic, with a glancing interest in a career as a professional baseball player. In the 1950s, after Sarah moved into her more ample Boston Back Bay quarters, Carrie Margaret was on the telephone from Fayetteville, Arkansas. "Why can't George come and stay with you?"

Acceding to her mother's demand, George arrived in Boston and moved in with Sarah for a time, while Sarah took considerable pains to find gainful employment for George. Finally, a kindly board member of Sarah's company, having learned of George's plight, found work for him in the mailroom of his medium-sized firm in a distant city. Now out of Sarah's hair, George was assigned menial chores, operating the duplicating machine, stuffing envelopes, and affixing postage.

By the time of Sarah's debut at the Met, George and his new wife were among the well-wishers, but the marriage soon ended. A second union with an older woman fared even worse. She left him as George became more confused and was eventually institutionalized. With Carrie Margaret's passing, Sarah's close associates hoped she would be free of such burdens. Instead, Sarah was a presence in George's remaining years and attended to his needs.

While Sarah maintained a public display of patience and forbearance with her mother, it was often her colleagues who found themselves the brunt of Sarah's unexpected rancor, particularly when they bore news Sarah was loath to hear. While planning her production of Mozart's *Abduction from the Seraglio* in her seventh season, she had occasion to speak with Warren Storey Smith, by then an esteemed Boston music critic. Hoping it was a "first," Sarah asked if the opera had ever been heard in Boston. When informed otherwise, Sarah became so testy that she snubbed him for some time thereafter.

Other of Sarah's peccadillos occasionally gave pause: her almost slav-ish habit to seek the company of those she most admired or those who exercised levers of power. When Edward Brooke, the African American senator from Massachusetts, was serving as treasurer of her board of trustees, at social functions Sarah would often refer to the senator as "Mr. President," even though few, if any, regarded him as a presidential hopeful. Likewise, when her company was on the ropes in the nineties, Sarah often expressed her delight when Bill Clinton, "a fellow Arkansan," became president. On one of her several visits to Yekaterin-burg, Sarah chanced to encounter Clinton while he was on an official state visit in the company of the then-president of Russia, Boris Yeltsin. In subsequent conversations, Sarah often referred to Clinton as "my Bill" when speaking of her current effort to engage HUD in an urban re-newal project in Boston that would rescue her theater. It was her way of suggesting a possible bond with those influential in wielding levers of power.

Sarah was no stranger to visits to the White House. During the John-son years, Sarah was invited to present Offenbach's *Voyage to the Moon* during an entertainment in the East Room honoring the president of Turkey. Sarah was most excited about meeting former secretary of state Dean Acheson. Puzzled by the admission, one of the performers in her group asked Sarah whom else she admired most. Without hesitation, Sarah replied, "Dean Acheson, Fritz Kreisler, and Jesus Christ, in that order."[8]

Sarah's primary focus was producing opera and bringing to her au-diences works she felt could be shown in a new and relevant light. When it came to press interviews, it was soon evident that there was not much else to tell about Sarah. She had no other interests and simply stated that opera was her all-consuming passion, one that left little time for other pursuits.

Within two weeks of Sarah's Massachusetts General Hospital stay, her condition began to improve. She was now breathing without the aid of a respirator, but a full recovery seemed far away. Seeing no alterna-tive, in a near split decision, her board voted to cancel the 1985 season. No further announcement was made before Sarah resumed her duties. Notice of the season's cancellation urged subscribers to contribute the cost of the lost ticket to financially aid the company. Still, the company's subsidiary educational and outreach endeavors would continue, in-cluding the already-planned Opera New England tour and Opera Ball.

On Valentine's Day, Sarah was discharged to the Boston Spaulding Rehabilitation Hospital, where she had convalesced for a full month, shedding forty-seven of her three hundred pounds. By mid-March she headed to Florida's Harbor Island to continue her recuperation but was still more delicate than she or the hospital had thought. Consequently, Sarah returned to Spaulding for an extended period of recovery.

Sarah completed her rehab by early May and returned to Boston but was cautious enough to rent a small apartment near the hospital. Later that month, a thinner but still overweight Sarah made her first public appearance at a press luncheon at the LaFayette Hotel, wearing a bright lavender dress with a sailor bow. She further claimed to be donning running shoes each morning in order to walk two miles a day, boasting that on the previous morning, she even commenced tennis lessons. Sarah dryly observed, "I am deeply aware of the special miracle granted to me that makes it possible to be here. I don't remember engaging in so much physical activity since I was in Girl Scout camp. I left after an encounter with quicksand. I haven't been near quicksand since, though I've skated on a lot of thin ice."[9] After further cracks about her tennis skills, or lack thereof, she stressed her renewed dedication to the company she had created, promising that she had learned lessons from the setback.

NOTES

1. Michael Steinberg, "Caldwell's *Falstaff* as a Dirty Old Man," *Boston Globe*, February 7, 1975, 18.

2. Michael Kaye (Opera Company of Boston staff member, 1970–1972), interview by the author, January 4, 2000.

3. James Billings, interview by the author, March 8, 2000.

4. Edgar Vincent (former Caldwell manager), interview by the author, March 15, 2000.

5. James Billings, interview by the author, March 8, 2000.

6. Ibid.

7. Herbert Senn, interview by the author, August 18, 2000.

8. Mac Morgan (baritone), interview by the author, December 16, 2000.

9. Richard Dyer, "Caldwell Back at Work with Opera Company," *Boston Globe*, May 2, 1985, 14.

16

SARAH'S
INDIAN SUMMER

After Sarah's near-fatal illness, she promised to cut back on any guest conducting, even admitting that she had tried to do too many things. Now, it was going to be different. Fund-raising, an arduous chore, was delegated to others during the rehearsal and performing phases of her work so that Sarah could concentrate on artistic matters. In a moment of whimsy, Sarah admitted, "I should have paid more attention to that parable about the loaves and the fishes, when I was in Bible school." Additional assistant stage directors were hired along with a "cover" conductor, who could step in should the need arise. One of her perks was a car and driver. She would no longer have to wonder where she had parked her car (often towed). As to her new home in Lincoln, Sarah told a reporter, "Now I'm only fifteen minutes from Copley Square."

There was more talk of establishing an endowment, a subject that never seemed to get off the ground. Everyone wanted to pitch in. Area restaurants were offering discounts on pretheater dinners to encourage attendance.

The canceled 1985 season left the company bereft of a $1.5 million projected cash flow that would have helped sustain it. Staff morale remained high, with some laboring on without pay. Sarah continued her accustomed roles as conductor and stage director. After five performances of Humperdinck's *Hansel and Gretel* for the holiday season, Sarah roused herself with rehearsals for a revival of her 1983 production of Puccini's *Turandot*, with its fabulous costumes much admired by the Boston public. Next followed the long-promised American premiere of Peter Maxwell Davies's *Taverner*, an event that brought back many of the out-of-town music critics. A further boost came with the company's first incursion into the operas of Leoš Janáček, his *Makropulos Case*.

For the Janáček opera, it was to Sarah's credit that she assembled a strong cast, including the company debut of German soprano Anja Silja in one of her signature roles, the flamboyant Emilia Marty. Not in the least daunted by the complexities of this nettlesome score, Sarah seemed to relish it, eliciting fine playing. Sarah's design team, Pond/Senn, did their homework, researching the Prague designs seen in the original Karel Čapek play. But what graced the stage of the Savoy was infinitely more elegant and atmospheric, eliminating the harshness of the original sets. Local costume designer Alfred Fiandaca attempted but did not always succeed in providing comparable costumes. The public response to Janáček's opera exceeded expectations for a work that was little known at the time. The last performance, a Sunday matinee, found the Savoy filled to 85 percent capacity.

With company finances in dire straits, only three operas were originally scheduled for the 1987 season, which Sarah said would provide more focus. Later, a fourth was added, Handel's *Giulio Cesare*, with the entire production team, director, and conductor brought intact from the State University of New York Purchase campus. Earlier, director Peter Sellars had done interesting theater work in the Boston community in partnership with Craig Smith, a conductor of concerts and choral works at Boston's Emmanuel Church. After recovering from her pneumonia, Sarah entered negotiations with the Sellars/Smith team to bring their *Giulio Cesare* production to Boston. It was the embodiment of the kind of innovative approach Sarah worked so hard to foster in the lyric theater.

Boston audiences showed an evident affection for Sellars and gave him a warmer reception than was accorded by the cold and hostile New York audience at Purchase, where *Giulio Cesare* fared less well at the box office. Local audiences' reactions to the Sellars/Smith duo ranged from "Who is this Craig Smith?" to "Where is the Emmanuel Church?" *Giulio Cesare* drew a younger audience, helping to restore a level of validation for the company. One of the obstacles that hobbled Sarah's fund-raising was her failure to understand that in both the public and private sectors, there was a natural reluctance to support an organization too closely allied to a particular individual. Imports such as the Sellars/Smith *Cesare* helped lessen that impression.

The company deficit now exceeded $4.5 million, a sum not only troublesome in itself but beyond any plan of attenuation. Since no one seemed to know what to do about it, the situation languished. One of the more enticing proposals bandied about by city officials was a projected $14 million bailout. Under this plan, the Boston Redevelopment Authority would apply for state funding, while the Massachusetts legislature responded with funds sufficient to buy the Savoy, which would be leased back to the Opera Company of Boston for a token sum. The plan called for the city to pay $7.8 million for the theater and another $6 million to restore it.

That was only part of the problem. The Savoy, after nine years of use, was in serious need of renovation. Engineers and conservators estimated the sum to exceed $10 million. At the time of purchase, limited resources were used only to effect emergency repairs. Meanwhile, the Mason Street expansion was on hold for lack of municipal approval and funds. If the legislature approved the deal, the needed improvements would fall to the state of Massachusetts.

As if immune from the financial chaos swirling about her, Sarah was full of bold ideas and possible projects. After her near-terminal bout with pneumonia, Sarah obtained permission from French composer Olivier Messiaen to stage the American premiere of his *St. Francis of Assisi*, but the work would entail a large orchestra and was therefore put on hold.

In the meantime, for her 1988 season, Sarah would offer Luigi Cherubini's *Medée*, previously promised subscribers. Sarah's penchant for travel and research led her to Greece, where she convinced composer Michael Christodoulides to write new recitatives in Greek to replace the music Bavarian composer Franz Lachner had written.

Medée was first produced in 1797 and contained patches of dialogue that later drew the attention of many composers and arrangers, including Lachner (1803–1890). But Cherubini's opera was originally wedded to heroic spoken lines, or classical Alexandrines, interspersed with sung parts. Once there were singers of the great classical tradition who could declaim the spoken lines. Musicologists and Francophiles had bemoaned their absence from the world's stages. Only they would have done justice to the score as Cherubini knew it, and they no longer existed.

With the passage of time, Ester Mazzoleni revived the role for La Scala in 1909 with Lachner's recitatives translated into Italian (*Medea*), making it the version most often performed. It became one of Maria Callas's calling cards. Before recording the opera, Callas had sung the role on the stage, first in Florence in 1953, and later in Venice, Rome, Dallas, and Paris. Sopranos such as Leyla Gencer, Magda Olivero, Eileen Farrell, and Leonie Rysanek followed suit.

Sarah's preference was for Cherubini's original *Medée*, shorn of Lachner's tamperings. It would resemble the original French version, to which new music would be added. However, the newly composed recitative would not be in a pseudo-nineteenth-century style flattering to Cherubini's score. Christodoulides' musical style would be electronic, a modern idiom. Into this mix would be added the taped voices of actors intoning classical Greek, to which the buskers mimed. Jonathan Richmond, writing for the *Christian Science Monitor*, reported, "Ultimately . . . the transitions between ancient Greek and French diluted rather than complemented the Cherubini work."[1] Sarah's trips to Greece notwithstanding, her assumption of a Greek connection was a tenuous one at best, for Cherubini's librettist, Francois Benoit Hoffmann, used as its origins the Latin dramatist Seneca and not the Greek play by Euripides. The dialogue could very well have been in Latin. But Lachner's Latin solution, in a version derived from Seneca, would probably not have pleased a number of Greek Americans living in the Boston area who Sarah had enlisted for financial backing.

Sarah's planned French Medée was Shirley Verrett. She had sung the demanding role at the Palais Garnier in Italian in 1986. But Sarah's production called for Ms. Verrett to share the stage with a competing "actress" Medée, who mimed spoken lines. Upon learning this, Verrett withdrew from the project, leaving Sarah stranded. Jon Vickers, who was to sing the role of Jason also deserted Sarah, feigning excuses, claiming he was not "physically, emotionally, or vocally up to the role." It would be left to Sarah to convince her house tenor, Joseph Evans, to step into the void on short notice.

Miraculously, *Medée* opened on January 22 with the atmospheric sets of John Cardella providing a suitable framework for the classical style of the piece. To her credit, Sarah restored all of the cuts, giving her audiences a chance to hear the complete score. Under her baton, the orchestra seemed well rehearsed and gave a propulsive reading of Cherubini's music. However, Josephine Barstow, Verrett's replacement, found herself in a tug-of-war with the actress Medée. Exhibiting true professionalism, Barstow delivered the goods. Although her French could best be described as "Franglais," Barstow's portrait ranged from delicate phrases to stentorian outbursts.

Critic Andrew Porter praised Barstow and was less critical of Sarah than the Boston and New York critics, who seemed to abhor Sarah's cut-and-pasted version of the score that they knew from the Callas recording. Porter added, "In most ways, this Boston *Medée* was the revelation of Cherubini's great opera that we have glimpsed again and again but have waited for decades to discover." And as to Sarah's conducting, he added, "Miss Caldwell may not have the baton competence of an Ozawa or a Mehta. She has something more important: instinct and understanding that lead listeners to the heart of a score. The power, the inventiveness, and the beauty of the music blazed." Of Joseph Evans's Jason, Porter noted, "Joseph Evans sang the role cleanly, clearly, and fully. It is time he learned to bear himself like a prince, not the boy next door."[2] Jeanne Ommerle proved herself to be a luminescent Dirce, while Markella Hatziano's mezzo offered a rich-sounding Neris. Jonathan Richmond of the *Christian Science Monitor* noted, "The most beautiful aria of the evening came from Markella Hatziano, singing Neris's 'Ah, nos peines seront communes.' The purity of her voice, profound grief, and introspective thought it communicated were most affecting."[3] If Porter's measured thumbs-up was a balm, Sarah's *Medée* aroused more controversy than anything she had ever attempted and brought upon her the harshest words yet from her critics and public.

Sarah's 1989 production of Leonard Bernstein's *Mass* was her last effort that could be ranked as a piece of innovative theater, originally serving as a *pièce d' occasion* for the 1971 Washington Kennedy Center opening. Mindful of the success Sarah had laid at his feet with her 1950 Tanglewood *Trouble in Tahiti*, Bernstein traveled to Boston for the premiere.

While *Trouble in Tahiti* dabbled in fifties topicality, *Mass* was mired in sixties street talk. It trafficked superficially in such things as the icons of the Latin Church and its liturgy. On stage was an odd assortment—a rock band, jazz players, and two hundred choristers. Very little of it was not amplified. Furthermore, it was eclectic, incorporating selections from the works of Bernstein and other composers. Many found it superficial, cloying, and in bad taste.

Bernstein fashioned his *Mass* by taking a leaf from Stravinsky's *Symphony of Psalms*, mounting it on a similar framework of the Catholic Mass, from "Kyrie eleison" to "Agnus dei." As for the text, Bernstein,

Stephen Schwartz, and Paul Simon cobbled together wording that resulted in such lines as (in the "Gloria") "half the people are stoned and the other half are waiting for the next election." There were also oblique but topical references to the Catholic Berrigan brothers, priests who had gone to jail in opposition to the Vietnam War. With this work, Bernstein tested the tenets of faith, depicting an ailing Church, unable to cope with matters of conscience and dissent. Was not the central figure, the celebrant, a surrogate for Leonard Bernstein? Had not Bernstein occasionally dabbled in radical chic, one from whom so much was expected?

Wisely, Sarah changed the focus from the celebrant to the other participants and their aspirations. Originally, the role was created by Alan Titus, a baritone. But Sarah wanted a tenor, Siegfried Jerusalem, for the part. However, he canceled at the last minute, leaving Sarah to scramble for a replacement. Previously, Sarah had the habit of delaying casting, saying in jest, "Oh, everyone is available at the last minute." This time, as luck would have it, she was not put to the test. A certain Welsh baritone, Richard Morris, was located. Not only was he the very embodiment of what Sarah was seeking, a handsome, strapping, man, but he somehow conveyed the right Christlike innocence, yet was still capable of portraying of a man on the edge of a mental breakdown, ready to shatter the cross and rend himself of his garments in a moment of desperation.

The excellent sets of the Pond/Senn team and the striking costumes of Carrie Robbins did much to bring off the piece, along with the sheer exuberance of the performance, which carried the day. The cost of providing costumes for the exceptionally large chorus would have defeated the project, as would have the question of where to place them on the shallow stage of the old vaudeville house. Herbert Senn suggested the use of translucent three-dimensional design panels behind which the choristers were arrayed in rows, clad in rented black choir robes. A flick of a switch made them materialize before the astonished eyes of the spectator, but otherwise invisible. The effect allowed Sarah to achieve one of her trademark moments of magic.

Following the curtain calls, Leonard Bernstein rushed up onstage, knelt down, and in a courtly gesture, kissed Sarah's hand in a show of deep gratitude for her valiant efforts. While there were many who argued that Bernstein's *Mass* was not technically an opera, most readily agreed—thanks to Sarah—it was one hell of a show!

Although buoyed by the unexpected success of *Mass*, by the time 1990 rolled around, Sarah was on the cusp of her last Boston season, her company tottering on the edge of financial ruin with little hope of rescue. Virtually nothing had been done (or could be done) to alleviate the company's finances, short of a massive bailout. As funds were gathered, casting would follow. Artists were summoned on relatively short notice. Continued borrowing had catapulted the company's debt to almost unmanageable fiscal levels. A new board president, Robert Cannon, worked through the previous season effecting certain changes. For one, he commenced the subscription drive earlier, claiming he had increased revenues by 50 percent. Disaffected subscribers were urged (without success) to return to the fold.

Company debts had ballooned to nearly $6 million and growing. Dissension erupted among Sarah's normally submissive board, resulting in several resignations. For years, Sarah had managed to play her cards right. Now, she was on thin ice, not only with her public, but also with her board. They relied on Sarah in all her capacities, with the realization that she held the aces, while they held the deuces. As if caught unexpectedly in a game of high-stakes poker, their choices were either to fold or to gamble on the next hand.

A transition committee would meet secretly with members of the Boston corporate world and private sources to see what could be done. What they heard was not positive. Resentment lingered over Sarah's singular management style and high-handedness, aggravated by the failure of the OCB board to rein her in and allow the company to achieve a sound financial footing. Therefore, fund-raising was at an impasse since few contributions were possible as long as Sarah remained in control. Robert Cannon and certain board members were emboldened to think in terms of other possibilities.

By 1990, in Boston and elsewhere, performing arts costs had risen dramatically to the point that it became increasingly difficult for various entities to sustain themselves, with each competing for its share of the fund-raising pie. One source of funding that offered hope was spurred on by the demise of the annual Met tour, but that organization was considering importing the New York City Opera. Fund-raising had become more fragmented than before.

The deteriorating Savoy Theater was of primary concern; with the failure of the Massachusetts legislature to allocate funds·to the "convention authority" to repair the theater, no other sizeable money source was available. Now there was a risk that the city inspectors might declare the theater unfit for health and safety reasons and shut it down. While the roof had been temporarily repaired, lingering ceiling water damage caused chunks of plaster to fall on the heads of patrons. A temporary solution was reached when the Pond/Senn team came up with a creative solution that would stave off the loss of the theater's entertainment license. It was to erect, paint, and fit into place a large ceiling canopy, or velarium.

In the meantime, a board power struggle led to the suspension of Robert Cannon. But the suspension was only temporary, as it was determined that he had done nothing wrong, and he was reinstated. Some were opposed to any additional borrowing. Feeding on the disarray, Cannon decided to strike out on his own with a company free of Caldwell's control. Central to this plan was to entice the municipal authority to buy the theater through a nonprofit corporation that would be set up to control it, with the usurping Cannon as its head. It would then put in place the artistic team of Sellars/Smith. It was suggested Sarah could be involved in a peripheral way, possibly mounting one production a season, adhering to strict budgetary constraints. Peter Sellars indicated his interest in the proposal but refused to take any personal initiative, out of deference to Sarah, whom he deeply admired and regarded as a friend.

Canon further claimed he had obtained a commitment from the erstwhile Boston Opera Association to cooperate. What Cannon did not appreciate at the time, and what Sarah knew all too well, was each Boston opera-producing entity had always functioned individually, playing more or less to its own constituency. Cannon was unable to succeed where others had also failed. He resigned and set up shop in a Boston office located in the city's Flower Market. At a press conference, he announced the formation of a new company with Peter Sellars and Craig Smith. In spite of the hoopla, press heraldry, and talk of future plans, the new enterprise never got off the ground.

Throughout, Sarah's posture was one of detachment, or feigned indifference to the politics swirling about her, while adopting the cloak of one who suffers for the sake of her calling, telling a *Globe* reporter, "I am an artist."

Just as Sarah's 1990 got under way, an explosion rocked the theater as fire erupted from inside a manhole located on Mason Street, filling the theater with smoke and sending a few staffers into the street. For several hours, the evening performance seemed to hang in the balance as doors were flung open to dissipate the fumes. The cause was reported to be electrical, although the exact sequence of events leading to the explosion was never fully explained. With full electrical service restored, the evening's performance of *Madama Butterfly* would proceed. Arriving patrons found the ticket office in a state of chaos due to lack of power, with the performance delayed some twenty minutes. Like so many of the recent difficulties besetting the company, the explosion and fire seemed to portend the close of an era. As the winter days passed, a cold chill hung in the air. The chill had its analog inside the theater. It was speculated that austere measures dictated a low thermostatic setting, or possibly it was the failure of the much-neglected heating system to generate sufficient BTUs. Also evident was a general feeling of malaise: reading a program became a trial, ceiling fixtures contributed little illumination, with burned-out bulbs not replaced. At intermission, crowds streamed toward the restrooms where many of the toilet stalls were boarded up. Occasionally, there was water on the floor. Faucets did not work.

Finances for the company's 1990 season were so chronically squeezed that anything beyond a bare-bones budget was not feasible. Subscribers were offered three operas instead of the customary four (and fewer performances). Sarah had again trotted out her much-admired production of *Madama Butterfly*, offering three different versions, offset by several sopranos who took on the title role. Richard Dyer referred to "a parade of Butterflies" from mid-January to March. The next offering was Mozart's *Magic Flute*, with sets by the Pond/Senn team and borrowed costumes.

Robert DiDomenica's *Balcony* ended the season with only two performances on June 14 and 17, the last opera of Sarah's company in that theater. A third performance was canceled due to poor box-office receipts. Although the reason was known, Sarah asserted in a letter to her dwindling subscriber base that the cancellation stemmed from the need for additional rehearsals for this complex work.

DiDomenica's *Balcony*, taken from the Jean Genet play, is a piece set in a "house of illusion" (brothel) while the real world outside is engulfed in chaos and revolution. The subject may not have been ideal for conservative Boston, particularly when four of the protagonists, a bishop, a general, a judge, and a brothel madam, are scarcely characters that arouse much sympathy. They are seen indulging in wish fulfillment of their fantasies involving power and sex.

Genet, like many playwrights before him, insisted on holding up a mirror to his audience. In the case of *The Balcony*, the image was not a flattering one. Sarah's staging, with her design team and costumes by Susan Tsu, coalesced in a compelling and realistic production. Mignon Dunn was Irma, the head madam. Leighton Kerner, writing for *The Village Voice*, noted, "I never realized Mignon Dunn . . . was capable of such relaxed but wounding humor. And predictably, the role's contralto range lay nicely for her still formidable voice."[4]

Susan Larson played the role of the tough prostitute, Carmen, and gave an impressive performance. Special praise was due Adele Nicholson, who had to act out some of the fantasies of the male characters. Noel Velasco, Spiro Malas, Richard Crist, and John Moulson offered fine portraits.

The opera was given with a short pause between the two parts instead of a full intermission, allowing the musical intensity to build. In spite of the dramatic possibilities inherent in the play, the tension led only to a muted conclusion when the audience is dismissed by Madame Irma, causing the opera to end with a whimper, instead of a bang. A lack of musical catharsis is hardly a characteristic one associates with the operas of Alban Berg, and coming from DiDomenica, who studied with a pupil of Berg, this was puzzling. DiDomenica's score left his audiences stranded. At no point in the opera did any of the characters reach a discernable epiphany or come to terms with their dilemma. Jazz elements were fused to atonal eruptions in the score. There were even scattered references to such diverse pieces as Bach's *Well-Tempered Clavier* and Glenn Miller's "In the Mood."

James R. Oestrich, writing for *The New York Times*, noted, "Mr. DiDomenica's *Balcony* is a wonderfully intelligent construct, overlaid with a lyrical and dramatic sensibility that makes searing emotional contact at many crucial points."[5] As to the worth of the piece, Richard Dyer, writing in the *Globe*, found the first three scenes "tough going." He attributed it to an assumption that "depiction of ugly things requires ugly music." He added, "Some of the vocal writing is exceptionally difficult. . . . Expository passage are almost always spoken, often accompanied by intricate percussion writing."[6] Ellen Pfeifer, reporting for the *Boston Herald*, noted, "Although some of the music fails to add anything to the already potent text, the best of it, particularly that written for Carmen, Madame Irma's favorite whore, does indeed enhance the words."[7] The boos of a few audience members did not override the generally positive reception the Boston public gave Robert DiDomenica's opera.

With the close of Sarah's last Boston season, the theater continued to be rented for an occasional rock concert that year, but by December, building-code violations caused the theater to be shuttered. Barring a miracle, it seemed, opera performances at the theater on Washington Street ended with "a fall" from *The Balcony*.

The loss of venue was the final blow. Many explained the demise of the company in terms of a noticeable decline in the product that eventually sent Sarah into a downward spiral. In the end, it was Caldwell's subscribers, they said, who were tired of being jerked around by opera cancellations and cast changes. Although the company managed to survive for a 1991 tour to Moscow with *The Balcony*, courtesy of U.S. taxpayers' money, dissension and defections from her board over an accumulated $8.5 million debt proved the last straw. One former board member volunteered, "Sarah left burn-out all over Boston."[8]

NOTES

1. Jonathan Richmond, "Caldwell's Vision vs. Fiscal Realism," *Christian Science Monitor*, January 29, 1988, 21.

2. Andrew Porter, "Musical Events," *New Yorker*, February 15, 1988, 93.

3. Jonathan Richmond, "Caldwell's Vision vs. Fiscal Realism."

4. Leighton Kerner, "Juice from Jean Genet," *Village Voice*, June 17, 1990, 85.

5. James R. Oestrich, "Jean Genet's *Balcony* Makes Debut as Opera." *New York Times*, June 17, 1990, 51.

6. Richard Dyer, "A Compelling *Balcony*," *Boston Globe*, June 15, 1990.

7. Ellen Peifer, "*Balcony*'s OPB High Point," *Boston Herald*, June 14, 1990.

8. Linda Cabot Black, interview by the author, October 15, 2001.

17

SARAH IN EXILE

With her exposure ever more limited, Sarah would be obliged to take advantage of any and every opportunity that came her way. Barely six months after the May 1991 reprise of her Moscow "Making Music Together" festival, Sarah led the opening concert of the symphony orchestra of Voronezh, Russia, an industrial city of eight hundred thousand souls close to the river Don. If Sarah Caldwell as conductor of Russian ensembles seemed an unlikely prospect, it was a move that was burnished through her former contacts with the Soviet Ministry of Culture.

It was only a short time after that Sarah was contacted by Boston University, the scene of her brilliant early workshop activities. They summoned her to conduct (but not direct) a student offering of Hans Werner Henze's *Elegy for Young Lovers*, a work thought to be beyond the capability of a fledgling effort. Unfortunately, the run of performances garnered mixed notices in spite of Sarah's input as conductor.

But by 1993, Caldwell was in Yekaterinburg, Russia, her transport to and from Boston courtesy of a generous Lufthansa Airlines. It was an undertaking that took her far from her home turf. Post-Soviet economic conditions were dire and Sarah's compensation nil, with only one commercial recording emerging from her efforts with her new ensemble.[1]

No sooner had she arrived than the difficulty musicians had in obtaining badly needed instrument parts (not easily accessible in post-Soviet Russia) became apparent. To her credit, Sarah did yeoman's service in an effort to rectify matters. Her luggage included extra violin bows and even aspirin. Through contacts back in Boston, Sarah arranged to have a harpsichord shipped off to Yekaterinburg, suggesting she had not given up on introducing new audiences to baroque opera.

While on her various Yekaterinburg sojourns between 1993 and 1997, the Philharmonic Society billeted Sarah among several small apartments and even assigned her a helpmate, one Eleana Shulyatyeva. Eleana spoke no English but moved in with Sarah, preparing her meals and attending to her laundry and various menial chores.

After orchestral rehearsals, Sarah often feted her Russian colleagues at local restaurants, picking up the tab in a spirit of generosity. Sarah ventured few, if any, Russian words, even in the most rudimentary situations, and relied on her assigned interpreter, Olga Voskoboinikova. Still, her Yekaterinburg hosts speculated Sarah understood more than she would allow, as if to "listen in" on what her Russian colleagues might be saying about her, thinking they were never the wiser.[2] It was a tack reminiscent of her onetime posture at OCB board meetings: "How else am I going to know what they're saying about me when they think I'm not listening?"

One of the more ambitious efforts of her Yekaterinburg sabbatical was a 1994 concert performance of Debussy's *Pelléas et Melisande*, then a novelty for her Russian audiences, featuring several artists formerly of her old company. Word of Sarah's activities occasionally surfaced in the *Globe*, but for the most part, little was ever mentioned or reported by the Boston media.

A late January 1996 visit offered the world premiere of Sergei Prokofiev's *Eugene Onegin*, an hour-and-twenty-minute narrative taken from Pushkin. Segments of the rehearsal and portions of the final performance were memorialized on film, *A Musical Adventure in Siberia with Sarah Caldwell*, by award-winning cinematographer Richard Leacock.[3] At Sarah's urging and promise of travel reimbursement by a financial angel, Leacock and his crew ventured to Yekaterinburg, where they were billeted in the most basic of accommodations. Formerly at MIT, in the sixties and seventies, Leacock had also worked for Sarah, providing arresting film sequences that were featured in several of her productions, while being already established as a cinéma vérité pioneer.

Before commencing the concert, Sarah turned from the podium and faced her audience. Via an interpreter she explained that the piece was banned in the Soviet time and was now having its world premiere. With cameras rolling, Sarah raised her baton while dressed in shamanlike attire and dangling beads, her face puffy with large bags under her eyes owing to her exuberant twenty-hour days in rehearsals with her ensemble. Sarah's Yekaterinburg colleagues marveled at her bright, luminous face and rosy cheeks, braced by the cold Siberian air, but the film captured her looking tired and haggard.

After viewing the film rushes of her Yekaterinburg performance, Sarah registered her displeasure, complaining she was shown as too hobbled and distraught. A decade on, Leacock's fifty-five-minute film was exhibited at the Fine Arts Museum in Boston and later at a Lincoln Center Film Society Awards presentation honoring Leacock. Following the Boston screening, Sarah reversed herself, withdrew her objections, and spoke glowingly of "Leacock's masterful work."[4]

As her Yekaterinburg experience drew to a close, Sarah's efforts might best be recalled in the way she reconfigured the seating for concert presentations at the hall, a spacious gallery of glass and mirrors. For the Prokofiev work, her approach allowed seating around circular tables from which refreshments were imbibed prior to the concert, rather than fixed seating rows facing the orchestra. Originally, society officials greeted with disdain her novel seating arrangement, but Sarah eventually won them over, and the practice continues to this day.

During, with her new Siberian venture, a May 1994 invitation roused Sarah to travel from her home in Lincoln to another faraway destination, Cape Town, South Africa, where she raised her baton over the Cape Philharmonic Orchestra on the nineteenth and twentieth of that month. The program featured Charles Ives's *Variations on America* (William Schuman's orchestration), Leonard Bernstein's Symphonic Dances from *West Side Story*, and Johannes Brahms's Symphony No. 1.

A possible January 1995 concert posed a question. Would Sarah serve gratis as conductor du jour for the financially ailing Florida Philharmonic while its regular conductor absented himself to engage in some last-minute fund-raising? Even though the ensemble later suffered financial collapse, it seemed an odd reversal of fortune for one who had so often sought to receive goods and services at little or no cost to herself. Yet believing it a rare opportunity to revive her American concert calendar, dormant for over a decade, and setting aside the ignominy, Sarah good-naturedly obliged. The offer, with hotel and travel reimbursement, came by way of a former OCB board member, now a South Florida resident and ardent supporter of the Florida "Phil." In any event, the conventional wisdom was that Sarah's podium presence would draw in the crowds.

Audiences in Boca Raton and Fort Lauderdale witnessed Handel's *Royal Fireworks Music*, followed by Prokofiev's *Peter and the Wolf*, narrated by baritone Thomas Stewart (paid for his services), concluding with Prokofiev's more complex Fifth Symphony.

The *Miami Herald*'s music critic, James Roos, judged Sarah's Handel a success, calling it "stylish," but found her hand with *Peter and the Wolf* to be "indifferent." Lastly, the Prokofiev symphony did not show either Sarah or the Florida Phil at their best. It would be Sarah's last U.S. concert gig.[5]

In August 1998, Sarah was summoned by two former players from her erstwhile OCB ensemble to the environs of Philadelphia at Swarthmore College. James Freeman, now artistic director of a seventeen-member chamber opera ensemble, would conduct a group euphemistically referred to as "Orchestra 2001." With Freeman's wife and father present, the occasion served as a family reunion for all concerned.

Following rehearsals, they performed the world premiere of an opera by one of their own Swarthmore professors, Thomas Whitman. The piece, *The Black Swan*, was taken from Thomas Mann's last opus, *Die Betrogene*, or "the deceived woman," and involved a middle-aged widow of some means who hires a handsome young male tutor to attend to her daughter.

Although Sarah had been invited to conduct and stage the piece, she ultimately demurred, favoring a more collaborative effort with her host, Freeman, who attended to matters in the pit.

Die Betrogene had its analog in another Mann novella, *Death in Venice*, but in *Die Betrogene* it is an older woman who is brought down by her infatuation with a young man. Sarah had not staged an opera in eight years. However, there was no slackening in her creative powers, as shown by her use of slides and projections that had observers praising her theatrical magic. Local critics deemed the effort a success.

As a part of her creative team, Sarah brought along her longtime design duo, Pond/Senn, who provided arresting props and visuals. It would serve as their last gig together.

Running concurrently with the two performances, a symposium titled "Opera in the Twentieth Century" invited Sarah's participation. At the conclusion, she spoke wistfully about her moribund company, asserting that it would be back in action the following year.

NOTES

1. Dmitri Shostakovich, *Cello Concerto no. 1 in E-flat*, Opus 107, William de Rosa (cello); Piano *Concerto no. 1 in C minor for Piano, Trumpet, and Strings*, *Opus 35*, Valentina Lisitsa (piano); Sarah Caldwell, Yekaterinburg Philharmonic Orchestra, Audiofon CD-72060 1996.

2. Olga Voskboinikova, interview by the author, November 25, 2007.

3. Leacock's film title, *A Musical Adventure in Siberia with Sarah Caldwell*, might arouse the ire of the citizens of Yekaterinburg, who regard their city as European, even if its geographical location places it to the east of the Ural Mountains, the accepted boundary between Europe and Asia/Siberia.

4. Richard Leacock, interview by the author, May 21, 2007.

5. Except for a concert in Puerto Rico in the mid-1990s (date unknown).

18

SARAH THE ENIGMA

Sarah was not one to reveal much of herself to anyone, maintaining her deadpan Buddha image for all the world to see. When she spoke to reporters, how much of it was accurate and how much was invented is difficult to say. The views of former friends and associates would not necessarily be helpful in unraveling the enigmas she presented. As is often the case with public figures, Sarah tended to compartmentalize her relationships. She was seen differently by different people, like a character from a Pirandello play, with each spectator convinced they saw something that did not particularly register with others. Rather than duplicity, it merely suggested that any general consensus about her was out of the question. Notwithstanding a personal image full of contradictions, there was a closet full of parchment that spoke of sixty-three honorary degrees bestowed on her, as well as a 1996 Medal of Honor presented by President Bill Clinton—a "fellow Arkansan" (as she would have it). Upon approaching her final days and beset with the infirmities of old age, she spoke enthusiastically of several projects still brimming in her mind. Sarah was not one to rest on her laurels, continuing to see her glass as half empty, rather than half full.

There was more to do.

But Sarah's mistakes or miscalculations could be judged as just as great as her successes. For many, her Boston company was viewed as her personal fiefdom, and that was not helpful. It was symptomatic of her failure to forge a broad-based organization. As a result, the Opera Company of Boston became a monument to Sarah rather than a living, breathing entity that would survive her. Was it her lack of business acumen or her failure to attend more closely to mundane matters that led her astray?

A contradictory argument ran that she enjoyed a favorable remunerative arrangement with her company for a number of years in the 1980s, salary and perks, a total value that was never less than 10 percent of the company's annual budget (assuming that the company's operations ended in the black, which was seldom the case). After her company folded, Sarah sold off a parcel of her property in Lincoln. With the proceeds, she purchased the Savoy Theater's first mortgage, thus ensuring an element of control over its future sale. Later, she shepherded the theater's listing onto the National Historic Registry. It would bar the theater from joining the parade of many of Boston's aging vaudeville houses that had fallen under the wrecking ball. Could it be that Sarah's early proficiency for mathematical calculation had escaped her? Was her ability to hold on to what she had accumulated the product of sound advice given her by financial advisors? All of this suggested another enigma.

Sarah's behavior could confound her admirers and, at the same time, confuse her detractors, as if to stay one step ahead of them. When a rumor surfaced that she was planning a particular course of action or about to make an important decision, her tack was to deny it, only to have it revealed she was pursuing it all along. The result was to strain relationships to the breaking point, leaving many in a state of dismay.

At her most innovative, as in the rehearsal phase, Sarah's work could be variable, if not erratic. In spite of the chaotic conditions that artists found while working with Sarah, many felt her staging ideas helped free them of bad habits that were not particularly communicative, thereby bringing them closer to their roles. Yet others maintained it was simply the product of infusing her artists with her passion for the medium, then harvesting the results.

To the dismay of her colleagues, Sarah was capable of creating last-minute crises, often as late as the final dress rehearsal, then berating the cast when she felt her vision had not taken shape. Only at the premiere would the work come together. But her habit of creating chaos often left her coworkers exhausted, even if exhilarated by the final outcome. Cast and chorus members were sometimes left in a state of suspended animation while endless rounds were spent awaiting Sarah's confused and poorly thought-out solutions involving basic blocking. To some, it signaled an overall lack of preparation and stagecraft. But setting aside these contradictions, many felt that it was her infectious love for the medium that carried the day.

It was often the nature of the business that artists were brought together in rehearsal and performance and then dispersed, leaving the relationship renewable with the next shared gig. On a more personal level, some artists who appeared regularly with the company found when they left that their connection with Sarah soon fizzled out. When one of her assistant conductors opted for a better opportunity, Sarah encouraged the move, only to criticize him as disloyal once he departed. Even trainees who thought they had established a lasting bond with Sarah could soon find that link quickly broken in an atmosphere of suspicion and mutual recrimination. Likewise, trainees who came to realize the danger of lingering under the tutelage of such a dominant figure would depart prematurely.

With the advent of old age, Sarah retreated to a kind of personal Valhalla of doomed gods and goddesses, albeit one of her own making. Like Wotan, she allowed a certain bitterness to cut through her better nature. On one occasion she confided she never really cared much for singers—she needed them and they needed her, and that was it!

Sarah seldom, if ever, used rough language. Like her mother, Carrie Margaret, Sarah was by instinct and demeanor a Southern woman. Still, Sarah's sharp tongue could easily wound others. Some were quick to point out her greater capacity for affection, often going the extra mile to placate or please an artist. Shirley Verrett, who appeared with the company in a number of roles, occasionally suffered serious allergic reactions to mold and smoke. Rather than risk a throat infection, Sarah undertook a number of precautions. She had Verrett's dressing room meticulously cleaned and lined with paper, including a pathway that extended all the way to where she would make her stage entrance.

From a distance Sarah was seen as subsumed by her endeavors, her accomplishments, and her failings. It was her dazzling brilliance and dedication, juxtaposed with her inconsistency and disinterest, that made her a human contradiction. Despite these conundrums, many felt privileged to be touched by her genius. As Helen Pond put it, "Nothing was worse than not working with Sarah."[1]

Like Athena of the Greek pantheon, Sarah initially sprang, not from Zeus, but from the forehead of Boris Goldovsky, with further burnishing by Walter Felsenstein. It is doubtful that, in her own mind, Sarah felt too tightly tethered to either of them. From Goldovsky came the emphasis on fully grounding performers in the art of stagecraft. With Felsenstein, it was a melding of the greater ensemble honed over weeks of toil. Instead of telling his performers what to do, Felsenstein would attempt to guide them by a psychological process so that they might discover the correct solution by themselves.[2] Sarah followed suit. But the financial constraints of plying her craft in the United States obliged her to be more free-form. Certain works did not lend themselves to Felsenstein's *Musiktheater* concept, works in which the singing aspect was merely a tradition and not a psychological necessity.

Not able to fully reconcile the two approaches, Sarah would pursue her own American style, aided by her manifold talents, a style that was a mélange of those of her mentors, while hoping to infuse her own moments of magic that would result in a more encompassing sense of lyric theater.

From this she sensed her calling, that opera, with all its complexities, was an arena in which she could play and affix her own individual stamp on the result. As was the case with her *Don Pasquale*, *The Bartered Bride*, and *Don Quichotte*, Sarah could stun audiences with her unique approach to standard repertoire, exploring a terra incognita not found by others, while attempting to give relevance to their daily lives. In so doing, she changed what a regional company could and should be in America. Her innovative approach was not unlike a movement that arose in Europe in the 1990s and was christened *Regietheater*, or "director's theater." In such a context, it is hard to imagine a Peter Sellars or a Francesca Zambello had there not been Sarah Caldwell. At her memorial service, the Rev. R. B. Haffenreffer, a family friend, declared, while concluding his eulogy, "She blazed a trail for so many. She was the first woman in the arts who smashed her head against a glass ceiling, and she broke it!"

As to her frequent bouts with narcolepsy, Sarah once admitted they were an embarrassment, often referring to the condition as "resting my eyes." Although warned by her physicians, Sarah regained her former weight and was occasionally seen eating junk food after her near-disastrous bout with double pneumonia. During the turmoil of the last days of her company, a former board member recalled stopping by the theater on Washington Street to personally tender her resignation. Sarah was seated behind her desk inside her *sanctum sanctorum* ready to devour a pile of glazed jelly doughnuts.[3]

Did her excessive eating habits stem from a psychological need to be viewed as a formidable presence on the podium, her sheer physical girth exerting authority over disparate and sometimes rancorous orchestral musicians? Others at regional opera conferences likened Sarah's habit of closing her eyes to the Fat Boy in Dickens's *Pickwick Papers*, who could fall asleep at the drop of any voice. Neurologists have since identified the condition as obesity hypoventilation syndrome, also known as the "Pickwickian syndrome." Instead of characterizing it as a vulgar demonstration of boredom, Sarah's defenders allowed, it was a result of her twenty-hour days involved in performing the myriad tasks essential to her work. They maintained that when Sarah was not the center of everyone's attention, it was only natural for her to drop into a deep, snoring slumber.

As time passed, Sarah's physical sturdiness was less robust. At airports she was often seen wheelchair bound. When asked, she averred it was only to facilitate being whisked through the customary formalities ahead of regular passengers.

With each passing year, death continued to cull away at the number of her onetime supporters and motley hangers-on. The death of one of her major financial backers foretold a comeback as unlikely. Relegated to the sidelines, rejected by the onetime "American Athens," her theater shuttered, and ignored for her real accomplishments, Sarah was denied the status of a *monstre sacré* in her own land. By the summer of 1999 she settled in Fayetteville, Arkansas, accepting the position of "distinguished professor and artistic director" of the music department's opera theater at the University of Arkansas.

It was not long before Sarah was bubbling with plans to expand the opera department's mandate as she had done many years ago at Boston University, but the faculty was less welcoming, with Sarah finding herself in the middle of a turf battle, other academics at the school nipping at her heels. Undeterred, Sarah was on the telephone to composers she had once championed, such as Robert DiDomenica, encouraging them to write works that she would find a way to produce at the school. With the limited resources allotted her, it would be difficult to fathom how she would be capable of accomplishing that—but then, the received wisdom was that one never counted Sarah out!

Determined to reassert at least the pretense of her status as an innovative force in opera at the university, she struggled valiantly against the odds, marshaling her students in preparation of various scenes from operas, sometimes given in the corridors of the school (to the astonishment of her academic colleagues).

One of Sarah's last efforts was a production of *Abstrakt Oper nr 1*, a thirty-four minute experimental piece by Boris Blacher. It had enjoyed a certain currency back in the 1950s and was well suited to a youthful ensemble. Sarah's choice was rooted in the past, since she had once dabbled with the score as far back as her BU opera workshop days in mounting a triple bill of Blacher's works.

Now, the economics of opera presentation at the school dictated a different approach. That was of little moment to Sarah, who was by nature loathe to repeat herself and felt capable of new insight and creative energy. Blacher's score was full of meaningless syllables, meant to create effect, not unlike Virgil Thompson and Gertrude Stein's *Four Saints in Three Acts*. With sets fashioned out of cardboard boxes and moved about economically by the chorus to suit the needs of a few brief scenes and an orchestra consisting mainly of brass and woodwinds and four singing parts, Sarah entranced her audience of faculty and students with Werner Egk's witty text. A clever use of lines followed, with a final whoop of a sliding trombone, suggesting flatulence more than anything else. With the aural and the visual coming together, it was again one of Sarah's moments of magic. It was to be Minerva's last effort, as if to serve as a proper valedictory: one that showed she was still capable of exploring new and unexpected pathways to bring off a difficult piece.

NOTES

1. Helen Pond, interview by the author, August 18, 2005.

2. Peter Paul Fuchs, ed., *The Music Theater of Walter Felsenstein* (New York: W.W. Norton & Co., 1975), 18.

3. Linda Cabot Black (former OCB board member), interview by the author, October 15, 2001.

EPILOGUE

Thank you, Sarah, for the intelligence you brought to your stage and for your willingness to let so many share in the thrill of creativity. I am so proud of you for the grace and sanity with which you faced the last few years. You didn't bear grudges, you never whined, and you refused to be an "old lady." Heaps of sincere praise flowed across newspaper pages around the world when you died. Your friends know, however, that you would give all that up in a minute for just one more show.

Once, just after I started to work for you, I rushed up to your dressing room after a performance when you were pleased with the way everything went. You did not hear me come in, but I remember you sitting at your desk with your head and arms leaning back, your eyes closed and a serene smile on your face. In all my life, I have never seen a woman more beautiful.

Jim Morgan, longtime friend and colleague
Quoted from the booklet distributed at the memorial service in Trinity Church, Boston, May 27, 2006

Note from the author: Sarah Caldwell spent her last years in declining health at her home in Freeport, Maine. She died of heart failure on March 23, 2006.

APPENDIX A

Annals of the Boston Opera Group and the Opera Company of Boston

(m) denotes a matinee performance.

1958—PRESEASON OPENER

Jun 18–21   Boston Arts Festival
Le Voyage dans la Lune **by Jacques Offenbach**

Conductor	Sarah Caldwell
Staging	Sarah Caldwell
English translation	Sarah Caldwell, Clyde Grisby, Eugene Haun
Scenery	Robert Fletcher
Costumes	Robert Fletcher
Lighting	Perma
Choreography	Robert Joffrey

King Cosmos	James Billings
Queen Popotte	Adelaide Bishop
Dr. Blastoff	Norman Kelley
Ensemble	Jean Kraft, Gwendolyn Bell, Pauline Gingras, Wilma Spence, Beatrice Tomkins, Diane Puffer, David Lloyd, Donald Gramm, Gerald Arpino, Thomas Beveridge, George Bishop, Clifford Crowther, Richard Gilley, Nels Jorgensen, John King, Luciene Oliver, Merle Puffer, Ray Smith, Gilbert Williams

1959—FIRST SEASON

Jan 29–30, Feb 1, 3, 5, 6,   Fine Arts Theater, Boston, MA
    8, 10, 12, 13, 15,
    16, 17, 19, 20, 22

La Bohème by Giacomo Puccini

Conductor	Sarah Caldwell
Staging	Sarah Caldwell
English translation	Sarah Caldwell, Boris Goldovsky
Scenery	David Hay
Costumes	Patricia Zipprodt
Lighting	Aristides Gazetas

Rodolfo	Charles K. L. Davis
Marcello	Robert Trehy
Mimi	Lois Marshall
Colline	Donald Gramm
Schaunard	Robert Mesrobian
Musetta	Adele Leigh/Judith Raskin/Beverly Bower
Benoit	James Billings
Alcindoro	Emil Renan
Parpignol	George Bishop/Raymond Smith
Waiter	George Kondek
Sergeant	Lucien Oliver
Custom official	Clifford Crowther

May 13, 15, 16, 18, 19,   Boston University Theater
    21, 22, 25, 26

Il Barbiere di Siviglia by Gioachino Rossini

Conductor	Sarah Caldwell
Staging	Sarah Caldwell
English translation	Boris Goldovsky
Scenery	Robert O'Hearn
Lighting	John Watts

Almaviva	Herbert Handt
Dr. Bartolo	Ralph Herbert
Don Basilio	Hugh Thompson
Figaro	Robert Trehy
Rosina	Phyllis Curtin
Berta	Eunice Alberts

May 27–30, Jun 1, 2   Boston University Theater
The Beggar's Opera by John Gay

Conductor	Sarah Caldwell
Staging	Sarah Caldwell
Scenery	Lester Polakov
Lighting	Lester Polakov
Costumes	Raymond Sovey
Choreography	Ruth Sandholm

Lucy Lockett	Patricia Neway
Macheath	Hugh Thompson
Mr. Peachum	Norman Kelley
Mrs. Peachum/Polly Peachum	Adelaide Bishop
Matt of the Mint	James Billings
Mr. Lockett	Robert Mesrobian
Mrs. Vixen	Geraldine Barretto
Mrs. Slammekin	Gwendolyn Bell
Suky Tawdry	Diane Puffer
Molly Brazen	Rosalind Hupp
Betty Doxy	Cherie Hughes
Jenny Diver	Joann Montesanti
Jemmy Twitcher	Charles Kondek
Robin of Bagshot	Merle Puffer
Wat Dreary	James Berg
Filch	Charles Bolender
Crook-Finger Jack	Thomas Kelley

1960—SECOND SEASON

Nov 9, 13, 15   Donnelly Memorial Theater, Boston, MA
Tosca by Giacomo Puccini

Conductor	Sarah Caldwell
Staging	Sarah Caldwell
Scenery	Robert Fletcher
Costumes	Robert Fletcher
Lighting	Gordon Micunis

Tosca	Lois Marshall
Cavaradossi	Thomas Hayward
Scarpia	Hugh Thompson

Angelotti	Robert Mesrobian
Sacristan	James Billings
Sciarrone	Robert Trehy
Spoletta	Clifford Crowther
Jailer	Joseph Kirkland>

Dec 9 (m), 11 (m), 13 (m)   Donnelly Memorial Theater, Boston, MA
    (prior to 14-week tour)

Le Voyage dans la Lune by Jacques Offenbach

Conductor	Sarah Caldwell
Staging	Sarah Caldwell
Scenery	Robert Fletcher
Costumes	Robert Fletcher
Lighting	Lewis Lehman
Choreography	Todd Bolender

King Cosmos	James Billings
Queen Popotte	Adelaide Bishop
Dr. Blastoff	Norman Kelley
Prince Caprice	Charles K. L. Davis
Fantasia	Jeanette Scovotti
King V'Lan IV	Emile Renan
Ensemble	Virginia Bitar, Ellen Faul, Claire Hurney, Christine Mayer, Lillian Messina, Jacquelynne Moody, Diane Puffer, Frank Carroll, Richard Christopher, Jon Crain, Leo Duggin, Robert Jepson, Richard A. Kenerson, John Mandia, Joseph Scott, Jack Sullivan

Columbia Artists Management Inc. (CAMI) arranged tour—Chicago, Milwaukee, Spokane, San Francisco, Kansas City, Dallas, Philadelphia, and others

Dec 27   Donnelly Memorial Theater, Boston, MA

Hansel and Gretel by Engelbert Humperdinck

Conductor	Osbourne McConathy
Staging	Sarah Caldwell
Scenery	Aristides Gazetas
Costumes	Aristides Gazetas
Lighting	Aristides Gazetas

Hansel	Jacquelynne Moody
Gretel	Edith Evans

Father	Chester Ludgin
Mother/witch	Ruth Kobart
Dew fairy/sandman	Diana Puffer

Jan 3–Apr 2
Le Voyage dans la Lune (second CAMI-arranged tour)

Apr 8, 11, 17   Donnelly Memorial Theater, Boston, MA
Carmen by Georges Bizet (two performances in French, one in English)
Conductor	Sarah Caldwell
Staging	Sarah Caldwell
Scenery	Will Steven Armstrong
Costumes	Will Steven Armstrong
Lighting	Will Steven Armstrong

Don José	Glade Peterson
Escamillo	Chester Ludgin
El Dancairo	Robert Mesrobian
El Remendado	Grant Williams
Zuniga	Jack Davison
Morales	Robert Trehy
Micaela	Maria di Gerlando
Frasquita	Geraldine Baretto
Mercedes	Corrine Curry
Carmen	Sophia Steffan

May 15   Boston Arena, Boston, MA
Carmen by Georges Bizet (abridged for children)
Conductor	Sarah Caldwell
Staging	Sarah Caldwell
Scenery	Will Steven Armstrong
Costumes	Will Steven Armstrong
Lighting	Will Steven Armstrong

Don José	Richard Cassily
Escamillo	Robert Trehy
El Dancairo	James Billings
Zuniga	Robert Mesrobian
Micaela	Lillian Messina
Carmen	Gloria Lane
Lilas Pastia	Ray Duffy

1961—THIRD SEASON

Nov 16, 18, 20   Donnelly Memorial Theater, Boston, MA
La Traviata **by Giuseppe Verdi (Italian and English performances)**
Conductor   Osbourne McConathy
Staging   Sarah Caldwell
Scenery   Wolfgang Roth
Costumes   Shirley Brown
Lighting   Wolfgang Roth

Violetta   Eva Likova (Nov 16, 18)
                                  Phyllis Curtin (Nov 20)
Alfredo Germont   John Alexander
Germont père   Igor Gorin
Gastone   Robert Bennett
Baron Douphol   Adib Fazah
Marquis d'Obigny   Justino Diaz
Flora   Eleanor Davis
Annina   Dolores Johnson
Dr. Grenvil   Robert Patterson
Gardener   William Flavin

Dec 7, 11, 14   Donnelly Memorial Theater, Boston, MA
Otello **by Giuseppe Verdi**
Conductor   Osbourne McConathy
Staging   Sarah Caldwell
Scenery   Wolfgang Roth
Costumes   Harold George and Olga Pertzoff
Lighting   Wolfgang Roth

Otello   Leonardo del Ferro
Iago   Tito Gobbi
Desdemona   Lucine Amara
Emilia   Eunice Alberts
Cassio   Howard Fried
Roderigo   William Flavin
Lodovico   Louis Sgarro
Montano   Robert Gregon
Herald   Robert Watson

Dec 31   Donnelly Memorial Theater, Boston, MA
Hansel and Gretel by Engelbert Humperdinck

Conductor	Osbourne McConathy
Staging	Sarah Caldwell
Scenery	Aristides Gazetas
Costumes	Aristides Gazetas
Lighting	Lewis Lehman

Hansel	Edith Evans
Gretel	Dolores Johnson
Father	Chester Ludgin
Mother	Eunice Alberts

Jan 25, 27   Donnelly Memorial Theater, Boston, MA
Falstaff by Giuseppe Verdi (in Italian)

Conductor	Sarah Caldwell
Staging	Sarah Caldwell
Costumes	Shirley Baron
Lighting	Lewis Lehman

Sir John Falstaff	James Pease
Fenton	Dino Formichini
Ford	Enzo Sordello
Dr. Caius	William Flavin
Bardolph	John King
Pistol	Lee Cass
Alice Ford	Adele Leigh
Nannetta	Jeanette Scovotti
Mistress Page	Edith Evans
Mistress Quickly	Eunice Alberts
Robin	Nym Cooke

Jan 30–Mar 11
La Bohème (CAMI tour)

Mar 15, 17   Donnelly Memorial Theater, Boston, MA
La Bohème by Giacomo Puccini

Conductor	Sarah Caldwell
Staging	Sarah Caldwell
Scenery	David Hays
Costumes	Patricia Zipprodt
Lighting	Lewis Lehman

Rodolfo	John Moulson
Marcello	Enzo Sordello
Mimi	Lois Marshall (Mar 15)
	Elaine Malbim (Mar 17, 19)
Musetta	Karol Lorraine
Colline	Rene Meville
Schaunard	William Beck
Alcindoro	Leonard Potter
Ensemble	Robert Trehy, Robert Gregori, Duff Redmond, Luis Sgarro

Apr 26, 28	Donnelly Memorial Theater, Boston, MA

Die Fledermaus by Johann Strauss II

Conductor	Arthur Fiedler
Staging	Sarah Caldwell
English translation	Ruth and Thomas Martin
Scenery	David Hays
Costumes	Shirley Baron
Lighting	David Hays
Choreography	E. Virginia Williams
	Sarah Leland and Earle Sieveling of the New York City Ballet

Gabriel von Eisenstein	William Olvis
Rosalinde	Gloria Lind
Adele	Jeanette Scovotti
Alfred	Thomas Hayward
Prince Orlofsky	Margaret Ruggero
Dr. Falke	Mac Morgan
Dr. Blind	Roland Gagnon
Frank	Richard Wentworth
Frosch	Ray Duffy

1962—FOURTH SEASON

Nov 11, 13	Vassar College, Poughkeepsie, NY

Command Performance by Robert Middleton (world premiere)

Nov 17, 18   Kresge Auditorium, MIT, Cambridge, MA
Command Performance (seven-piece chamber opera)
Conductor   Robert Middleton (at the piano)
Staging   Sarah Caldwell
Scenery   Alexander Pertzoff
Costumes   Raymond Sovey
Lighting   Raymond Sovey

Sultan   Ezio Flagello
Prime minister   Thomas Hayward
Organ builder/Janissary   James Billings
Queen Elizabeth   Blanche Thebom
Lady Anne   Doris Yarik
Dorina   Patricia Brooks
Ensemble   Robert Trehy, Jack Wilton

Feb 28, Mar 2   Donnelly Memorial Theater, Boston, MA
Manon by Jules Massenet (minus Transylvania scene)
Conductor   Osbourne McConathy
Staging   Sarah Caldwell
Scenery   Robert Fletcher
Lighting   Lewis Lehman
Choreography   E. Virginia Williams

Chevalier des Grieux   John Alexander
Le Compt de Grieux   Norman Treigle
Lescaut   Robert Trehy
Guillot-Morfonatine   Robert Schmorr
De Brétigny   Mac Morgan
Manon Lescaut   Beverly Sills
Pousette   Karol Lorraine
Javotte   Geraldine Barretto
Rosette   Laurel Miller
Maid   Nalora Steele
Innkeeper   James Billings
Guardsmen   Irving Schuman, Paolo D'Allesandro
Sergeant   Maurice Carbonneau
Porter of the seminary   Rene Rancourt
Ensemble   Irving Shuman, Robert Trehy

Mar 11   Donnelly Memorial Theater, Boston, MA
Die Meistersinger von Nürnberg **by Richard Wagner (in German; abridged for children)**

Mar 14, 16   Donnelly Memorial Theater, Boston, MA
Die Meistersinger von Nürnberg
Conductor   Laszlo Halasz
Staging   Sarah Caldwell
Scenery   Alexander Pertzoff
Costumes   Goldstein & Co.
Lighting   Lewis Lehman
Choreography   E. Virginia Williams

Eva   Jutta Mayfarth
Walther von Stolzing   Marion Alch
Hans Sachs   Paul Schöffler
Veit Pogner   Giorgio Tozzi
Vogelgesang   Robert Bennett
Nachtigall   Williams Buck
Beckmesser   James Billings
David   Thomas Hayward
Kothner/night watchman   Robert Trehy
Balthasar Zorn   Robert Schmorr
Eisslinger   John King
Moser   Richard Conrad
Ortell   Paul Hickfang
Schwartz   Maurice Charbonneau
Hans Foltz   Keith Cota
Magdalena   Eunice Alberts

Mar 25   Donnelly Memorial Theater, Boston, MA
Rigoletto **by Giuseppe Verdi**
Conductor   Sarah Caldwell
Staging   Sarah Caldwell
Scenery   Robert Fletcher
Costumes   Richard Baldridge
Lighting   Lewis Lehman

Rigoletto   Enzo Sordello
Duke of Mantua   Thomas Hayward
Gilda   Marguerita Gignac
Maddalena   Elaine Bonazzi

Count Monterone/Sparafucile	Richard Cross
Count Ceprano	Justino Diaz
Countess Ceprano/Giovanna	Geraldine Barretto
Matteo Borsa	James Billings
Marullo	William Beck
Pages	Carol Poppenger, Irving Shuman

1963—FIFTH SEASON

Dec 2	Wellesley High School Auditorium, Wellesley, MA
Dec 5	Harvard Square Theater, Cambridge, MA
Dec 6	Winchester High School Auditorium, Winchester, MA

Madama Butterfly by Giacomo Puccini

Conductor	Sarah Caldwell
Staging	Sarah Caldwell
English translation	Ruth and Thomas Martin
Scenery	Ming Cho Lee
Costumes	Patricia Zipprodt
Lighting	Ming Cho Lee

Cio-Cio-San	Taeko Tsukamoto
Lieutenant Pinkerton	Thomas Hayward
Suzuki	Umeko Shindo
Sharpless	John Reardon
Goro	James Billings
Kate Pinkerton	Corrine Curry
Prince Yamadori/the Bonze	Leonard Potter
Imperial Commissioner	Seigo Matsuda
Cio-Cio-San's mother	Sumiko Yatsuhasi
Official registrar	Etsuro Motoyama
The aunt	Kumi Seki
Uncle Yakuside	Ikuo Ohmori

Feb 1, 3	Donnelly Memorial Theater, Boston, MA

Il Barbiere di Siviglia by Gioachino Rossini

Conductor	Osbourne McConathy
Staging	Sarah Caldwell
Scenery	Raymond Sovey

Costumes	Raymond Sovey
Lighting	Raymond Sovey
Almaviva	Dino Formichini
Dr. Bartolo	Donald Gramm
Don Basilio	Arnold Voketatis
Figaro	Enzo Sordello
Fiorello/the sergeant	James Billings
Ambrogio	Karol Kostka
Rosina	Mattiwilda Dobbs
Berta	Eunice Alberts

Feb 15, 23   Donnelly Memorial Theater, Boston, MA
Faust by Charles Gounod

Conductor	Osbourne McConathy
Staging	Sarah Caldwell
Scenery	Alexander Pertzoff
Lighting	Lewis Lehman
Faust	Thomas Hayward
Mephistopheles	Norman Treigle
Marguerite	Beverly Sills
Valentin	Arthur Budney
Siebel	Corrine Curry
Wagner	James Hurst
Martha	Eunice Alberts

1964—SIXTH SEASON

Jan 17   Donnelly Memorial Theater, Boston, MA
Lulu by Alban Berg (two-act version; in English; U.S. East Coast premiere)

Conductor	Osbourne McConathy
Staging	Sarah Caldwell
Scenery	Rudolf Heinrich
Costumes	Rudolf Heinrich
Lighting	Rudolf Heinrich
Lulu	Joan Carroll
Gräfin Geschwitz	Blanche Thebom
Painter	David Lloyd
Dr. Schön	Ramon Vinay

Alwa	Frank Poretta
Schigolch	Joshua Hecht
Animal trainer	Spiro Malas
Wardrobe mistress/schoolboy	Edith Evans
Prince	Julian Patrick
Theater director	Robert Schmorr
Jack the Ripper	Karol Kostka
Clown	Ray Duffy

Jan 29   Donnelly Memorial Theater, Boston, MA

The Magic Flute by Wolfgang Amadeus Mozart

Conductor	Sarah Caldwell
Staging	Sarah Caldwell
English adaptation	Charles Kondek
Spoken dialogue	Eugene Haun
Scenery	Lloyd Burlingame (courtesy of Peabody Institute)
Costumes	Fred Voelpel

Tamino	Frank Poretta
First lady	Ruth Vecchione
Second lady	Marlena Kleinma
Third lady	Dorothy Cole
Papageno	Martyn Green
Queen of the Night	Beverly Sills
Monastatos	James Billings
Pamina	Natanya Davrath
Sarastro	Chester Watson
The speaker	Spiro Malas
First priest	Karol Kostka
Second priest	Harry Hallenbeck
First man in armor	Ralph Racuso
Second man in armor	James Berg

Feb 12   Donnelly Memorial Theater, Boston, MA

I Puritani by Vincenzo Bellini

Conductor	Richard Bonynge
Staging	Sarah Caldwell
Scenery	Lloyd Burlingame
Costumes	Fred Voelpel

Lord Gaultiero Walton	Chester Watson

Elvira	Joan Sutherland
Sir Giorgio Walton	Spiro Malas
Lord Arthur Talbott	Charles Craig
Sir Riccardo Forth	Richard Cross
Sir Benno Robertson	James Stewart
Queen Henrietta	Dorothy Cole

Feb 21   Donnelly Memorial Theater, Boston, MA

Madama Butterfly by Giacomo Puccini

Conductor	Laszlo Halasz
Staging	Sarah Caldwell
Scenery	Ming Cho Lee
Costumes	Patricia Zipprodt
Lighting	Robert Brand

Cio-Cio-San	Camilla Williams
Lieutenant Pinkerton	Thomas Hayward
Suzuki	Edith Evans
Sharpless	Chester Watson
Goro	Mauro Lampi
Kate Pinkerton	Elizabeth McCarty
Prince Yamadori/the Bonze	Chester Watson
Imperial Commissioner	Ronald Gerbrands
Official registrar	Karol Kostka
Trouble	Billy Forester

Mar 11   Donnelly Memorial Theater, Boston, MA

L'Elisir d'Amore by Gaetano Donizetti

Conductor	Sarah Caldwell
Staging	Sarah Caldwell
Scenery	Tadeusz Gesek
Costumes	Richard Baldridge
Lighting	Robert Brand

Nemorino	Dino Formichini
Adina	Beverly Sills
Belcore	Ercole Bertolino
Dulcamara	Gemi Beni
Giannetta	Lenya Gabriele

1965—SEVENTH SEASON

Donnelly Memorial Theater is renamed The Back Bay Theater.

Jan 11, 13   Back Bay Theater
Die Entführung aus dem Serail by Wolfgang Amadeus Mozart
Conductor   Sarah Caldwell
Staging   Sarah Caldwell
English translation   Charles Kondek
Scenery   Helen Pond and Herbert Senn
Costumes   Fred Voelpel

Konstanze   Beverly Sills
Blonde   Lynn Blair
Belmonte   Donald Grobe
Pedrillo   David Lloyd
Osmin   Guus Hoekman
Pasha Selim   Karol Kostka

Feb 5, 7   Back Bay Theater
Semiramide by Gioachino Rossini
Conductor   Richard Bonynge
Staging   Sarah Caldwell
Scenery   Helen Pond and Herbert Senn
Costumes   Fred Voelpel
Lighting   Thomas Skelton

Semiramide   Joan Sutherland
Arsace   Marilyn Horne
Oroe/Ghost of Nino   Guus Hoekman
Assur   Joseph Rouleau
Azema   Nalora Steele
Idreno   André Montal
Ensemble   Chapin Davis

Feb 21   Back Bay Theater
Intolleranza by Luigi Nono (U.S. premiere)
Conductor   Bruno Maderna
Staging   Sarah Caldwell
Scenery   Josef Svoboda
Costumes   Jan Skalicky

Lighting	Josef Svoboda
Television sequences	Greg Harney

Refugee	Lawrence White
Refugee's companion	Beverly Sills
Friend of the refugee	Margaret Ruggero
Tortured man	Guus Hoekman,
Algerian	Ercole Bertolino

Mar 10, 12	Back Bay Theater

Les Contes d'Hoffmann by Jacques Offenbach (in English)

Conductor	Sarah Caldwell
Staging	Siegfried Schoenbaum
Scenery	Rudolf Heinrich
Costumes	Rudolf Heinrich (courtesy of Komische Oper Berlin)
Lighting	Rudolf Heinrich

Hoffmann	David Lloyd
Lindorf/Coppelius/Dr. Miracle/ Dapertutto	John Reardon
Olympia/Antonia/Giulietta/ Stella	Beverly Sills
Nicklausse	Edith Evans
Voice of Antonia's mother	Eunice Alberts
Crespel	Guus Hoekman
Andrès/Cochenille/Frantz/ Pittichinaccio	James Billings
Schlemil/Spalanzani	Karol Kostka
Luther	Nicholas Cosindas
Hermann	Harris Poor
Nathaniel	Richard Firmin

May 10, 12	Back Bay Theater

Boris Godunov by Modest Mussorgsky (in English; original version without Polish Act and Kromy Forest)

Conductor	Sarah Caldwell
Staging	Sarah Caldwell
Scenery	Rudolf Heinrich
Costumes	Raymond Sovey and Henry Heyman
Lighting	David Reppa

Boris Godunov	George London
Fyodor	Mildred Allen
Xenia	Maxine Makas
The old nurse/hostess	Eunice Alberts
Shuisky	Norman Kelley
Pimen	Guus Hoekman
Dimitri the pretender	David Lloyd
Ensemble	James Joyce, Harris Poor, Clayne Robeson, Joseph Sopher, Ernest Triplett

In late October of 1965, the Boston Opera Group is rechristened The Opera Company of Boston.

1966—EIGHTH SEASON

Feb 18, 21   Back Bay Theater
Don Giovanni by Wolfgang Amadeus Mozart (Prague version)

Conductor	Sarah Caldwell
Staging	Sarah Caldwell
Scenery	Oliver Smith
Costumes	Stanley Simmons
Lighting	John Harvey

Don Giovanni	William Dooley
Leporello	Donald Gramm
Donna Anna	Beverly Sills
Donna Elvira	Brenda Lewis
Don Ottavio	Michel Sénéchal
Zerlina	Laurel Hurley
Masetto	Robert Trehy
Commandatore	Ernest Tripplett (Act I)
	McHenry Boatwright (Act II)

Mar 16, 18   Back Bay Theater
Boris Godunov by Modest Mussorgsky (in Russian; second revival; without Polish Act and Kromy Forest)

Conductor	Sarah Caldwell
Staging	Sarah Caldwell
Scenery	Rudolf Heinrich
Costume supervision	Henry Heymann
Lighting	John Harvey

Boris Godunov	Boris Christoff
Fyodor	Nancy Williams
Xenia	Maxine Makas
The old nurse/hostess	Eunice Alberts
Shuisky	Norman Kelley
Tschelkalov	George Fourie
Pimen	Boris Carmelli
Dimitri the pretender	David Lloyd
Varlaam	Donald Gramm
Missail	Jack Bates

Apr 4, 6	Back Bay Theater

Hippolyte et Aricie by Jean-Philippe Rameau (U.S. stage premiere)

Conductor	Osbourne McConathy
Staging	Sarah Caldwell
Scenery	Helen Pond and Herbert Senn
Costumes	Patricia Zipprodt
Lighting	John Harvey
Choreography	E. Virginia Williams and The Boston Ballet

Aricie	Beverly Sills
Hippolyte	Plácido Domingo
Phaedra	Jeannine Crader
Oenone/huntress	Maxine Makas
Diane	Carole Bogard
Theseus	George Fourie
Pluton	Boris Carmelli
Chief fury of the underworld	Norman Kelley
Ensemble	John Ferrante, Marvin Hayes, Joseph Sopher

Apr 27, May 1	Back Bay Theater

La Bohème by Giacomo Puccini

Conductor	Vincent La Selva
Staging	Sarah Caldwell
Scenery	Rudolf Heinrich
Costumes	Rudolf Heinrich
Lighting	Rudolf Heinrich and John Harvey

Rodolfo	Plácido Domingo
Marcello	Peter Glossop
Mimi	Renata Tebaldi
Colline	Boris Carmeli

Musetta	Adele Leigh
Benoit/Alcindoro	Robert Mesrobian

Nov 28
Moses und Aron by Arnold Schoenberg (performance for students)

Nov 30, Dec 2   Back Bay Theater
Moses und Aron by Arnold Schoenberg (U.S. premiere)

Conductor	Osbourne McConathy
Staging	Sarah Caldwell
English translation	Allen Forte
Scenery	Oliver Smith
Costumes	Stanley Simmons
Lighting	John Harvey
Choreography/mime coaching	Claude Kipnis

Moses	Donald Gramm
Aron	Richard Lewis
Young girl	Maxine Makas
Invalid woman	Eunice Alberts
Young man	Harry Theyard
Another man	Robert Trehy
Naked youth	John Bates
A priest	Ernest Triplett
Ensemble	Maurice Charbonneau, William Conlon, David Ham, David Hatfield, Andrew Poulemenos, Herbert Scott-Gibson

1967—NINTH SEASON

Feb 6, 8, 15   Back Bay Theater
Don Giovanni by Wolfgang Amadeus Mozart (second revival)

Conductor	Richard Bonynge
Staging	Sarah Caldwell
Scenery	Oliver Smith
Costumes	Stanley Simmons
Lighting	John Harvey

Don Giovanni	Justino Diaz
Leporello	Donald Gramm
Donna Anna	Joan Sutherland

Donna Elvira	Margarita Elkins
Don Ottavio	Lauren Driscoll
Zerlina	Hugette Tourangeau
Masetto	Robert Trehy
Commendatore	Ernest Triplett (Act I)
Statue commendatore	Herbert Scott-Gibson (Act II)

Feb 24, 27, Mar 6   Back Bay Theater
Otello by Giuseppe Verdi (*La Bohème* originally scheduled)

Conductor	Osbourne McConathy
Staging	Ramon Vinay and Sarah Caldwell
Scenery	Robert O'Hearn
Costumes	Stanley Simmons
Lighting	John Harvey

Otello	Claude Heater
Iago	Ramon Vinay
Desdemona	Renata Tebaldi
Emilia	Dorothy Cole
Cassio	Harry Theyard
Roderigo	William Denbaugh
Lodovico	David Ham

Mar 29, 31, Apr 2   Back Bay Theater
The Rake's Progress by Igor Stravinsky (*Der Freischütz* originally scheduled)

Conductor	Sarah Caldwell
Staging	Sarah Caldwell
Scenery	Helen Pond and Herbert Senn
Costumes	Helen Pond and Herbert Senn
Lighting	John Harvey
Wigs and makeup	Gottfried Schiller
Choreography	Killer Joe Piro, "King of the Discotheques"
Special kinetic visuals	Jackie Cassen and Rudi Stern

Tom	Alexander Young
Anne	Doris Yarik
Nick Shadow	Raymond Herincx
Trulove	Robert Mesrobian
Mother Goose	Eunice Alberts/Geraldine Barretto
Baba the Turk	John Ferrante

Sellem/keeper of the madhouse	James Billings
Boy	Albert Flake

May 7, 14   Back Bay Theater

Duke Bluebeard's Castle (in Hungarian) and *The Miraculous Mandarin* (a pantomime) by Béla Bartòk

(This was intended as a Bartòk trilogy but the ballet *The Wooden Prince* was canceled).

Conductor	János Kulka
Staging	Sarah Caldwell
Scenery	Dinah Kipnis
Lighting	Nananne Porcher
Pantomime staging	Claude Kipnis

Bluebeard	Guus Hoekman
Judith	Solga Szongi
Pantomime principal soloist	Claude Kipnis
Ensemble	Laurie Gould, Tom Andriano, Lance Henriksen, Don Stomavik

May 21, 27, 28 (originally   Back Bay Theater
       scheduled for Mar 13,
       15, 20)

Tosca by Giacomo Puccini

Conductor	Vincent La Selva
Staging	Ray Duffy/Charles Kondek
Scenery	Rudolf Heinrich
Costumes	Sonia Lowenstein
Lighting	Peter Hunt

Tosca	Jean Fenn
Cavaradossi	Daniele Barioni
Scarpia	Cesare Bardelli
Angelotti	Robert Trehy
Sacristan/jailer	James Billings
Sciarrone	Harris Poor
Spoletta	Jack Bates/Chapin Davis
Shepherd	Trudie Pepin

Der Freischütz (postponed)

1968—TENTH SEASON

Feb 11, 14   Back Bay Theater
Tosca by Giacomo Puccini

Conductor	Osbourne McConathy
Staging	Sarah Caldwell
Scenery	Rudolf Heinrich
Costumes	Rudolf Heinrich
Lighting	Rudolf Heinrich

Tosca	Beverly Bower
Cavaradossi	Ray Arbizu
Scarpia	George Fourie
Angelotti	Ronald Hedlund
Sacristan	James Billings
Sciarrone	Charles Koehn
Spoletta	Robert Petersen
Jailer	Thomas Jamerson
Shepherd	James Crawley

Feb 23   Back Bay Theater
Lulu by Alban Berg

Conductor	Sarah Caldwell
Staging	Sarah Caldwell
Scenery	Robin Wagner

Lulu	Louise Budd
Gräfin Geschwitz	Eunice Alberts
Painter	Anastasios Vrenios
Dr. Schön	Donald Gramm
Alwa	Thomas Rall
Schigolch	Charles Koehn
Wardrobe mistress	Jacqueline Pierce
Schoolboy	Rosalyn Wykes
Athlete	James Billings
Ensemble	David Hall, Ronald Hedlund, Karol Kostka, Robert Peterson

Mar 2   Back Bay Theater
Carmen by Georges Bizet

Conductor	Henry Lewis
Staging	Sarah Caldwell

Scenery	Oliver Smith
Costumes	Peter Hall
Lighting	Peter Hunt
Choreography	Ciro

Don José	Glade Peterson
Escamillo	Bruce Yarnell
El Dancairo	Robert Peterson
El Remendado	James Billings
Zuniga	Charles Koehn
Morales	Thomas Jamerson
Micaela	Carole Bogard
Frasquita	Katherine Christiensen
Mercedes	Linda Phillips
Carmen	Marilyn Horne

Mar 9   Back Bay Theater

La Traviata by Giuseppe Verdi

Conductor	Richard Bonynge
Scenery	Franco Zeffirelli
Staging	Peter Hall
Choreography	E. Virginia Williams and The Boston Ballet

Violetta	Joan Sutherland
Alfredo	Anastios Vrenios
Germont père/Baron Douphol	Robert Hedlund
Flora	Jacqueline Pierce
Annina	Nell Evans
Dr. Grenville	Thomas Jamerson
Ensemble	Barry Ingram, Clayton Ivey, Charles Koehn, Raphael Lebron

Mar 12   Back Bay Theater

Falstaff by Giuseppe Verdi

Conductor	Sarah Caldwell
Staging	Sarah Caldwell
Scenery	Oliver Smith
Costumes	Lewis Brown
Lighting	Jean Rosenthal

Falstaff	Peter Glossop
Fenton	Anastios Vrenios

Ford   Ronald Hedlund
Dr. Caius   Ray Arbizu
Bardolph   James Billings
Pistol   Charles Koehn
Alice Ford   Beverly Bower
Nannetta   Carole Bogard
Mistress Page   Margaret Yauger
Mistress Quickly   Eunice Alberts

1969—ELEVENTH SEASON

Jan 10, 12   Shubert Theater, Boston, MA
Béla Bartòk trilogy: *Duke Bluebeard's Castle*, *The Miraculous Mandarin*, a pantomime, and *The Wooden Prince*, a ballet (U.S. premiere of the three performed together)
Conductor   János Kulka
Staging   Sarah Caldwell
Scenery   Dinah Kipnis (*Bluebeard*)
                            George Blass (*Wooden Prince* and *Mandarin*)
Costumes   Dinah Kipnis (*Bluebeard*)
                            Judith Gombar (*Wooden Prince* and *Mandarin*)
Choreography   Imre Eck with principals of Hungary's Ballet
                            Sopianae and the corps of the Boston Ballet

Bluebeard   Guus Hoekman
Judith   Olga Szonyi

Jan 29, 31, Feb 2   Shubert Theater, Boston, MA
***Lucia di Lammermoor* by Gaetano Donizetti**
Conductor   Sarah Caldwell
Staging   Sarah Caldwell
Scenery   Helen Pond and Herbert Senn
Costumes   Jan Skalicky
Lighting   John Harvey

Enrico Ashton   James Farrar
Lucia   Beverly Sills
Edgardo   Jaroslav Kachel
Arturo   Salvador Novoa

Raimondo	Donald Gramm
Alice	Eunice Alberts

Mar 31, Apr 2, 4, 13   Shubert Theater, Boston, MA
Macbeth by Giuseppe Verdi (original 1847 version)
Conductor	Osbourne McConathy
Staging	Sarah Caldwell
Scenery	Rudolf Heinrich
Costumes	Rudolf Heinrich
Lighting	Rudolf Heinrich

Lady Macbeth	Hannelore Kushe
Macbeth	Kostas Paskalis
Banquo	Simons Estes
Macduff	Salvador Novoa
Gentlewoman	Barbara Wallace
Ensemble	James Bigelow, Lawrence Beauregard, Jerry Helton

Apr 9, 11, 14, 18   Shubert Theater, Boston, MA
Le Nozze di Figaro by Wolfgang Amadeus Mozart (in English)
Conductor	Sarah Caldwell
Staging	Sarah Caldwell
Scenery	Rudolf Heinrich
Costumes	Rudolf Heinrich
Lighting	Rudolf Heinrich

Count Almaviva	John Darrenkamp
Figaro	Simon Estes
Dr. Bartolo	Herbert Beattie
Don Basilio/Don Curzio	Norman Paige
Cherubino	Lauretta Young
Antonio	Allen Wentt
Countess	Grace de la Cruz,
Susanna	Carole Bogard
Marcellina	Gwendolyn Killebrew
Barbarina	Cheryl Gibbs

May 18
Montezuma by Roger Sessions (canceled)

Dec 1969
OCB Symphony Hall gala featuring Eleanor Steber, Blanche Thebom, and Beverly Sills

1970—TWELFTH SEASON

Jan 28, 30, Feb 1   Kresge Auditorium, MIT, Cambridge, MA
Der Fliegende Holländer **by Richard Wagner**
Conductor   Sarah Caldwell
Staging   Sarah Caldwell
Scenery   Helen Pond and Herbert Senn
Costumes   Sean Kenny (on loan from Covent Garden)
Lighting and projections   Carol Hoover
Film sequences   Richard Leacock, MIT film department

Daland   Giorgio Tozzi
Senta   Phyllis Curtin
Eric   Richard Martell
Mary   Eunice Alberts
Steersman   Grayson Hirst
Dutchman   Thomas Stewart

Feb 21, 23   Cousens Gymnasium, Tufts University, Medford, MA
La Fille du Régiment **by Gaetano Donizetti**
Conductor   Roland Gagnon
Staging   Sarah Caldwell
Scenery   Helen Pond and Herbert Senn
Costumes   Sandro Sequi
Lighting   Carol Hoover

Marie   Beverly Sills
Sulpice   Donald Gramm
Tonio   Grayson Hirst
Marquise de Birkenfeld   Muriel Greenspon
Hortensio   Gemi Beni
Duchess de Krankenthorpe   Trudie Pepin

Apr 11, 12   Rockwell Cage, MIT, Cambridge, MA
The Good Soldier Schweik **by Robert Kurka**
Conductor   Sarah Caldwell
Staging   Sarah Caldwell
Scenery   Helen Pond and Herbert Senn
Film sequences   Richard Leacock, MIT film department
Televised sequences   Thomas J. Knott

Schweik	Norman Kelley
Lieutenant Lutash	Donald Gramm
Ensemble	Eunice Alberts, Geraldine Baretto, Mary Jennings, Angeline Katranis-Lakis, Nalora Steele, Frank Hofmeister, Mac Morgan, Andrew Foldi, Karol Kostka, Naymond Thomas, Jack Bates, Nicholas Cosindas Benjamin Cox, Chapin Davis, Nym Cook

May 7, 10   Savoy Theater, Boston, MA

The Fisherman and His Wife by Gunther Schuller (world premiere)

Conductor	Gunther Schuller
Staging	Sarah Caldwell
Scenery	Helen Pond and Herbert Senn

Televised on WGBH-TV, as shot in the studio

Fisherman	David Lloyd
Fisherman's wife	Muriel Greenspon
The cat	Louise Budd
The fish	Donald Gramm

Jun 3, 5, 7 (m)   Kresge Auditorium, MIT, Cambridge, MA

***Rigoletto* by Giuseppe Verdi**

Conductor	Sarah Caldwell
Staging	Sarah Caldwell
Scenery	Helen Pond and Herbert Senn

Rigoletto	Vern Shinall
Duke of Mantua	John Alexander
Gilda	Benita Valente
Maddalena	Eunice Alberts
Sparafucile	Donald Gramm
Giovanna	Geraldine Barretto
Count Monterone	Michael Devlin
Marullo	Sean Barker

1971—THIRTEENTH SEASON

Feb 24, 26   Cyclorama Hall, a.k.a. the Flower Market, Boston, MA

Louise by **Gustave Charpentier**

Conductor	Osbourne McConathy
Staging	Sarah Caldwell
Scenery	Helen Pond and Herbert Senn
Costumes	Robert Mackey and Larry Mills
Lighting	Molly Friedel

Louise	Carol Neblett
Her mother	Eunice Alberts
Julien	John Alexander
Louise's father	Donald Gramm

Mar 31, Apr 2
Aida with **Elinor Ross (canceled)**

Mar 31, Apr 2	Cousens Gymnasium, Tufts University, Medford, MA

La Finta Giardiniera by **Wolfgang Amadeus Mozart**

Conductor	Sarah Caldwell/Richard Woitach
Staging	Sarah Caldwell
English translation	Eugene Haun
Scenery	Marsha Louis Eck
Baroque proscenium for Tufts gym	Helen Pond and Herbert Senn
Costumes	Suzanne Mess
Lighting	Marcia Madeira

Nardo	George Livings
Serpetta	Catherine Christiansen
Gardner	Carole Bogard
Arminda	Alice Marie Nelson
Ramiro	Edith Evans
Ensemble	David Holloway, Gimi Beni

On June 11, 1971, the Opera Company of Boston moved to the Orpheum/Aquarius Theater. Subsequent performances are in this theatre, unless otherwise indicated.

Jun 11, 13
Norma by **Vincenzo Bellini**

Conductor	Sarah Caldwell
Staging	Sarah Caldwell
Scenery	Helen Pond and Herbert Senn
Costumes	Robert Mackey and Larry Mills

Lighting	Molly Friedel
Pollione	John Alexander
Oroveso	Donald Gramm
Norma	Beverly Sills
Adalgisa	Beverly Wolff
Clothilde	Eunice Alberts
Flavio	George Livings

1972—FOURTEENTH SEASON

Feb 3

La Prise de Troie by Hector Berlioz

Conductor	Sarah Caldwell
Staging	Sarah Caldwell
Scenery	Helen Pond and Herbert Senn
Costumes	Suzanne Mess
Lighting	Gilbert Hemsley
Special effects	Esquire Joachem
Choreography	Billy Wilson

Cassandra/ghost of Cassandra	Maralin Niska
Ascanius	Cheryl Bibbs
Hecuba	Jan Curtis
Polyxenes	Nalora Steele
Aeneas	Ronald Dowd
Coroebus	Louis Quilico
Pantheus	Gimi Beni
Ghost of Hector/Priam	Herbert Beattie
Trojan soldier	Rene Milville
Greek captain	Terence Tobias
Helenus	Marshall Reiner
Andromache	Leslie Holmes
Astynax	Alton Hegarty
Dido	Regine Créspin
Anna	Eunice Alberts
Iopas/Hylas	Grayson Hirst
Narbal/Mercury	Ronald Hedlund
Ghost of Priam	Richard Crist
First sentry	Frank Hoffmeister
Second sentry	Naymond Thomas

Dancers from the National Center for African
American Artists

Feb 4
Les Troyens a Carthage by Hector Berlioz
Same crew, cast and characters as *La Prise de Troie* above

Feb 6
La Prise de Troie et les Troyens by Hector Berlioz (U.S. premiere of
unabridged version)
Same crew and cast as Feb 3

Apr 5, 9
Tosca by Giacomo Puccini

Conductor	Osbourne McConathy
Staging	Sarah Caldwell
Scenery	Helen Pond and Herbert Senn
Costumes	Rudolf Heinrich

Tosca	Maralin Niska
Cavaradossi	Nicolai Gedda
Scarpia	Donald Gramm

May 12, 14
La Traviata by Giuseppe Verdi

Conductor	Sarah Caldwell
Staging	Sarah Caldwell
Scenery	Helen Pond and Herbert Senn
Lighting	Gilbert Hemsley

Violetta	Beverly Sills
Alfredo	Stuart Borrows
Germont père	Peter Glossop
Baron Douphol	Ralph Griffin

1973—FIFTEENTH SEASON

Jan 26, 28
The Bartered Bride by Bedřich Smetana (in English)

Conductor	Sarah Caldwell
Staging	Sarah Caldwell

Scenery	Lester Polakov
Costumes	Jan Skalicky
Lighting	Gilbert Hemsley
Choreography	Vlastimil Jilek

Krušina	Fred Teschler
Ludmilla	Jan Curtis
Mařenka	Mary Costa
Vašek	James Atherton
Jenik	Miroslav Svejda
Kečal	Jaroslav Horàček
Ringmater of a troupe of circus artists	Alan Crofoot
Esmeralda	Linda Houpt
Ensemble	Emmett Kelly, Sr., of the Ringling Bros. Circus

Feb 16, 18

La Fille du Régiment by Gaetano Donizetti (in English)

Conductor	Sarah Caldwell
Staging	Sarah Caldwell
Scenery	Beni Montressor
Lighting	Gilbert Hemsley
Choreography	Vlastimil Jilek

Marie	Beverly Sills
Sulpice	Spiro Malas
Tonio	Enrico diGiuseppe
Marquise de Birkenfeld	Muriel Greenspon
Hortensio	Naymond Thomas
Corporal	Fred Teschler
Peasant	Hans-Jürgen Wachsmuth
Duchess de Krackenthorpe	Kitty Carlisle Hart

Apr 13, 15

Aufstieg und Fall der Stadt Mahagonny by Kurt Weill and Bertolt Brecht

Conductor	Sarah Caldwell
Staging	Sarah Caldwell
Scenery	Helen Pond and Herbert Senn
English translation	Arnold Weinstein and Lys Symonette
Costumes	Patricia Zipprodt/Domingo Rodriguez
Lighting	Gilbert Hemsley
Projections	Lester Polakov

Leokadja Begbick	Carolyn James
Fatty	Raymond Manton
Trinity Moses	Robert Mosley
Jenny	Leonore Morvaya
Jimmy Mahoney	Richard Kness
Jacob Schmidt	R. G. Webb
Ensemble	Robert Trehy, Philip Steele, Michael Trimble

May 22, 24
Don Carlos by Giuseppe Verdi (U.S. premiere of the original French version)

Conductor	Sarah Caldwell
Staging	Sarah Caldwell
Scenery	Donald Oenslager (on loan from San Antonio Opera Festival)
Costumes	Andreas Nomikos
Lighting	Duane Schuler

Elisabetta de Valois	Edith Tremblay
Princess Eboli	Michele Vilma
Don Carlos	John Alexander
Rodrigo, Marquess of Posa	William Dooley
Philip II, King of Spain	Donald Gramm
The Grand Inquisitor	Fred Teschler
Monk	Michael Trimble

1974—SIXTEENTH SEASON

Feb 20, 22, 24 (m)
Don Quichotte by Jules Massenet

Conductor	Sarah Caldwell
Staging	Sarah Caldwell
Scenery	Helen Pond and Herbert Senn
Costumes	Hugh Sherrer
Lighting	Robert Tomkins

La belle Dulcinée	Mignon Dunn
Don Quichotte	Noel Tyl
Sancho Panza	Donald Gramm
Pedro	Joann Yockey
Garcias	Teresa Treadway
Ténébrun	Ralph Griffin

Rosinante, the horse	Tony Molock
Grison, the donkey	Henry Chapin
Ensemble	Timothy Nolen, David Sundquist, Pete Kessel, Eloise Watt

Apr 3, 5, 7
Madama Butterfly by Giacomo Puccini (third revival; announced for Anna Moffo)

Conductor	Sarah Caldwell
Staging	Sarah Caldwell
Scenery	Ming Cho Lee
Costumes	Hugh Sherer
Lighting	John Michael Deegan

Cio-Cio-San	Maralin Niska
Lieutenant Pinkerton	John Alexander
Suzuki	Eunice Alberts
Sharpless	Ralph Griffin
Goro	Alan Crofoot
The Bonze	Naymond Thomas

May 8, 10, 12
War and Peace by Sergei Prokofiev (U.S. stage premiere)

Conductor	Sarah Caldwell
Staging	Sarah Caldwell
Scenery	Helen Pond and Herbert Senn
Costumes	Margaret Harris
Lighting	Patricia Collins
Choreography	E. Virginia Williams and The Boston Ballet

Prince Andrey Bolkonsky	Lenus Carlson
Natasha Rostova	Arlene Saunders
Sonya	Edith Evans
Pierre (Count Pyotr Bezukhov)	William Neil
Princess Bolkonskaya	Eunice Alberts
Hélène Bezukhova	Jan Curtis
Prince Anatol Kuragin	Joseph Evans
Dolokhov/Field-Marshal Mikhail Kutuzov	Donald Gramm
Napoleon Bonaparte	James Billings
Ensemble	David Evitts, Philip Steele, Harry Dworchak, Alan Crofoot, John Davies

Jun 1, 3, 6
Il Barbiere di Siviglia by Gioachino Rossini
Conductor   Sarah Caldwell
Staging   Sarah Caldwell
Scenery   Helen Pond and Herbert Senn
Costumes   Jan Skalicky
Lighting   Gilbert Hemsley

Almaviva   Bruce Brewer
Dr. Bartolo   Donald Gramm
Don Basilio   Fred Teschler
Figaro   Alan Titus
Fiorillo   Ralph Griffen
Ambrogio   Nicholas Muni
Rosina   Beverly Sills
Berta   Jan Curtis
Notary   David Gorin
Soldiers   Frank Hoffmeister, John Davis, Alexander
                       Stevenson, Richard Crist

1975—SEVENTEENTH SEASON

Feb. 5, 7, 9
Falstaff by Giuseppe Verdi
Conductor   Sarah Caldwell
Staging   Sarah Caldwell
English translation   Andrew Porter
Scenery   Helen Pond and Herbert Senn
Costumes   John Lehmeyer
Lighting   Gilbert Hemsley

Falstaff   Donald Graham
Fenton   Joseph Evans
Ford   William Justus
Dr. Caius   Douglas Perry
Bardolph   James Billings
Pistol   Gimi Beni
Alice Ford   Joann Yockey
Nannetta   Barbara Hendricks
Mistress Page   Nancy Williams
Mistress Quickly   Muriel Costa-Greenspon
Host of the Garter Inn Nicholas Muni

Mar 19, 21, 23
Così fan tutte by Wolfgang Amadeus Mozart

Conductor	Sarah Caldwell
Staging	Sarah Caldwell
Scenery	Helen Pond and Herbert Senn
Costumes	Jan Skalicky
Lighting	Gilbert Hemsley
Fiordiligi	Heather Thompson
Dorabella	Maria Ewing
Ferrando	William Harness
Guglielmo	Richard Stilwell
Don Alfonso	Alan Baker/Robert Trehy
Despina	Karen Hunt

May 3, 5, 7
Benvenuto Cellini by Hector Berlioz (U.S. premiere)

Conductor	Sarah Caldwell
Staging	Sarah Caldwell
Scenery	Helen Pond and Herbert Senn
Costumes	Beni Montressor (courtesy of Covent Garden)
Lighting	Steve Ross
Choreography	E. Virginia Williams
Pope Clement VII	Donald Gramm
Balducci	Gimi Beni
Teresa	Patricia Wells
Benvenuto Cellini	Jon Vickers
Ascanio	Nancy Williams
Francesco	Joseph Evans
Bernardino/Pompeo	Ralph Griffin
Fieramosca	John Reardon
Innkeeper	David Evitts
A metalworker	David Waite
Cassandro	Hank Chapin

Jun 2, 5, 7
I Capuleti ed i Montecchi by Vincenzo Bellini

Conductor	Sarah Caldwell, William Fred Scott
Staging	Sarah Caldwell
Scenery	Helen Pond and Herbert Senn
Costumes	Yasmina Bozin
Lighting	Steve Ross

Giulietta	Beverly Sills
Romeo	Tatiana Troyanos
Tebaldo	Joseph Evans
Capellio	Herbert Beattie
Lorenzo	Robert Trehy

1976—EIGHTEENTH SEASON

Feb 15, 17, 19
Fidelio by Ludwig van Beethoven

Conductor	Sarah Caldwell
Staging	Sarah Caldwell and David Gorin
Scenery	Helen Pond and Herbert Senn
Costumes	Yasmina Bozin
Lighting	Gilbert Hemsley

Florestan	Jon Vickers
Leonora/Fidelio	Teresa Kubiac
Don Fernando	Mac Morgan
Don Pizzaro	Richard Van Allen
Rocco	Donald Gramm
Marcellina	Magdalena Falewicz
Jacquino	Joseph Evans

Mar 31, Apr 2, 4
Montezuma by Roger Sessions (U.S. premiere)

Conductor	Sarah Caldwell
Staging	Sarah Caldwell
Scenery	Helen Pond and Herbert Senn
Costumes	Delfina Vargas (courtesy of Mexico's Ballet Folklorico)
Lighting	Gilbert Hemsley
Choreography	Amalia Hernandez

Young Bernal Diaz	Alexander Stevenson
Bernal Diaz	Donald Gramm
Cortez	Brent Ellis
Montezuma	Richard Lewis/John Moulson
Malinche	Phyllis Bryn-Julson/Pamela Kuceniuc
Jeronimo Aguilar/veteran	Alan Crofoot
Cuaximati	Eunice Alberts

The Caicique of Cempoalla/	Douglas Perry
the lord of Tacuba/.	
Cacamatzin	
Cuaunhtemoc	David Evitts
Netzahualcoyotl	Severino Barbiere
Pedro de Alvarad	Joseph Evans
Friar Almedo de la Merced	William Fleck
Voice of a Spanish soldier/	Clyde Battles
Guidela/Teuhtlilli	
Itlamal	Deborah O'Brien

May 12, 14, 16
La Fanciulla del West by Giacomo Puccini (in English)

Conductor	Sarah Caldwell
Staging	Sarah Caldwell
Scenery	Helen Pond and Herbert Senn
Costumes	Jane Papanek
Lighting	Gilbert Hemsley

Minnie	Arlene Saunders
Jack Rance	Giorgio Tozzi
Dick Johnson	William Lewis
Nick (bartender)	Alan Crofoot
Sid	Edward Huls/Jason Byce
Handsome	Jack Bates
Harry	David Waite
Joe	Antonio Barasorda
Happy	Jonathan Prescott
Larkens	Eric Halvarson
Ashby	Monte Jaffe
Billy Jackrabbit	Nicholas Cosindas
Wowkie	Eunice Alberts
Jake Wallace	Robert Peterson
Courier	William Cashman
José Castro	Richard Crist

Jun 2, 4, 6
Macbeth by Giuseppe Verdi (1865 version)

Conductor	Sarah Caldwell
Staging	Sarah Caldwell
Scenery	Helen Pond and Herbert Senn
Costumes	Jane Greenwood and Janet Papanek

Lighting　　　　　　　　　Stephen Ross
Choreography　　　　　　Stuart Sebastian

Lady Macbeth　　　　　　Shirley Verrett
Macbeth　　　　　　　　Ryan Edwards
Banquo　　　　　　　　Giorgio Tozzi
Macduff　　　　　　　　Joseph Evans
Duncan　　　　　　　　Jay Bragdon
Gentlewoman　　　　　　Elizazbeth Phinney
Malcolm　　　　　　　　Antonio Barasorda
Physician　　　　　　　David Evitts
Messenger　　　　　　　Eric Halfvarson

1977—NINETEENTH SEASON

Mar 5, 8, 11, 13
Ruslan and Ludmilla by Mikhail Glinka (U.S. première)
Conductor　　　　　　　Sarah Caldwell
Staging　　　　　　　　Sarah Caldwell
English translation　　　　Francis Dalvin
Scenery　　　　　　　　Helen Pond and Herbert Senn
Costumes　　　　　　　Carrie Robbins
Lighting　　　　　　　　John Michael Deegan
Choreography　　　　　　Ben Stevenson.
Naina's aerial act credited "Flying by Foy" illusionist

Svetozar　　　　　　　William Fleck
Ludmilla　　　　　　　Jeanette Scovotti
Ruslan　　　　　　　　Victor Braun
Ratmir　　　　　　　　Eunice Alberts
Farlaf　　　　　　　　Giorgio Tozzi
Gorislava　　　　　　　Marianna Christos
Finn　　　　　　　　　John Moulson
Naina　　　　　　　　Edith Evans
Bayan　　　　　　　　Joseph Evans

Mar 19, 22, 25, 27
La Bohème by Giacomo Puccini (in English, from Opera New England tour circuit)
Conductor　　　　　　　William Fred Scott
Staging　　　　　　　　Sarah Caldwell

Scenery	Rudolf Heinrich and John Lehmeyer
Lighting	Ralph J. Tompkins

Rodolfo	Jack Trussel
Marcello	Ron Holgate
Mimi	Magdelena Falewicz
Colline	John Davies/William Fleck
Schaunard	Ralph Griffin
Benoit/Alcindoro	Alan Crofoot
Musetta	Marianna Christos
Parpignol	William Cashman

Apr 24, 26, 28, 30
Rigoletto by Giuseppe Verdi (replaced *Sonnambula* with Beverly Sills)

Conductor	Sarah Caldwell
Staging	Sarah Caldwell
Scenery	Douglas W. Schmidt
Costumes	Carrie Robbins
Lighting	Gilbert Hemsley

Rigoletto	Richard Fredericks
Duke of Mantua	Joseph Evans
Gilda	Beverly Sills
Maddalena	Suzanne Marsee
Sparafucile	James Johnson
Giovanna	Jeanine Kelley
Count Monterone	Michael Burt
Borsa	Alan Crofoot
Maurillo	Jason Byce

Jun 2, 5, 7, 10
Orfeo ed Euridice by Christoph Willibald Gluck (in Italian)

Conductor	Sarah Caldwell
Staging	Sarah Caldwell
Scenery	Helen Pond and Herbert Senn
Costumes	John Lehmeyer
Lighting	John Michael Deegan
Choreography	Ben Stevenson

Orfeo	Shirley Verrett
Euridice	Benita Valente
Amor	Marianna Christos

Jun 8, 9, 11
Orphée aux Enfers **by Jacques Offenbach (in English)**

Conductor	Osbourne McConathy, Kent Nagano, and William Frederick Scott
Staging	Sarah Caldwell with Arthur Fiedler, Donald Gramm, J. Balme, P. Eisenberg, and D. Gorin
Scenery	Helen Pond and Herbert Senn
Costumes	John Lehmeyer
Lighting	John Michael Deegan
Choreography	Ben Stevenson

Pluto	Joseph Evans
Professor Orpheus	Donald Gramm
John Styx	Fred Gwynn
Mercury	Ron Holgate
Mars	Matthew Murray
Jupiter	Alan Crofoot
Morpheus	Raymond Herdin
Eurydice	Maralin Niska
Diana	Jan Curtis
Miss Public Opinion	Margaret Hamilton/Geraldine Barretto
Venus	Marianna Cristos
Cupid	Leigh Munro
Juno	Eunice Alberts
Minerva	Cynthia DuPont
Ceres	Nalora Steele
Vesta	Geraldine Barretto
Vulcan	Randall Scheri
Bacchus	Matthew Doley
Apollo	Jonathan Prescott
Neptune	John Kern

1978—TWENTIETH SEASON

Feb 15, 17, 19 (m), 24
Stiffelio **by Giuseppe Verdi (U.S. stage premiere; scheduled for Anna Moffo)**

Conductor	Sarah Caldwell
Staging	Sarah Caldwell
Scenery	Zach Brown

| Costumes | John Lehmeyer |
| Lighting | Gilbert Hemsley |

Stiffelio	Roelof Oostwoud/Richard Taylor
Lena	Anna Moffo/Leigh Munro
Stankar	Brent Ellis
Dorotea	Theresa Treadway
Raffaele	Dean Rhodus
Jorg	William Fleck
Federico	Pietro Pozzo

May 1, 8, 15, 21
Tosca (intended for Shirley Verrett; canceled)

May 24, 26 (m), 28
Damnation of Faust by Hector Berlioz (in English)

Conductor	Robert Shaw
Staging	Sarah Caldwell
Scenery	Eugene Lee
Costumes	Fran Lee

Marguerite	Evelyn Lear
Faust	Alberto Remedios
Mephistopheles	Donald Gramm
Brander	Lenus Carlson

May 8, 31, Jun 1, 4 (m)
Don Pasquale by Gaetano Donizetti

Conductor	Sarah Caldwell
Staging	Sarah Caldwell
Scenery	Helen Pond and Herbert Senn
Costumes	John Lehmeyer
Lighting	John Michael Deegan

Don Pasquale	Donald Gramm
Dr. Malatesta	Alan Titus
Ernesto	Joseph Evans
Norina	Beverly Sills
Notary	Alan Crofoot
Servant	Angelina Katranis

In 1979, the Opera Company of Boston is installed in their new permanent home, the Savoy Theater, which is then renamed The Opera House. Subsequent performances are in this theater, unless otherwise indicated.

Nov 1, 3, 5 (m), 8
Tosca by Giacomo Puccini

Conductor	William Frederick Scott
Staging	Sarah Caldwell
Scenery	Rudolf Heinrich
Costumes	Constance Mellon
Lighting	Rudolf Heinrich
Tosca	Magda Olivero
Cavaradossi	William Johns
Scarpia	Giorgio Tozzi
Angelotti	Robert Trehy
Sacristan	William Fleck
Sciarrone	John Kern
Spoletta	Jack Bates

1979—TWENTY-FIRST SEASON

Feb 9, 11, 16, 18
Mazeppa (canceled)

Mar 21, 23 (in Italian), Mar 25, 30 (in English)
Falstaff by Giuseppe Verdi

Conductor	Sarah Caldwell
Staging	Sarah Caldwell
Scenery	Helen Pond and Herbert Senn
Costumes	Julie Kaihoj-Anderson and Suzanne Mess
Lighting	Gilbert Hemsley
Falstaff	Donald Gramm/Richard Fredericks
Ford	Richard Fredericks/Ryan Edwards
Fenton	Joseph Evans
Dr. Caius	Ragnar Ulfung
Bardolph	James Billings
Pistol	William Fleck
Alice Ford	Catherine Wilson
Nannetta	Leigh Munro

Mistress Page	Jan Curtis
Mistress Quickly	Eunice Alberts

Apr 4, 8, 13, 20
La Vide Breve by **Manuel de Falla**

Conductor	Sarah Caldwell
Staging	Sarah Caldwell and Claude Kipnis
Scenery	Helen Pond and Herbert Senn
Costumes	Allen Charles Klein
Lighting	Gilbert Hemsley
Choreography	Maria Benitez

Salud	Vitoria de los Angeles/Elizabeth Phinney
Paco	Evelio Esteve
Abuela	Carolyn James
Beda Bolanco	Eunice Alberts
Ensemble	Maryanne Telese, Sarah Williams, Aaron Bergell, Peter Cody, William Fleck, Ralph Griffin, Peter Hume

Apr 4, 8, 13, 20
El Retablo de Maese Pedro by **Manuel de Falla**

Conductor	Sarah Caldwell
Staging	Sarah Caldwell and Claude Kipnis
Scenery	Diana Kipnis
Costumes	Diana Kipnis
Lighting	Gilbert Hemsley

Don Quixote	Ryan Edwards
Mimes	Melodie Arterberry, Michael Atwell, Jimmy Bueschen, John Collins, Stephan Driscoll, Annie Louis, Drucilla Markle, David Morse, Jody Scalise
Ensemble	Aaron Bergell, Scott Rigby

Apr 12, 14 (m) May 1, 8
Il Barbiere di Siviglia by **Gioachino Rossini**

Conductor	Sarah Caldwell
Staging	Sarah Caldwell
Scenery	Helen Pond and Herbert Senn
Costumes	Jan Skalicky
Lighting	Gilbert Hemsley

Almaviva	Joseph Evans
Dr. Bartolo	Donald Gramm
Don Basilio	William Fleck
Figaro	Richard Fredericks/Alan Titus
Fiorello	James Tyseka
Ambrogio	Nicholas Muni
Rosina	Beverly Sills
Berta	Jan Curtis

May 18, 20, 22, May 25 (m)
The Ice Break by Sir Michael Tippett (U.S. premiere)

Conductor	Sarah Caldwell
Staging	Sarah Caldwell
Scenery	Helen Pond and Herbert Senn
Costumes	Marcia Dixcy and Polly P. Smith
Lighting	Gilbert Hemsley
Film sequences	Richard Leacock, MIT film department
Choreography	Tally Beatty

Lev	Richard Fredericks
Nadia	Arlene Saunders
Yuri	Jake Gardner
Gayle	Leigh Munro
Nurse	Cynthia Clarey
Olympion	Curtis Rayam
Police lieutenant	Naymond Thomas
Astron	Adele Nicholson/Jeffrey Gall (countertenor)

Nov 2, 11
Madama Butterfly by Giacomo Puccini (Opera New England touring production)

Conductor	William Fred Scott
Staging	Sarah Caldwell
Scenery	Ming Cho Lee
Costumes	Hugh Sherer

Cio-Cio- San	Sung Sook Lee
Lieutenant Pinkerton	Joseph Evans
Suzuki	Eunice Alberts
Sharpless	Ralph Griffin
Kate Pinkerton	Leslie Holmes
Prince Yamadori	Jack Bates

The Bonze	Lawrence Thomas
Imperial Commissioner	William Cashman
Official registrar	Robert Viau
Trouble	Daniel Condon
Uncle Yakuside	Matthew Dooley

Dec 7–9, 12, 14, 15
Hansel and Gretel by Engelbert Humperdinck

Conductor	Sarah Caldwell
Staging	Sarah Caldwell
Scenery	David Sharir
Costumes	David Sharir
Lighting	Timothy Buckman

Hansel	Evelyn Petros
Gretel	Leigh Munro
Father	Ronald Hedlund
Mother	Jan Curtis
Dew fairy/sandman	Adele Nicholson
Witch	Virginia Boomer

1980—TWENTY-SECOND SEASON

Jan 25, 27 (m), 31, Feb 3 (m)
Die Fledermaus by Johann Strauss II

Conductor	Sarah Caldwell
Staging	Sarah Caldwell
Scenery	Helen Pond and Herbert Senn
Costumes	Ray Diffen
Lighting	Gilbert Hemsley
Choreography	Graciela Daniele

Gabriel von Eisenstein	Alan Titus
Rosalinde	Beverly Sills
Adele	Constanza Cuccaro
Alfred	Joseph Evans
Orlofsky/Frosch	Robert Trehy
Falke	Donald Gramm
Dr. Blind	Michael Hume
Frank	Victor Borge
Ida	Elena Gambulos

Apr 18, 20 (m), 24, 27 (m)
Der Fliegende Holländer by **Richard Wagner**

Conductor	Sarah Caldwell
Staging	Sarah Caldwell
Scenery	David Sharir
Costumes	David Sharir
Lighting	Gilbert Hemsley
Special effects	Esquire Joachem
Film sequences	Richard Leacock

Daland	William Wildermann
Senta	Elisabeth Payer-Tucci
Erik	Edward Sooter/John Moulson
Mary	Eunice Albert
Steersman	Vincent Cole
Dutchman	Simon Estes

May 9, 11 (m), 15, 18 (m)
War and Peace by **Sergei Prokofiev (revival)**

Conductor	Sarah Caldwell
Staging	Sarah Caldwell
Scenery	Helen Pond and Herbert Senn
Lighting	Gilbert Hemsley
Special effects	Esquire Joachem
Choreography	Stephen Driscoll

Prince Andrey Bolkonsky	Brent Ellis
Natasha	Magdalena Falewicz/Elizabeth Hynes
Sonya/Matfroysha/Vasilisa	Adele Nicholson
Count Ilya Rostov/Napoleon *Bonaparte*	Michael Rippon
Maria Dmitrievna Akhrosimova	Eunice Alberts
Pierre (Count Pyotr Bezukhov)	John Moulson
Princess Bolkonsky	Suzanne Brenning
Hélène Bezukhova	Jan Curtis
Prince Anatol Kuragin	Joseph Evans
Dolokhov/Field Marshall *Mikhail Kutuzov*	Donald Gramm
Mme. Peronskaya	Elisabeth Phinney
A house maid	Nancy Karen Green
Dunyasha	Claudette Peterson
The czar's mistress	Sheryl Mirsky

Matvyev	Robert Trehy
Denisov	David Evitts
First staff officer	Curtis Rayam
Second staff officer	Ralph Griffin
Czar Nicholas I	Stephen Driscoll
Fyodor/footman	Michael Hume
Tikhon	William Dansby
Orderly	Kenneth Raynor
Kutuzov's aide-de-camp	Michael Magiera

May 29, Jun 1 (m), 5, 8 (m)
***Aida* by Giuseppe Verdi**

Conductor	Sarah Caldwell
Staging	Sarah Caldwell
Scenery	Helen Pond and Herbert Senn
Costumes	Ray Diffen
Lighting	Gilbert Hemsley
Choreography	Sam Kurkjian

Aida	Shirley Verrett
Amneris	Elizabeth Connell
Amonasro	David Arnold
Radames	James McCracken
Ramfis	Ferruccio Furlanetto
King	William Dooley
High priestess	Elizabeth Phinney
Messenger	Michael Magiera

1981—TWENTY-THIRD SEASON

Feb 20, 22, 26, Mar 1
***Faust* by Charles Gounod**

Conductor	Sarah Caldwell
Staging	Sarah Caldwell
Scenery	David Sharir
Costumes	David R. Roberts
Lighting	Robby Monk

Faust	John Alexander
Mephistopheles	Donald Gramm
Marguerite	Diana Soviero

Valentin	Håkan Haggegård
Siebel	Kerry McCarthy
Wagner	Jan Opalach
Martha	Eunice Alberts

Mar 20, 22, Apr 2, 5
Der Rosenkavalier by Richard Strauss

Conductor	William Frederick Scott
Staging	Sarah Caldwell
Scenery	Helen Pond and Herbert Senn
Costumes	Ray Diffen
Lighting	Michael R. Moody

Princess von Werdenberg *(Marschallin)*	Arlene Saunders
Baron Ochs	Donald Gramm
Octavian	Tatiana Troyanos/Delia Wallis
Herr von Faninal	Robert Trehy
Sophie	Jeanne Ommerle
Marianne	Elizabeth Phinney
Valzacchi	David Lloyd
Annina	Eunice Alberts
Commissary of police/notary	Bruce Kramer
Vendor of animals/landlord/ *major domo of Faninal*	Harry Danner
Italian singer	Riccardo Calleo
Three orphans	Sue Ellen Kuzma, Diane Cole, Nancy Kern Green
Milliner	Geraldine Barretto

Apr 24, 26, 30, May 3
Rigoletto by Giuseppe Verdi

Conductor	Sarah Caldwell
Staging	Sarah Caldwell
Scenery	Douglas Schmidt
Costumes	Carrie Robbins
Lighting	Michael R. Moody

Rigoletto	Brent Ellis
Duke of Mantua	Ryszard Karczykowsky
Gilda	Ashley Putnam
Maddalena	Rosalind Elias

Monterone/Sparafucile	Fred Teschler
Count Ceprano	Giullermo Poteri
Countess Ceprano/Giovanna	Rochelle Zuroff
Borsa	Michael Hume
Marullo	Jay Willoughby
Herald	Mark Aliapoulis

May 21, 24 (m), 28, 31 (m)
Otello by Giuseppe Verdi (performing edition by Alfredo Zedda)

Conductor	Sarah Caldwell
Staging	Sarah Caldwell
Scenery	Helen Pond and Herbert Senn
Costumes	Ray Diffen
Lighting	Michael R. Moody
Special effects	Esquire Joachem and Greg Meeh

Otello	James McCracken
Iago	John Reardon
Desdemona	Shirley Verrett
Emilia	Jennifer Barron
Cassio	Roelof Oostwoud
Roderigo	Michael Hume
Ludovico	Fred Teschler
Montano	Jay Willoughby
Herald	Mark Aliapoulis

1982—TWENTY-FOURTH SEASON

Feb 4, 6, 7 (m)
Die Soldaten by Bernd Alois Zimmermann (in English; U.S. premiere)

Conductor	Sarah Caldwell
Staging	Sarah Caldwell
Assistant director	Lisi Oliver
Scenery	David Sharir
Costumes	David Sharir
Lighting	Michael Moody
Film sequences	Richard Leacock
Choreography	Carmen de Lavallade

Marie	Phyllis Hunter
Charlotte	Beverly Morgan

Wesener's elderly mother	Eunice Alberts
Stolzius	Joseph Evans
Stolzius's mother	Kirsten Meyer
Countess de la Roche	Rose Marie Freni
Desportes	William Cochran
Major Mary	John Brandstetter
Pirzel	Joaquin Romaguerrta
Major Haudy	Timothy Noble
Wesener	Richard Crist
Eisenhardt	John Moulson
First young officer	Noel Velasco
Second young officer	Nicholas Savarin
Third young officer	Thomas Silverborg
Colonel	Robert Honeysucker
Count de la Roche	Otonel Gonzaga
Servant to the countess	George Kott

Feb 25, 28, Mar 4, 7
Aida by Giuseppe Verdi

Conductor	Sarah Caldwell
Staging	Sarah Caldwell
Scenery	Helen Pond and Herbert Senn
Costumes	Ray Diffen
Lighting	Michael R. Moody
Choreography	Thom Molinaro

Aida	Shirley Verrett
Amneris	Joann Grillo/Mignon Dunn
Amanasro	David Arnold
Radames	James McCracken
Ramfis	Philip Booth
King	Frank Ventriglia
Priestess	Sarah Reese
Messenger	Noel Velasco

Apr 2, 4 (m), 8, 11 (m)
La Bohème by Giacomo Puccini

Conductor	Sarah Caldwell
Staging	Sarah Caldwell
Scenery	Rudolf Heinrich
Costumes	Ray Diffen and Timothy Miles
Lighting	Deidre Taylor

Rodolfo	Noel Velasco
Marcello	Lenus Carlson
Mimi	Sarah Reese
Colline	Philip Booth
Schaunard	Vernon Hartman
Benoit/Alcindoro	Robert Falk
Musetta	Jan Ommerle
Parpignol	George Kott
Sergeant	Michael Morizi
Custom officer	Mark Aliapoulis

A musicians' strike was settled by May 18, but not in time for rehearsals for Carl Maria von Weber's Der Freischütz, *causing the scheduled performances of May 21, 23, 27, and 30 to be canceled.*

Jun 13 (m), 16, 18, 20 (m)
Orphée aux Enfers by Jacques Offenbach (in English)

Conductor	Sarah Caldwell
Staging	Sarah Caldwell
Scenery	Helen Pond and Herbert Senn
Costumes	Ray Diffen and Timothy Miles
Lighting	Michael R. Moody
Choreography	James Starbuck

Pluto	Robert Orth
Professor Orpheus	James Billings
John Styx	Sid Caesar
Mercury	Noel Velasco
Mars	Mark Jackson
Jupiter	Harlan Foss
Morpheus	Robert Viau
Eurydice	Leigh Munro
Diana	Adele Nicholson
Miss Public Opinion	Imogene Coca
Venus	Sarah Reese
Cupid	Jan Ommerle
Juno	Eunice Alberts
Minerva	Angelina Lakis
Ceres	Nalora Steele
Vesta	Geraldine Barretto
Iris	Andrea Bradford
Liberty	Beda Polanco

Vulcan	Mark Aliapoulios
Bacchus	George Kot
Neptune	David Huggins

1983—TWENTY-FIFTH SEASON

Feb 18, 20 (m), 24, 27 (m)
Carmen by Georges Bizet

Conductor	Sarah Caldwell
Staging	Sarah Caldwell
Scenery	Helen Pond and Herbert Senn
Costumes	Ray Diffen and Timothy Miles
Lighting	Michael Moody

Don José	James McCracken/Harry Theyard
Escamillo	John Reardon/Brent Ellis
El Dancairo	Robert Orth
El Remandado	Noel Velasco
Zuniga	James Rensink
Micaela	Sarah Reese
Frasquita	Linda Wall
Mercedes	Patricia McCaffrey
Carmen	Régine Crespin
Innkeeper	Ray Duffy

Apr 17 (m), 19, 22, 24 (m)
Invisible City of Kitezh by Nikolai Rimsky-Korsakov

Conductor	Neville Dove
Staging	Sarah Caldwell
Scenery	Robert O'Hearn
Costumes	Timothy Miles
Lighting	Michael Moody

Prince Vsevolod	Noel Velasco
Prince Yuri	Donald Gramm
Fevronia	Sarah Reese
Alkonost	Eunice Alberts
Servant/Sirin	Adele Nicholson
Bard	James Rensink
Grishka	John Moulson

Beartamer	Steven Schnurman
Bedyai	Harry Dworchak
Buirndai	Gamaliel Viray
Nobleman	George Kott
Ensemble	Mark Aliapoulios, Robert Viau

May 19, 22 (m), 26, 29 (m)
Norma by Vincenzo Bellini

Conductor	Sarah Caldwell
Staging	Sarah Caldwell
Scenery	Helen Pond and Herbert Senn
Costumes	Ray Diffen and Timothy Miles
Lighting	Graham Walne

Pollione	Joseph Evans
Oroveso	Donald Gramm
Norma	Shirley Verrett
Adalgisa	Rosemary Freni
Clothilde	Sarah Reese
Flavio	James Rensink

Nov 13, 18, 22, 27 (m), Dec 4 (m) (Dec 4 scheduled by popular demand)
Turandot by Giacomo Puccini

Conductor	Sarah Caldwell
Staging	Sarah Caldwell
Scenery	Ming Cho Lee
Lighting	Graham Walne
Costumes and props	Wang Linyou (courtesy of Central Opera Theater of Beijing, China)
Choreography	Yao Li's Kung Fu Academy

Turandot	Eva Marton
Emperor Altoum	Michael Hume
A Mandarin	James Rensink
Liu	Sarah Reese
Calaf	James McCracken
Timur	Harry Dworchak
The Prince of Persia	Michael Olsen
Ping	James Rensink
Pang	Steven Schnurman
Pong/the Emperor Altoum	Noel Velasco
The executioner	J. Scott Brumit

Dec 4
Der Freischütz (canceled)

1984—TWENTY-SIXTH SEASON

Jan 15 (m), 22 (m), 27
Der Freischütz **by Carl Maria von Weber (sung in German with English surtitles; first use of surtitles by company)**

Conductor	Sarah Caldwell
Staging	Sarah Caldwell
Scenery	Helen Pond and Herbert Senn
Costumes	Timothy Miles
Lighting	Graham Walne
Special effects	Esquire Joachem and Gregory Meeh
Choreography	Stephen Driscoll
Prince Ottokar	Robert Trehy
Max	John Moulson
Caspar	William Wildermann
A hermit/Samiel	Roger Roloff
Agathe	Sarah Reese
Aennchen	Ariel Rubstein

Feb 24, 26, 29, Mar 4
Silver Anniversary Opera Gala featuring Shirley Verrett, James McCracken, Ruth Welting, and others

Apr 6, 8, 11, 18
Madama Butterfly **by Giacomo Puccini (fourth revival of 1963 production)**

Conductor	Sarah Caldwell
Staging	Sarah Caldwell
Scenery	Ming Cho Lee
Costumes	Patricia Zipprodt
Lighting	Graham Walne
Cio-Cio-San	Veronika Kincses
Lieutenant Pinkerton	Joseph Evans
Suzuki	Eunice Alberts
Sharpless	Cornelius Opthof
Goro	Noel Velasco

Kate Pinkerton/Geraldine Barretto	Robin Weisel-Capsouto
Prince Yamadori/Uncle Yakuside	James Rensink
Imperial Commissioner	Michael Morizio
The Bonze	William Wildermann
Official registrar	George Kott
Sorrow	Brendan Picker

May 11, 13, 16, 20
Taverner by Peter Maxwell Davies (canceled)

May 18, 20 (m)
Il Barbiere di Siviglia by Gioachino Rossini (not originally scheduled for that season)

Conductor	Sarah Caldwell
Staging	Sarah Caldwell
Scenery	Helen Pond and Herbert Senn
Costumes	Jan Skalicky
Lighting	Graham Walne
Surtitles	Lisi Oliver

Almaviva	Joseph Evans
Dr. Bartolo	Spiro Malas
Don Basilio	Claude Corbeil
Figaro	Robert Orth
Fiorello	Robert Wilbur
Ambrogio	Elliot J. Cohen
Rosina	Ruth Welting
Berta	Robin Weisel-Capsouto
Musicians and soldiers	Michael Morizio, William Cashman, Ray Karns

Jun 1, 3, 5
Don Giovanni by Wolfgang Amadeus Mozart

Conductor	Jonathan Shames
Staging	Sarah Caldwell
Scenery	Oliver Smith
Costumes	Stanley Simmons, coordinated by Christine Holmes
Lighting	Graham Walne

Don Giovanni	Claude Corbeil
Leporello	Spiro Malas
Donna Anna	Sarah Reese
Donna Elvira	Carol Gutnecht
Don Ottavio	Noel Velasco
Zerlina	Julia Lovett
Masetto/Commendatore	James Sergi

Nov 30, Dec 2, 5, 9
Les Contes d'Hoffmann by Jacques Offenbach

Conductor	Neville Dove
Staging	Bliss Hebert
Scenery	Gunther Schneider-Siemssen
Costumes	Gunther Schneider-Siemssen
Lighting	Graham Walne
Surtitles	Lisi Oliver

Hoffmann	John Alexander
Nicklausse/Muse	Adele Nicholson
Lindorf/Coppelius/Dr. Miracle/ Dappertutto	Justino Diaz
Olympia	Ruth Welting
Nathaniel	Issac Kriger
Antonia	Sarah Reese
Giulietta/Stella	Madelyn Renée
Luther/Crespel/ Schlemil	Richard McKee
Andrès/Cochenille/Frantz/ Pittichinaccio	David Eisler
Hermann	Michael Morizio

1985—TWENTY-SEVENTH SEASON (ABBREVIATED SEASON DUE TO SARAH CALDWELL'S NEAR-FATAL ILLNESS)

Dec 5, 7, 8, 14, 15
Hansel and Gretel by Engelbert Humperdinck

Conductor	Sarah Caldwell
Staging	Sarah Caldwell
Scenery	David Sharir
Lighting	Graham Walne

Hansel	Rose Marie Freni
Gretel	Jeanne Ommerle

Father	Chester Ludgin
Mother	Pamela Gaily
Dew fairy/sandman	Adele Nicholson

1986—TWENTY-EIGHTH SEASON

Jan 20, 23, 26 (m)
Turandot by Giacomo Puccini

Conductor	Sarah Caldwell
Staging	Sarah Caldwell
Scenery	Ming Cho Lee
Lighting	Graham Walne
Costumes and props	Wang Linyou (courtesy of Central Opera Theater of Beijing, China)
Choreography	Yao Li's Kung Fu Academy

Turandot	Eva Marton
Emperor Altoum	J. Scott Brumit
Liu	Sarah Reese
Calaf	János Nagy
Timur	Spiros Malas
Ping	James Rensick
Pang	Steven Schnurman
Pong	Noel Velasco

Mar 9 (m), 12, 14, 16 (m)
Taverner by Peter Maxwell Davies (U.S. premiere)

Conductor	Sarah Caldwell
Staging	Sarah Caldwell
Scenery	David Sharir
Costumes	Carrie Robbins
Lighting	Graham Walne
Choreography	Stephan Driscoll (Yao Li's Kung Fu Academy)

Taverner	John Moulson
Jester	Alan Oke
White Abbot	Raimund Herincx
Cardinal	Noel Velasco
Rose Parrowe	Rosemary Freni
Priest	Jeffrey Gall
Choirboy	Jared Lawton

King	Andrew Gallagher
Black monk	George Kott
White monk	Kyle Bradford

May 11 (m), 16, 18 (m), 20
The Makropulos Case by Leoš Janáček

Conductor	Sarah Caldwell
Staging	Sarah Caldwell
Scenery	Helen Pond and Herbert Senn
Costumes	Fiandaca
Lighting	Graham Walne

Emilia Marty	Anja Silja
Albert Gregor	William Cochran
Vitek	Noel Velasco
Kristina	Cynthia Clarey
Jaraslav Prus	Chester Ludgin
Janek	Jon David Gruett
Dr. Kolenaty	Richard Fredericks
Stagehand	James Billings
Charwoman	Mary Westbrook-Geha
Hauk-Sendak	John Langston
Chambermaid	Pamela Gailey

Jun 4, 8 (m), 11
Tosca by Giacomo Puccini (replaced Cherubini's *Médée*)

Conductor	Sarah Caldwell
Staging	Sarah Caldwell
Scenery	John Yeck (props borrowed from Opera New England)
Costumes	Ray Diffen
Lighting	Graham Walne
Surtitles	Lisi Oliver

Tosca	Shirley Verrett
Cavaradossi	Joseph Evans
Scarpia	Charles Long
Angelotti	Hugh Givens
Sacristan	James Billings
Sciarrone	Michael Morizio
Spoletta	Geore Kott
Shepherd	Pamela Gailey

1987—TWENTY-NINTH SEASON

Jan 23, 25, 28, Feb 1 (m)
Il Trovatore **by Giuseppe Verdi**

Conductor	Sarah Caldwell
Staging	Sarah Caldwell
Scenery	Helen Pond and Herbert Senn
Costumes	Ray Diffen
Lighting	Graham Walne

Count di Luna	Garbis Boyagian
Ferrando	Jeffrey Wells
Manrico	Bruno Sebastian
Ruiz	George Kott
Lenora	Stefka Evstatieva
Azucena	Stefanie Toczyska

Feb 13, 15 (m), 19, 22 (m)
Giulio Cesare **by George Frideric Handel**

Conductor	Craig Smith
Staging	Peter Sellars
Scenery	Elaine Spatz-Rabinhowitz and Dunya Ramicova
Costumes	Elaine Spatz-Rabinhowitz and Dunya Ramicova
Lighting	James Ingall

Giulio Cesare	Jeffrey Gall
Cornelia	Mary Westbrook-Geha
Sesto Pompeo	Lorraine Hunt
Cleopatra	Susan Larson
Ptolmey	Drew Mintner
Achilla	James Maddalena
Nireno	Cheryl Cobb
Curio	Herman Hildebrand

Mar 25, 29 (m) Apr 3, 5 (m)
Madama Butterfly **by Giacomo Puccini (fourth revival)**

Conductor	Sarah Caldwell
Staging	Sarah Caldwell
Scenery	Ming Cho Lee
Costumes	Ray Diffen

Lighting   Graham Walne
Surtitles   Lisi Oliver

Cio-Cio-San   Sarah Reese
Lieutenant Pinkerton   Joseph Evan
Suzuki   Markella Hatziano
Sharpless   Chester Ludgin
Goro   Noel Velasco
Kate Pinkerton   Andrea Bradford
Prince Yamadori   George Kott
The Bonze   Keith Frederic Howard
Official registrar   Darrell Pestano
Trouble   Atia Walker
Yakside   J. Scott Brumitt

May 6, 10, 17
Don Pasquale by Gaetano Donizetti (Médée postponed)
Conductor   Sarah Caldwell
Staging   Sarah Caldwell
Scenery   Helen Pond and Herbert Senn
Costumes   John Lehmeyer
Lighting   Graham Walne

Don Pasquale   Chester Ludgin
Malatesta   Robert Orth
Ernesto   Joseph Evans
Norina   Jeanne Ommerle
Notary   George Kott

1988—THIRTIETH SEASON

Jan 22, 24 (m), 31 (m)
Médée by Luigi Cherubini (in French with classical Greek dialogue)
Conductor   Sarah Caldwell
Staging   Sarah Caldwell
Scenery   John Gardella
Costumes   George Ziakis
Surtitles   Lisi Oliver

Médée   Josephine Barstow
Médée (speaking role)   Antigony Valakou

Jason	Joseph Evans
Glauce (Dirce)	Jeanne Ommerle
Creon	George Pappas
Neris	Markella Hatziano
First maid's servant	Jayne West
Second maid's servant	Melody Horton

Mar 12, 16, 20, 27
Dead Souls by Rodion Shchedrin, based on the novel by Nikolai Gogol (U.S. premiere)

Conductor	Dzhansug Kahidze
Scenery	Valery Leventhal

Chickikov	Igor Morozov
Mizhuev	Richard Crist
Korobochka	Nina Gaponova
A social climber	Sarah Reese
Plyushkin	Galina Borisova
Maslennilov	Emily Rawlins/Eunice Alberts
Sobakevich	Boris Morosov
Ensemble	Chester Ludgin, Noel Velasco, William Fleck

Apr 22, 24 (m), 27
The Threepenny Opera by Kurt Weill and Bertolt Brecht

Conductor	Joel Thome
English translation	Marc Blitzstein
Scenery	Helen Pond and Herbert Senn
Costumes	Marcia K. McDonald
Lighting	Graham Walne
Surtitles	Lisi Oliver

Macheath	John Brandstetter
Mr. Peachum	Chester Ludgin
Mrs. Peachum	Phyllis Curtin
Polly Peachum	Jeanne Ommerle
Lucy	Emily Rawlins
Jenny	Sarah Reese
Filch	Stephan Driscoll
Tiger Brown	Richard Crist
Street Singer	Keith Buterbauge

257

May 15 (m), 18, 20, 22 (m)
La Traviata by Giuseppe Verdi
Conductor   Sarah Caldwell
Staging   Sarah Caldwell
Scenery   William Pitkin
Costumes   Wayne Newton
Lighting   Graham Walne
Surtitles   Lisi Oliver

Violetta   Catherine Lamy
Alfredo   Noel Velasco
Germont pére   John Brandstetter
Gaston   George Kott
Baron Douphol   Roger Saylor
Marquis d'Obigny   Raymond Karnes
Flora   Rose Marie Freni
Annina   Andrea Bradford
Dr. Grenvil   Richard Crist
Gardner   Frank Levar

1989—THIRTY-FIRST SEASON

Jan 19, 22, 29
Mass by Leonard Bernstein
Conductor   Sarah Caldwell
Staging   Sarah Caldwell
Scenery   Helen Pond and Herbert Senn
Costumes   Carrie Robbins
Choreography   Patricia Birch

Celebrant   Richard Morris

Mar 2, 5 (m), 12 (m)
Aida by Giuseppe Verdi
Conductor   Sarah Caldwell
Staging   Sarah Caldwell
Scenery   Helen Pond and Herbert Senn
Costumes   Ray Diffen

Aida   Shirley Verrett
Amneris   Markella Hatziano

Amanasro	David Arnold
Radames	Franco Bonanome
Ramfis	Barseg Tumanyan

Apr 13, 16 (m), 23 (m)
Der Rosenkavalier by Richard Strauss

Conductor	William Fred Scott
Staging	Lisi Oliver
Scenery	Helen Pond and Herbert Senn
Costumes	Ray Diffen
Lighting	John McLain

Princess von Werdenberg (*Marshallin*)	Gwyneth Jones/Kay Griffel
Baron Ochs	William Wildermann
Octavian	Delia Wallis
Herr Von Faninal	Chester Ludgin
Sophie	Jeanne Ommerle
Italian tenor	Tonio Di Paolo
Valzacchi	John Moulson

Jun 1, 4 (m), 9, 11 (m)
La Bohème by Giacomo Puccini (revival of 1966 production)

Conductor	Sarah Caldwell
Staging	Sarah Caldwell
Associate director	Esquire Joachem
Scenery	Rudolf Heinrich
Costumes	Ray Diffen
Lighting	John McClean
Surtitles	Lisi Oliver

Rodolfo	Tonio Di Paolo
Marcello	Vladimir Chernov
Mimi	Ilona Tokody
Colline	Kevin Langan/James Courtney
Schaunard	James Busterud
Benoit/Alcindoro	James Billings
Musetta	Sarah Reese
Parpingnol	Christoper Vettel
Sergeant	John Clarke
Customs officer	D. Robert Maher

1990—THIRTY-SECOND SEASON

Jan 25, 28
Madama Butterfly (Puccini's final version; fifth revival of Ming Cho Lee production)

Conductor	Sarah Caldwell
Staging	Sarah Caldwell
Scenery	Ming Cho Lee/Ray Diffen production

Cio-Cio-San	Yoko Wantanabe
Lieutenant Pinkerton	Joseph Evans
Suzuki	Markela Hatziano
Sharpless	Chester Ludgin
Goro	Noel Velasco
The Bonze	George Kott

Feb 4, 11
Madama Butterfly (Brescia version)
Same crew and cast as January 25, 28, except:

Cio-Cio-San	Patricia Craig
Lieutenant Pinkerton	Tonio Di Paolo

Mar 11, 18, Apr 21, 29
Madama Butterfly (La Scala version)
Same crew and cast as January 25, 28, except:

Cio-Cio-San	Catherine Lamy

May 8, 11, 18
The Magic Flute by Wolfgang Amadeus Mozart (in English)

Conductor	Sarah Caldwell
Staging	Sarah Caldwell
Scenery	Helen Pond and Herbert Senn
Costumes	Rudolf Heinrich
Lighting	John Michael Deegan

Tamino	Joseph Evans
Papageno	Richard Paul Fink
Queen of the Night	Penelope Walmsley-Clark
Monostatos	Noel Velasco
Pamina	Jeanne Ommerle
Sarastro	Stefan Szkafarowsky
Speaker	Thomas Stewart/Chester Ludgin

Jun 14, 17
The Balcony by Robert DiDomenica (world premiere)

Conductor	Sarah Caldwell
Staging	Sarah Caldwell
Scenery	Helen Pond and Herbert Senn
Costumes	Susan Tsu
Lighting	John McClain

Irma	Mignon Dunn
Woman	Mary Westbrook-Geha
Girl	Adele Nicholson
Bishop	Spiro Malas
Judge	Richard Crist
Executioner	Richard Paul Fink
General	John Brandsteter
Chief of police	John Moulson
Roger	Noel Velasco

APPENDIX B

Annals of Opera New England

(m) denotes a matinee performance.

Cast lists are as shown at first mention in a given season; only changes are noted subsequently. Also, performances for Opera New England of Northeastern Connecticut were held in Woodstock, Connecticut, unless otherwise noted.

1974–1975 TOUR

Oct 28	Opera New England of Northeastern Connecticut, Woodstock, CT: Anniston College Cultural Arts Center
Nov 7	Opera League of New Hampshire, Manchester, NH: Palace Theater
Nov 16	Opera New England of Darien, Connecticut, Darien, CT: Darien High School Auditorium

Madama Butterfly by Giacomo Puccini (in English)

Conductor	Sarah Caldwell
Staging	Sarah Caldwell
Scenery	Ming Cho Lee
Costumes	Hugh Sherrer
Lighting	John Michael Deegan

Cio-Cio-San	Joann Hockey
Lieutenant Pinkerton	Joseph Evans
Suzuki	Edith Evans
Sharpless	Ralph Griffin

Goro	David Wait
Kate Pinkerton	Jan Curtis
Yamadori	Jake Bates
The Bonze	John Davies
Imperial Commissioner	David Gorin
Uncle Yakuside	Karol Kostka
Trouble	Eddie Meade

Nov 4   Opera New England of Maine, Portland, ME: City Hall Auditorium

Madama Butterfly
Same crew and cast as 10/28, except:

Suzuki	Eunice Alberts
Sharpless	David Evitts

Nov 9   Opera Worcester, Worcester, MA: Worcester State College Auditorium

Madama Butterfly
Same crew and cast as 10/28, except:

Sharpless	David Evitts

Apr 1	Opera New England of Maine
Apr 5	Opera New England of Darien
Apr 8	Opera Worcester
Apr 14	Opera League of New Hampshire

Così fan tutte by Wolfgang Amadeus Mozart

Conductor	Sarah Caldwell
English translation	Ruth and Thomas Martin
Scenery	Helen Pond and Herbert Senn
Costumes	Jan Skalicky

Fiordiligi	Heather Thompson
Dorabella	Nancy Williams
Ferrando	Joseph Evans
Guglielmo	Will Parker
Don Alfonso	Alan Barker
Despina	Kate Hurney

Apr 12   Opera New England of Northeastern Connecticut, Woodstock, CT: Mansfield Training School, Longley Auditorium

Così fan tutte
Same crew and cast as 4/1, except:
Fiordiligi   Elizabeth Finney
Guglielmo   Ralph Griffin

1974-1975 CHILDREN'S OPERA PROGRAM

Oct 29 (m)   Opera New England of Northeastern Con-
                               necticut
Nov 6 (m)   Opera League of New Hampshire
Nov 9 (m)   Opera Worcester
Nov 15 (m)   Opera New England of Darien, Connecticut
The Jumping Frog of Calaveras County by Lukas Foss
Conductor   David Bishop
Staging   Sarah Caldwell
Scenery   John Michael Deegan

Lulu   Jan Curtis
Smiley   Neil Rosenschein
Uncle Henry   Ralph Griffin
Stranger   John Ostendorf
Guitar player   David Evitts
First craps shooter   David Waite
Second craps shooter   John Davies

Apr 12   Opera New England of Northeastern Con-
                               necticut
Apr 15   Opera League of New Hampshire
The Fisherman and His Wife by Gunther Schuller
Fisherman   Larry Hoenig
Fisherman's wife   Jan Curtis
The cat   Susan Roberts
The fish   Ralph Griffin
Brothers Grimm   David Gorin and Nicholas Muni

1975-1976 TOUR

Oct 24   Opera New England of Maine
Nov 1   Opera New England of Darien

Il Barbiere di Siviglia by Gioachino Rossini (in English)

Conductor	Sarah Caldwell with William Fred Scott, harpsichordist
Staging	Sarah Caldwell with William Fred Scott
Scenery	John Michael Deegan

Almaviva	Joseph Evans
Dr. Bartolo	William Fleck
Don Basilio	John Stephen
Figaro	Ralph Griffin
Fiorello	Gary Gowen
Ambrogio	David Gorin
Rosina	Susanne Marsee
Berta	Jan Curtis

Oct 25	Opera League of New Hampshire
Nov 6	Opera Worcester
Nov 12	Opera New England of Greater Brockton, Brockton, MA

Il Barbiere di Siviglia
Same crew and cast as 10/24, except:

Figaro	David Evitts

Oct 31	Opera New England of Northeastern Connecticut, Woodstock, CT: Anniston College Cultural Arts Center
Nov 2 (m)	Opera New England of Darien

Il Barbiere di Siviglia
Same crew and cast as 10/24, except:

Almaviva	Neil Rosenschein
Figaro	David Evitts
Rosina	Diane Barone

May 1	Opera New England of Bridgeport, Bridgeport, CT: Mertens Theater, Bernhard Center, University of Bridgeport
May 8	Opera League of New Hampshire
May 21	Opera New England of Greater Brockton, Brockton, MA: Brockton High School Auditorium

La Fanciulla del West by Giacomo Puccini

Conductor	Sarah Caldwell
Staging	Sarah Caldwell
English translation	Ruth and Thomas Martin
Scenery	Helen Pond and Herbert Senn
Costumes	Janet Papanek

Minnie	Arlene Saunders
Jack Rance	Giorgio Tozzi
Dick Johnson	William Lewis
Bartender	Alan Crofoot
Wells Fargo agent	Monte Jaffe

May 2   Opera New England of Bridgeport, Bridgeport, CT: Mertens Theater, Bernhard Center, University of Bridgeport

La Fanciulla del West

Same crew and cast as 5/1, except:

Conductor	William Fred Scott
Minnie	Pamela Kucenic
Dick Johnson	Aaron Bergell

May 4   Opera New England of Northeastern Connecticut, Woodstock, CT: Manning Training School, Longley Auditorium

La Fanciulla del West

Same crew and cast as 5/1, except:

Dick Johnson	Aaron Bergell

May 22   Opera Worcester

La Fanciulla del West

Same crew and cast as 5/1, except:

Conductor	William Fred Scott

1975–1976 CHILDREN'S OPERA PROGRAM

Oct 6 (m)	Opera New England of Greater Brockton
Oct 7 (m)	Opera Worcester
Oct 31 (m)	Opera New England of Northeastern Connecticut

Nov 3 (m)   Opera New England of Darien
Nov 9 (m)   Opera New England of Maine
Le Voyage dans la Lune by Jacques Offenbach (in English)
Conductor   William Fred Scott
Staging   Sarah Caldwell

King Cosmos   Robert Mesrobian
Queen Popotte   Cynthia duPont
Dr. Blastoff   John Stephens
Prince Caprice   Neil Rosenschein
Fantasia   Elizabeth King
King V'Lan   Ralph Griffin

Nov 12 (m)   Opera Worcester
The Fisherman and His Wife by Gunther Schuller
Conductor   William Fred Scott
Staging   Sarah Caldwell
Scenery   John Michael Deegan
Costumes   Barbara Devio

Fisherman   Larry Hoenig
Fisherman's wife   Jan Curtis
The cat   Susan Roberts
The fish   Ralph Griffin

1976–1977 TOUR

Nov 13   Opera New England of Maine
La Bohème by Giacomo Puccini (in English)
Conductor   Sarah Caldwell
Staging   Sarah Caldwell
Scenery   Rudolf Heinrich
Costumes   Rudolf Heinrich
Lighting   Robert Tomkins

Rodolfo   Joseph Evans
Marcello   Jake Gardner
Mimi   Joann Yockey
Colline   William Fleck
Schaunard   Matthew Murray
Musetta   Julia Lovett

Benoit/Alcindoro	Ralph Griffin
Parpignol	William Cashman

Dec 3 — Opera New England of Northeastern Connecticut, Danielson, CT: Killingly High School Auditorium

La Bohème

Same crew and cast as 11/13, except:

Rodolfo	Robert Moulson

Dec 7 — Opera League of New Hampshire

La Bohème

Same crew and cast as 11/13, except:

Rodolfo	Melvyn Poll
Marcello	Matthew Murray
Benoit/Alcindoro	Alan Crofoot

Dec 4, 5 — Opera New England of Darien

La Bohème

Same crew and cast as 11/13, except:

Conductor	William Fred Scott
Rodolfo	Melvin Poll/Robert Moulson
Marcello	Matthew Murray/Jake Gardner
Mimi	Joann Yockey/Barbara Hocher
Schaunard	Ralph Griffin
Benoit/Alcindoro	Alan Crofoot
	Chorus of Ox Ridge School

Dec 11 — Opera Worcester

La Bohème

Same crew and cast as 11/13, except:

Conductor	William Fred Scott
Rodolfo	Robert Moulson
Colline	Ralph Griffin
Schaunard	William Fleck

Dec 15 — Opera New England of Greater Brockton

La Bohème

Same crew and cast as 11/13, except:

Conductor	William Fred Scott
Benoit/Alcindoro	Alan Crofoot
Parpignol	Fred Capodilupo

Apr 3	Opera New England of Cape Cod, Sandwich, MA
Apr 8	Opera New England of Maine
Apr 13	Opera Worcester
Apr 15	Opera New England of Greater Brockton
May 2	Opera New England of Northeastern Connecticut

Rigoletto by Giuseppe Verdi (in English)

Conductor	Sarah Caldwell
Staging	Sarah Caldwell
Rigoletto	Adib Fazah
Duke of Mantua	Joseph Evans
Gilda	Leigh Munro
Maddalena	Jan Curtis
Sparafucile	James Johnson
Count Monterone	Michael Burt

Apr 16	Opera League of New Hampshire

Rigoletto
Same crew and cast as 4/3, except:

Duke of Mantua	Aaron Bergell

May 7	Opera New England of Bridgeport, Connecticut

Rigoletto
Same crew and cast as 4/3, except:

Conductor	William Fred Scott

May 8	Opera New England of Bridgeport, Connecticut

Rigoletto
Same crew and cast as 4/3, except:

Conductor	John Balme

May 8 (m)	Opera New England of Bridgeport, Connecticut

Rigoletto
Same crew and cast as 4/3, except:
Conductor   David Gorin

1976–1977 CHILDREN'S OPERA PROGRAM

Nov 3   Opera New England of Northeastern Con-
                                    necticut
Nov 4, 5   Opera New England of Darien
Il Trionfo dell'Onore by Alessandro Scarlatti (in English)
Cast list unavailable

Feb 4   Opera New England of Northeastern Con-
                                    necticut
Second Hurricane by Aaron Copland
Cast list unavailable

1977–1978 TOUR

Oct 14   Opera New England of Northeastern Con-
                                    necticut
Oct 19   Opera Worcester
Oct 23   Opera New England of Bridgeport, Connecti-
                                    cut
Oct 25   Opera League of New Hampshire
Le Nozze di Figaro by Wolfgang Amadeus Mozart
Conductor   William Fred Scott
Staging   Sarah Caldwell
English translation   Edward Dent
Scenery   Lester Polakov

Count Almaviva   Ralph Griffin
Figaro   Richard Barrett
Dr. Bartolo   William Fleck
Don Basilio/Don Curzio   Alexander Stevenson
Cherubino   Eunice Alberts
Antonio   Matthew Dooley
Countess   Mariana Christos
Susanna   Leigh Munro

| Marcellina | Evelyn Petros |
| Barbarina | Sue Ellen Kuzma |

Mar 31	Opera League of New Hampshire
Apr 2	Opera Worcester (in English)
Apr 4	Opera New England of Maine
Apr 7	Opera New England of Northeastern Connecticut

Tosca by Giacomo Puccini

| Conductor | William Fred Scott |
| Staging | Sarah Caldwell |

Tosca	Claudia Lindsey
Cavaradossi	Thomas O'Leary
Scarpia	Ronald Holgate
Angelotti	Matthew Murray
Sacristan	William Fleck
Sciarrone	Robert Honeysucker
Spoletta	Chapin David
Jailer	John Kern
Shepherd	Geraldine Baretto

| Apr 8 | Opera New England of Darien |

Tosca

Same crew and cast as 3/31, except:

| Conductor | Sarah Caldwell |

| Apr 10 | Opera New England of Greater Brockton |

Tosca

Same crew and cast as 3/31, except:

Conductor	Sarah Caldwell
Tosca	Eileen Schauler
Shepherd	Geraldine Barretto

1977-1978 CHILDREN'S OPERA PROGRAM

Dec 2 (m)	Opera New England of Darien
Dec 5 (m)	Opera New England of Northeastern Connecticut
Dec 8 (m)	Opera New England of Greater Brockton
?	Opera New England of Cape Cod

Feb 7, 8, 9 (m) Opera New England of Bridgeport, Connecticut

The Jumping Frog of Calaveras County by Lukas Foss
Cast list unavailable

Mar 25 Opera New England of Northeastern Connecticut

The Impresario by Wolfgang Amadeus Mozart
Cast list unavailable except:

Ensemble	Leigh Munro, Claudette Peterson, Michael Hume

1978–1979 TOUR

Oct 7	Opera League of New Hampshire
Oct 9	Opera Worcester
Oct 15	Opera New England of Northeastern Connecticut

La Fille du Régiment by Gaetano Donizetti (in English)

Conductor	William Fred Scott
Staging	Sarah Caldwell
Scenery	Judie A. Juracek

Marie	Claudette Peterson
Sulpice	Michael Rippon
Tonio	Peter Jeffries
Marquise de Birkenfeld	Jan Curtis
Hortensio	William Fleck
Duchess de Krankenthorpe	Eugenia Rawlins

Oct 19 Opera New England of Greater Brockton

La Fille du Régiment
Same crew and cast as 10/7, except:

Conductor	Sarah Caldwell
Tonio	Abram Morales

Nov 11 Opera New England of Darien

La Fille du Régiment
Same crew and cast as 10/7, except:

Marie	Maryanne Telese

| *Sulpice* | William Fleck |
| *Tonio* | Abram Morales |

| Apr 18 | Opera New England of Greater Brockton |

Falstaff by Giuseppe Verdi

Conductor	William Fred Scott
Staging	Sarah Caldwell
English translation	Andrew Porter
Scenery	Helen Pond and Herbert Senn

Falstaff	Ronald Hedlund
Fenton	Joseph Evans
Ford	Ralph Griffin
Dr. Caius	Michael Magierea
Bardolph	Larry Bakt
Pistol	William Fleck
Alice Ford	Catherine Wilson
Nannetta	Leigh Munro
Mistress Page	Jan Curtis
Mistress Quickly	Eunice Alberts

| Apr 21 | Opera New England of Northeastern Connecticut |

Falstaff

Same crew and cast as 4/18, except:

| *Bardolph* | John Krovany |

| May 3 | Opera New England of Maine |

Falstaff

Same crew and cast as 4/18, except:

| *Ford* | David Arnold |

| May 7 | Opera League of New Hampshire |

Falstaff

Same crew and cast as 4/18, except:

Ford	David Arnold
Bardolph	John Krovany
Mistress Page	Jan Curtis

| May 12 | Opera New England of Stratford, Connecticut: American Shakespeare Festival Theatre |

Falstaff (same crew and cast as 4/18)

1978-1979 CHILDREN'S OPERA PROGRAM
CHRISTMAS/HOLIDAY PROGRAM

Dec 3	Opera New England of Bridgeport, CT: Mertens Theater, Bernhard Center, University of Bridgeport
Dec 7 (m), 8	Opera New England of Northeastern Connecticut, Putnam, CT: Putnam Middle School Auditorium
Dec 8	Opera New England of Bridgeport, CT: Ridgefield High School
?	Opera New England of Cape Cod

Hansel and Gretel **by Engelbert Humperdinck (in English)**

Conductor	John Balme
Staging	Sarah Caldwell
Scenery	David Sharir
Costumes	David Sharir

Hansel	D'Anna Fortunato
Gretel	Claudette Peterson
Father	William Fleck
Mother	Victoria Vergara
Sandman/dew fairy	Ellen McLain
Witch	Eunice Alberts

Dec 13	Opera New England of Maine

Hansel and Gretel

Same crew and cast as 12/3, except:

Hansel	Evelyn Petros
Gretel	Janice Hall
Father	Noel Tyl
Witch	Jan Curtis

Dec 17	Opera New England of Greater Brockton

Hansel and Gretel

Same crew and cast as 12/3, except:

Hansel	Evelyn Petros

1979-1980 TOUR

Oct 26	Opera New England of Northeastern Connecticut

Oct 30   Opera New England of Greater Brockton
Nov 9   Opera League of New Hampshire

Madama Butterfly by Giacomo Puccini

Conductor	William Fred Scott
Staging	Sarah Caldwell
Scenery	Ming Cho Lee
Costumes	Hugh Sherrer

Cio-Cio-San	Sung Sook Lee
Lieutenant Pinkerton	Joseph Evans
Suzuki	Eunice Alberts
Sharpless	Ralph Griffin
Goro	Michael Hume
Kate Pinkerton	Leslie Holmes
Prince Yamadori	Jack Bates
The Bonze	Lawrence Thomas
Imperial Commissioner	William Cashman
Uncle Yakuside	Mathew Dooley

Apr 21   Opera League of New Hampshire
May 3   Opera New England of Northeastern Connecticut
May 13   Opera New England of Maine
May 19   Opera New England of Greater Brockton

Die Fledermaus by Johann Strauss II (in English)

Conductor	William Fred Scott
Staging	Sarah Caldwell

Gabriel von Eisenstein	Ralph Griffin
Rosalinde	Eleanor Berguist
Adele	Claudette Peterson
Alfred	Harry Danner
Prince Orlofsky	Suzanne Brenning
Dr. Falke	Michael Rippon
Blind	Michael Hume
Frosch	Jim Morgan
Ida	Elena Gamboulis

1979-1980 CHILDREN'S OPERA PROGRAM

Nov 26, 29	Opera New England of Ridgefield and Stamford, CT: Ridgefield Auditorium
?	Opera New England of Cape Cod
Apr 25	Opera New England of Stratford, CT: American Shakespeare Festival Theatre

The Impresario by Wolfgang Amadeus Mozart

Impresario	Michael Hume
Mme. Herz	Elena Gambulos
Mlle. Silberklang	Sally Arenson

1980-1981 TOUR

Oct 22	Opera League of New Hampshire
Oct 29	Opera New England of Greater Brockton
Nov 7	Opera New England of Northeastern Connecticut, Danielson, CT: Killingly High School Auditorium

Der Vampyr by Heinrich Marschner (in English)

Lord Ruthven	Brent Ellis
Sir Edgar Aubry	James Atherton
Sir Berkeley	Bruce Kramer
Lord Berkeley's daughter	Paula Seibel
Sir Humphrey's daughter	Pamela Rucenac
Vampire master	Peter Lightfoot

Apr 29	Opera New England of Cape Cod
May 4	Opera Worcester (canceled)
May 13	Opera New England of Maine
May 15	Opera New England of Greater Brockton
May 16	Opera New England of Stratford, Connecticut
May 17	Opera New England of Bangor, Maine

Don Pasquale by Gaetano Donizetti (in English)

Conductor	David Montgomery
Staging	Sarah Caldwell
Scenery	Helen Pond and Herbert Senn
Costumes	John Lehmeyer

Don Pasquale	Gemi Beni
Dr. Malatesta	Ralph Griffin

Ernesto	Joseph Evans
Norina	Diane Barone
Notary	George Kott
Major-domo	Mark Keppel

May 9	Opera New England of Northeastern Connecticut, Killingly High School Auditorium
May 14	Opera League of New Hampshire

Don Pasquale
Same crew and cast as 4/29, except:

Norina	Jeanne Ommerle

1980-1981 CHILDREN'S OPERA PROGRAM

Nov 12, 13	Opera New England of Northeastern Connecticut
?	Opera New England of Cape Cod

Die Prinzessin auf der Erbse by Ernst Toch (in English)
Cast list unavailable

1981-1982 TOUR

Nov 7	Opera New England of Bangor, Maine
?	Opera New England of Cape Cod

Il Barbiere di Siviglia by Gioachino Rossini (in English)

Conductor	Sarah Caldwell
Staging	Sarah Caldwell

Almaviva	Gerald Grahame
Dr. Bartolo	Carlos Chausson
Don Basilio	Michael Burt
Figaro	William McGraw
Fiorello	Rodney Miller
Rosina	Evelyn Petros
Berta	Rebecca Mercer-White

Nov 13	Opera League of New Hampshire

Il Barbiere di Siviglia
Same crew and cast as 11/7, except:

Figaro	Vernon Hartman

Apr 20   Opera New England of Maine
La Bohème by Giacomo Puccini (in English)
Conductor   Neville Dove
Staging   Sarah Caldwell

Rodolfo   Noel Velasco
Marcello   David Evitts
Mimi   Sarah Reese
Colline   Philip Booth
Shaunard   Vernon Hartman
Musetta   Jan Ommerle
Benoit/Alcindoro   George Kott

Apr 23   Opera New England of Northeastern Connecticut

May 1   Opera League of New Hampshire
La Bohème
Same crew and cast as 4/20, except:
Musetta   Gloria Carone

1982–1983 TOUR

Nov 5   Opera League of New Hampshire
Nov 7   Opera New England of Northeastern Connecticut

Nov 13   Opera New England of Maine
La Traviata by Giuseppe Verdi
Conductor   Steven Stein
Staging   Sarah Caldwell

Violetta   Sarah Reese
Alfredo   Noel Velasco
Germont père   David Parsons
Baron Douphol   William McFarland
Dr. Grenvil   James Rensink

Apr 27   Opera New England of Maine
May 1   Opera New England of Cape Cod
May 6   Opera New England of Northeastern Connecticut

May 8   Opera New England of Bangor, Maine
May 14   Opera New England of Stamford, Connecticut

Die Entführung aus dem Serail by Wolfgang Amadeus Mozart (in English)
Conductor   Neville Dove
Staging   Sarah Caldwell

Konstanze   Catherine Caccavallo
Blonde   Claudette Peterson
Belmonte   Joseph Evans
Pedrillo   Keith Olsen
Osmin   Philip Booth
Pasha Selim   Robert Bloodworth

Apr 29   Opera League of New Hampshire
Die Entführung aus dem Serail
Same crew and cast as 4/27, except:
Belmonte   Noel Velasco
Pedrillo   Richard Crist
Osmin   Herbert Beattie

1982–1983 CHILDREN'S OPERA PROGRAM

?   Opera New England of Northeastern Con-
                                    necticut
?   Opera New England of Cape Cod
The Frog Who Became a Prince and *Zetabet* by Edward Barnes
Cast list unavailable

1983–1984 TOUR

Oct 14   Opera League of New Hampshire
Oct ?   Opera New England of Northeastern Con-
                                    necticut
Oct 22   Opera New England of Maine
Orphée aux Enfers by Jacques Offenbach (in English)
Conductor   Neville Dove
Staging   Sarah Caldwell

Professor Orpheus   Robert Orth
Jupiter   James Rensink

Morpheus	Noel Velasco
Eurydice	Jeanne Ommerle
Miss Pubic Opinion	Kathryn Grayson
Cupid	Evelyn Petros
Juno	Eunice Alberts
Apr 25	Opera League of New Hampshire
Apr 26	Opera New England of Maine
Apr 27	Opera League of New Hampshire
May 4	Opera New England of Northeastern Connecticut

Don Giovanni by Wolfgang Amadeus Mozart

Don Giovanni	Robert Trehy
Leporello	James Rensink
Donna Anna	Sarah Reese
Don Ottavio	Noel Velasco

1983–1984 CHILDREN'S OPERA PROGRAM

Nov 9, 10	Opera New England of Northeastern Connecticut
?	Opera New England of Cape Cod

The Impresario by Wolfgang Amadeus Mozart
Cast list unavailable

1984–1985 TOUR

Oct 26	Opera League of New Hampshire
Oct 28	Opera New England of Cape Cod
Nov 2	Opera New England of Northeastern Connecticut

Tosca by Giacomo Puccini

Tosca	Katherine Ciesinski
Cavaradossi	Noel Velasco
Scarpia	Rodney Stenborg
Angelotti/Sciarrone	Joseph McKee
Sacristan	James Billings
Spoletta	Ross Price

| May 3 | Opera New England of Northeastern Connecticut |
| May 10 | Opera League of New Hampshire |

La Fille du Régiment by Gaetano Donizetti (in English)

1984–1985 CHILDREN'S OPERA PROGRAM

| ? | Opera New England of Cape Cod |

La Voyage dans la Lune
Cast list unavailable

1985–1986 TOUR

| Oct 18 | Opera League of New Hampshire |
| Nov 2 | Opera New England of Northeastern Connecticut |

Les Pêcheurs de Perles by Georges Bizet (in English)

| Conductor | Jonathan Shames |
| Staging | Sarah Caldwell |

Leila	Joyce Guyer
Nadir	Paul S. Adkins
Zurga	David Arnold
Nourabad	J. B. Davis

Apr 18	Opera New England of Natick, Massachusetts
Apr 30	Opera New England of Torrington, Connecticut
May 2	Opera New England of Northeastern Connecticut
May 8	Opera Worcester
May 9	Opera League of New Hampshire
May 17	Opera New England of Bangor, Maine

Madama Butterfly by Giacomo Puccini

Conductor	James Brenner
Staging	Sarah Caldwell
Scenery	Ming Cho Lee

| *Cio-Cio-San* | Lea Jorgenson |
| *Lieutenant Pinkerton* | Stephen Smith |

Suzuki	Eunice Alberts
Sharpless	Steven Tachell
Goro	Michael Hume
Kate Pinkerton	Abbie Jenn Sher
Prince Yamadori	George Kott
The Bonze	J. Scott Brumit

May 4   Opera New England of Cape Cod
Madama Butterfly
Same crew and cast as 4/18, except:
Cio-Cio-San   Louisa Jonason

1985–1986 CHILDREN'S OPERA PROGRAM

Nov 18, 19   Opera New England of Northeastern Con-
                                        necticut, Danielson, CT: Killingly High
                                        School/Mansfield Middle School
?   Opera New England of Cape Cod
La Fille du Régiment by Gaetano Donizetti (in English)
Cast list unavailable

1986–1987 TOUR

Nov 1   Opera New England of Northeastern Con-
                                        necticut
Nov 7   Opera League of New Hampshire
Rigoletto by Giuseppe Verdi
Conductor   Michael Barrett
Staging   Sarah Caldwell

Rigoletto	Mark Rucker
Duke of Mantua	Paul Hartfiel
Gilda	Maureen O'Flynn
Maddalena	Jan Curtis
Monterone/Sparafucile	Brian Phipps
Count Ceprano	Charles Bosselman

May 2   Opera New England of Northeastern Con-
                                        necticut

May 8   Opera League of New Hampshire
May 9   Opera New England of Cape Cod
Don Pasquale by Gaetano Donizetti
Conductor   Theodore Ganger
Staging   Sarah Caldwell
Scenery   Helen Pond and Herbert Senn
Costumes   John Lehmeyer

Don Pasquale   Thomas Hammons
Dr. Malatesta   Eugene Perry
Ernesto   Gary Harger
Norina   Jeanine Thames
Notary   George Kott

1986-1987 CHILDREN'S OPERA PROGRAM

?   Opera New England of Cape Cod
?   Opera New England of Northeastern Con-
                               necticut
The Jumping Frog of Calaveras County by Lukas Foss
Cast list unavailable

1987-1988 TOUR

Oct 23   Opera New England of Natick, Massachusetts
Oct 25   Opera New England of Cape Cod
Oct 28   Opera Worcester
Oct 30   Opera League of New Hampshire
Nov 5   Opera New England of Northeastern Con-
                               necticut
Le Nozze di Figaro by Wolfgang Amadeus Mozart (in English)
Conductor   Theodore Ganger
Staging   Sarah Caldwell

Count Almaviva   Randolph Messing
Figaro   Stephan Len White
Dr. Bartolo/Antonio   Richard Crist
Don Basilio   David Ronis
Cherubino   Dorene Falcett

Countess	Judith Burbank
Susanna	Maureen O'Flynn
Marcellina	Barbara McCalister

May 6	Opera League of New Hampshire
May 14	Opera New England of Cape Cod, Sandwich, MA: Sandwich High School

The Threepenny Opera by Kurt Weill and Bertolt Brecht

Conductor	Joe Thome
Staging	Stephan Driscoll, associate director
English translation	Marc Blitzstein
Scenery	Helen Pond and Herbert Senn
Costumes	Marcia K. MacDonald
Lighting	Michael Fastoso
Surtitles	Lisi Oliver

Macheath	Keith Buterbaugh
Mr. Peachum	Stephan Driscoll
Mrs. Peachum	Rose Marie Freni
Polly Peachum	Jeanne Ommerele
Lucy	Pamela Hinchman
Jenny	Emily Rawlins
Filch	Carl Kraenzel
Street singer/Tiger Brown	Richard Crist

1987-1988 CHILDREN'S OPERA PROGRAM

Nov 16	Opera New England of Bridgeport, Connecticut, Bridgeport, CT: Klein Memorial Auditorium
?	Opera New England of Cape Cod
?	Opera New England of Northeastern Connecticut

Hansel and Gretel by Engelbert Humperdinck
Cast list unavailable

1988-1989 TOUR

Oct 30, Nov 1	Opera New England of Cape Cod
Nov 4	Opera League of New Hampshire

Nov 5   Opera New England of Northeastern Con-
                                   necticut
Il Barbiere di Siviglia by Gioachino Rossini (in English)
Almaviva   Noel Velasco
Dr. Bartolo   Richard Crist
Don Basilio   Gerard Edery
Figaro   Vernon Hartman
Rosina   Melanie Helton
Berta   Andrea Bradford

May 6   Opera New England of Northeastern Con-
                                   necticut
May 12   Opera League of New Hampshire
May 13   Opera New England of Cape Cod
La Traviata by Giuseppe Verdi
Violetta   Karen Acampora
Alfredo   Gabriel Sade
Germont père   Charles Robert Stephens
Flora   Jan Curtis

1989–1990 TOUR

May 5   Opera New England of Northeastern Con-
                                   necticut
May 9   Opera Worcester
May 11   Opera League of New Hampshire
La Bohème by Giacomo Puccini
Conductor   Robert Kapilow
Staging   Lisi Oliver
Scenery   Rudolf Heinrich
Costumes   Rudolf Heinrich

Rodolfo   Noel Velasco
Marcello   Stephan Lusmann
Mimì   Maureen O'Flynn
Colline   Howard Wilkinson
Schaunard   Michael Sokol
Musetta   Judith Gray
Benoit/Alcindoro   George Kott

1989-1990 CHILDREN'S OPERA PROGRAM

Nov 2, 3   Opera New England of Northeastern Con-
                    necticut, Danielson, CT: Killingly High
                    School/Mansfield Middle School

The Jumping Frog of Calaveras County, by **Lukas Foss**
Cast list unavailable

APPENDIX C

Annals of the American National Opera Company

1967–1968 TOUR

(m) denotes a matinee performance.

Sept 15 — Clowes Hall, Butler University, Indianapolis, IN

***Falstaff* by Giuseppe Verdi**

Conductor	Sarah Caldwell
Staging	Sarah Caldwell
Scenery	Oliver Smith
Costumes	Lewis Brown
Lighting	Jean Rosenthal

Falstaff	Peter Glossop
Fenton	Anastasios Vrenios
Ford	George Fourie
Dr. Caius	Ray Arbizu
Bardolph	James Billings
Pistol	Charles Koehn
Alice Ford	Beverly Bower
Nannetta	Benita Valente
Mistress Page	Joanna Simon
Mistress Quickly	Betty Allen

Sept 16   Clowes Hall, Butler University, Indianapolis,
                                    IN

Lulu by Alban Berg
Conductor   Osbourne McConathy
Staging   Sarah Caldwell
English translation   Arthur Jacobs
Scenery   Robin Wagner
Costumes   Frank Thompson
Optical projections   Milton Olshin

Lulu   Louise Budd
Gräfin Geschwitz   Joanna Simon
Painter   Anastasios Vrenios
Dr. Schön   Donald Gramm
Alwa   Thomas Rall
Schigolch   Andrew Foldi
Animal trainer   William Whiteside
Schoolboy   Rosalind Wykes
Wardrobe mistress   Jeanette Walters
Prince/servant   Frank Hoffmeister
Dr. Goll/theater director   Karol Kostka

Sept 19   Clowes Hall, Butler University, Indianapolis,
                                    IN

Tosca by Giacomo Puccini
Conductor   Jonel Perlea
Staging   Sarah Caldwell
Scenery   Rudolf Heinrich
Costumes   Rudolf Heinrich
Lighting   Jean Rosenthal

Tosca   Marie Collier
Cavaradossi   Ray Arbizu
Scarpia   George Fourie
Angelotti   Bruce Yarnell
Sacristan   Robert Peterson
Sciarrone   Harris Poor
Spoletta   Thomas Jamerson
Jailer   Thomas Carey
Shepherd   Betsy Norden

Sept 20   Clowes Hall, Butler University, Indianapolis,
                                    IN

Lulu
Same as Sept 16 except:
Lulu   Patricia Cullen

Sept 22   Clowes Hall, Butler University, Indianapolis,
                                        IN

Falstaff (in English)
Same as Sept 15 except:
Falstaff   Andrew Foldi
Ford   Ronald Hedlund
Nannetta   Carole Bogard

Sept 23   Clowes Hall, Butler University, Indianapolis,
                                        IN

Tosca
Same as Sept 19 except:
Tosca   Beverly Bower

Sept 25   Shea's Buffalo Theater, Buffalo, NY
Falstaff (in English)
Same as Sept 15 except:
Falstaff   Andrew Foldi
Nannetta   Carole Bogard
Mistress Page   Margaret Yauger
Mistress Quickly   Eunice Alberts

Sept 26 (m)   Shea's Buffalo Theater, Buffalo, NY
Falstaff (two acts, in Italian, for children)
Same as Sept 15

Sept 26   Shea's Buffalo Theater, Buffalo, NY
Lulu
Same as Sept 16 except:
Lulu   Patricia Cullen

Sept 27   Shea's Buffalo Theater, Buffalo, NY
Sept 28   Eastman Theater, Rochester, NY
Sept 30   Middletown High School, Middletown, NY
Tosca
Same as Sept 19 except:
Tosca   Beverly Bower

Oct 2   Loew's State Theater, Syracuse, NY

Falstaff
Same as Sept 15 except:

Falstaff	Robert Petersen
Ford	Ronald Hedlund
Nannetta	Carole Bogard
Mistress Page	Margaret Yauger
Mistress Quickly	Nell Evans

Oct 3 — Procter's Theater, Schenectady, NY

Falstaff **(in English)**
Same as Sept 15 except:

Falstaff	Robert Petersen
Mistress Ford	Jeannette Walters

Oct 6 — Brooklyn Academy of Music, Brooklyn, NY

Lulu
Same as Sept 16 except:

Lulu	Patricia Cullen

Oct 7 (m) — Brooklyn Academy of Music, Brooklyn, NY

Falstaff **(same as Sept 15)**

Oct 7 — Brooklyn Academy of Music, Brooklyn, NY

Oct 9 — Veterans Memorial Auditorium, Columbus, OH

Tosca **(same as Sept 19)**

Oct 12 — Wisconsin Union Theater, University of Wisconsin, Madison, WI

Lulu
Same as Sept 16 except:

Lulu	Patricia Cullen

Oct 13 — Wisconsin Union Theater, University of Wisconsin, Madison, WI

Falstaff **(in Italian)**
Same as Sept 15 except:

Ford	Ronald Hedlund
Alice Ford	Jeanette Walters
Nannetta	Carole Bogard
Mistress Page	Margaret Yauger
Mistress Quickly	Eunice Alberts

Oct 14 (m)   Wisconsin Union Theater, University of Wisconsin, Madison, WI

Tosca (in English, special matinee for high school and college students)
Same as Sept 19

Oct 14   Wisconsin Union Theater, University of Wisconsin, Madison, WI

Tosca
Same as Sept 19 except:
Tosca   Beverly Bower

Oct 16   Masonic Auditorium, Detroit, MI
***Tosca* (same as Sept 19)**

Oct 17   Masonic Auditorium, Detroit, MI
***Falstaff* (same as Sept 15)**

Oct 18   Civic Opera House, Chicago, IL
***Tosca* (same as Sept 19)**

Oct 19   Civic Opera House, Chicago, IL
Lulu
Same as Sept 16 except:
Lulu   Patricia Cullen

Oct 20   Civic Opera House, Chicago, IL
Falstaff
Same as Sept 15 except:
Nannetta   Carole Bogard

Oct 21   Civic Opera House, Chicago, IL
Lulu
Same as Sept 16 except:
Lulu   Patricia Cullen
Dr. Schön   Edmund Hurshell
Schigolch   Charles Koehn

Oct 22 (m)   Civic Opera House, Chicago, IL
***Falstaff* (in English)**
Same as Sept 15 except:
Ford   Ronald Hedlund

Oct 24	Assembly Hall, University of Illinois, Champaign, IL

Falstaff
Same as Sept 15 except:
Falstaff   Robert Petersen
Nannetta   Carole Bogard

Oct 26	Kiel Auditorium, St. Louis, MO

Falstaff
Same as Sept 15 except:
Ford   Ronald Hedlund

Oct 27	Kiel Auditorium, St. Louis, MO

Lulu
Same as Sept 16 except:
Lulu   Patricia Cullen

Oct 28 (m)	Kiel Auditorium, St. Louis, MO

Tosca (same as Sept 19)

Oct 30	Jones Hall, Little Rock, AR

Tosca
Same as Sept 19 except:
Shepherd   James Crawley

Oct 31	Jones Hall, Little Rock, AR

Falstaff (same as Sept 15)

Nov 2	Tivoli Theater, Chattanooga, TN

Tosca (same as Sept 19)

Nov 3	Civic Auditorium, Knoxville, TN

Falstaff (same as Sept 15)

Nov 4	Civic Auditorium, Knoxville, TN

Tosca (same as Sept 19)

Nov 6	Coffee Auditorium, Florence, AL

Tosca
Same as Sept 19 except:
Conductor   Vincent La Selva
Cavaradossi   Michele Molese
Scarpia   Peter Glossop

Nov 7	Tuscaloosa High School Auditorium, Tuscaloosa, AL

Falstaff (in English)
Same as Sept 15 except for:
Falstaff   Edmund Hurshell
Ford   Ronald Hedlund

Nov 8	Municipal Auditorium, Birmingham, AL

Falstaff
Same as Sept 15

Nov 9	Municipal Theater, Mobile, AL

Tosca (same as Sept 19)

Nov 10	Municipal Auditorium, New Orleans, LA

Lulu
Same as Sept 16 except:
Lulu   Patricia Cullen

Nov 11	Municipal Auditorium, New Orleans, LA

Tosca
Same as Sept 19 except:
Cavaradossi   Michele Molese
Shepherd   James Crawley

Nov 14	Back Bay Theater, Boston, MA

Falstaff
Same as Sept 15 except:
Ford   Ronald Hedlund
Nannetta   Carole Bogard
Mistress Page   Margaret Yauger

Nov 15	Back Bay Theater, Boston, MA

Falstaff
Same as Sept 15 except:
Falstaff   Robert Petersen
Ford   David Hall
Dr. Caius   Thomas Jamerson
Mistress Quickly Eunice Alberts

Nov 16	Back Bay Theater, Boston, MA

Falstaff
Same as Sept 15 except:
Ford   Ronald Hedlund

Nov 17   Back Bay Theater, Boston, MA
Lulu
Same as Sept 16 except:
Lulu   Patricia Cullen

Nov 19   Back Bay Theater, Boston, MA
Lulu (same as Sept 16)

Mar 16   University Concert Hall, Albuquerque, NM
Carmen by Georges Bizet
Cast list unavailable except for:
Escamillo   Bruce Yarnell
Carmen   Gloria Lane

Mar 17   University Concert Hall, Albuquerque, NM
Tosca (same as Sept 19)

Mar 20   Grady Gammage Auditorium, Arizona State
                                            University, Tempe, AZ

Tosca by Giacomo Puccini
Conductor   Osbourne McConathy
Staging   Sarah Caldwell
Scenery   Rudolf Heinrich
Costumes   Rudolf Heinrich
Lighting   Jean Rosenthal

Tosca   Lucine Amara
Cavaradossi   Thomas Rall
Scarpia   George Fourie
Angelotti   Ronald Hedlund
Sacristan   James Billings
Spoletta   Robert Petersen
Jailer   Thomas Jamerson
Shepherd   Betsy Norden

Mar 21   Grady Gammage Auditorium, Arizona State
                                            University, Tempe, AZ

The Rake's Progress by Igor Stravinsky

Conductor	Robert Craft
Staging	Sarah Caldwell
Scenery	Helen Pond and Herbert Senn
Wigs and makeup	Gottfried Schiller
Choreography	Killer Joe Piro, "King of the Discotheques"

Tom Rakewell	Ragnar Ulfung
Anne Trulove	Benita Valente
Nick Shadow	Donald Gramm
Trulove	Charles Koehn
Mother Goose	Nell Evans
Baba the Turk	John Ferrante
Sellem/keeper of the madhouse	James Billings

Mar 22	Grady Gammage Auditorium, Arizona State University, Tempe, AZ

Carmen by Georges Bizet

Conductor	Henry Lewis
Staging	Sarah Caldwell
Scenery	Oliver Smith
Lighting	Peter Hunt
Choreography	Ciro

Don José	Thomas Rall
Escamillo	Bruce Yarnell
El Dancairo	Robert Petersen
El Remendado	Barney Ingram
Morales	Thomas Jameson
Micaela	Carole Bogard
Frasquita	Louise Budd
Mercedes	Linda Phillips
Carmen	Gloria Lane
Innkeeper	Ray Duffy

Mar 25	Dorothy Chandler Pavilion, Los Angeles, CA

Falstaff by Giuseppe Verdi

Conductor	Sarah Caldwell
Scenery	Oliver Smith
Costumes	Lewis Brown
Lighting	Jean Rosenthal

Falstaff	Robert Petersen
Fenton	Anastasios Vrenios
Ford	Ronald Hedlund
Dr. Caius	David Hall
Bardolph	James Billings
Pistol	Charles Koehn
Alice Ford	Beverly Bower
Nannetta	Benita Valente
Mistress Page	Margaret Yauger
Mistress Quickly	Eunice Alberts

Mar 26   Dorothy Chandler Pavilion, Los Angeles, CA
Tosca
Same as March 20 except:
Tosca   Beverly Bower

Mar 27   Dorothy Chandler Pavilion, Los Angeles, CA
The Rake's Progress (same as March 21)

Mar 29   Dorothy Chandler Pavilion, Los Angeles, CA
Carmen
Same as March 22 except:
Don José   Chris Lacona
El Remendado   Robert Petersen

Mar 30 (m)   Dorothy Chandler Pavilion, Los Angeles, CA
Tosca (same as March 20)

Mar 30   Dorothy Chandler Pavilion, Los Angeles, CA
Falstaff (same as March 25)

Mar 31   Dorothy Chandler Pavilion, Los Angeles, CA
Carmen (same as March 22)

Apr 1   Dorothy Chandler Pavilion, Los Angeles, CA
Falstaff (same as March 25)

Apr 2   Dorothy Chandler Pavilion, Los Angeles, CA
The Rake's Progress
Same as March 21 except:
Trulove   Ronald Hedlund

Apr 3	Dorothy Chandler Pavilion, Los Angeles, CA

Tosca
Same as March 20 except:

Tosca	Beverly Bower
Cavaradossi	Ray Arbizu

Apr 4	Civic Theater, San Diego, CA (presented as part of the San Diego Opera season)

The Rake's Progress
Same as March 21 except:

Anne Trulove	Carole Bogard

Apr 5	Civic Theater, San Diego, CA

***The Rake's Progress* (same as March 21)**

Apr 6 (m)	Dorothy Chandler Pavilion, Los Angeles, CA

***Falstaff* (same as March 25)**

Apr 6	Dorothy Chandler Pavilion, Los Angeles, CA

***Carmen* (same as March 22)**

BIBLIOGRAPHY

The following is a select list of books and articles consulted in the course of my research. I am grateful to the authors and publishers of those quoted, as identified in the source notes.

BOOKS

Ashbrook, William. *Donizetti*. London: Cassel, 1965.

Brown, David. *Musorgsky: His Life and Works*. New York: Oxford University Press, 2002.

Budden, Julian. *The Operas of Verdi*. 3 vols. New York: Oxford University Press, 1978.

Cairns, David. *Berlioz*. Vol. 2, *Servitude and Greatness*. Berkeley: University of California Press, 2000.

Carner, Mosco. *Puccini: A Critical Biography*. Letchworth, Hertfordshire, U.K.: Duckworth, 1958, pp. 120–137.

Clapham, John. *Smetana*. New York: Octagon Books, 1972.

Clement, Felix, and Pierre Larousse. *Dictionnaire des opéras*. 2 vols. Paris, 1906. New York: Da Capo Press, 1969.

Curtis, Mina. *Bizet and His World*. New York: Alfred A. Knopf, 1958.

David, Ronald. *Opera in Chicago*. New York: Appleton-Century, 1966.

Eaton, Quaintance. *The Boston Opera Company*. New York: Appleton-Century, 1965, pp. 280–281.

Ferris, Alexander. *Jacques Offenbach*. New York: Charles Scribner & Sons, 1980.

Fitzgerald, Gerald. *Annals of the Metropolitan Opera, 1883–1985*. Boston: G.K. Hall & Co., 1989, p. 4-A.

Fuchs, Peter Paul, ed. *The Music Theater of Walter Felsenstein.* New York: W.W. Norton & Co., 1975.

Goldovsky, Boris. *Bringing Opera to Life.* Englewood Cliffs, N.J.: Prentice Hall, 1968

Goldovsky, Boris. *My Road to Opera.* Boston: Houghton Mifflin Co., 1979.

Harding, James. *Massenet.* London: J.M. Dent & Sons, 1970.

Harewood, Earl of. *Kobbe's Complete Opera Book.* London: Bodley Head, 1976.

Irvine, Delmar. *Massenet.* Portland, Ore.: Amadeus Press, 1994.

Omstead, Andrea. *Conversations with Roger Sessions.* Boston: Northeast University Press, 1987.

Prausnitz, Frederick. *Roger Sessions.* New York: Oxford University Press, 2002.

Reich, Willi. *Schoenberg: A Critical Biography.* New York: Praeger Publishers, 1968.

Robinson, Harlow. *Sergei Prokofiev: A Biography.* Boston: Northeast University Press, 1987.

Sokol, Martin L. *The New York City Opera: An American Adventure.* New York: Macmillan Publishing, 1981, pp. 456, 458, 489, 493.

Soubies, Albert, and Charles Malherbe. *Histoire de l'opera-comique, 1840–1887.* Paris: Librarie Marpen & Flammarion, 1892–1893.

Steptoe, Andrew. *The Mozart–Da Ponte Operas.* Oxford, U.K.: Clarendon Press, 1988.

Weinstock, Herbert. *Vincenzo Bellini.* New York: Alfred A. Knopf, 1971.

White, Eric Walter. *Tippett and His Operas.* London: Barrie Jenkins, 1979.

PLAY TEXT

de Molina, Tirso. "The Trickster of Seville," published in *Spanish Drama.* A. Flores, ed. New York: Bantam, 1962.

Harrison, Tony. *Le Roi s'amuse/The Prince's Play* by Victor Hugo. London: Farber & Farber, 1996.

MAGAZINES

Time
Newsweek
LIFE
New York Magazine
The New Yorker
Saturday Review of Literature
Boston Magazine

Opera magazine (London)
Opera News (New York)
Opera International (Paris)

NEWSPAPERS

Boston Globe
Boston Herald
Christian Science Monitor
New York Times
New York Daily News
New York Post
Village Voice (New York)
Washington Post
Washington Star
Miami Herald
Chicago Tribune
Chicago Sun-Times
Cleveland Plain Dealer
Houston Chronicle
Houston Post
Dallas Morning News
Los Angeles Times
St. Louis Post-Dispatch
Kansas City Star
Arkansas Gazette (Little Rock)
Indianapolis Star
Buffalo (N.Y.) Courier Express
Buffalo (N.Y.) Evening News
Syracuse (N.Y.) Herald-Journal
Middletown (N.Y.) Times Herald Record
Rochester (N.Y.) Democrat and Chronicle
Albany (N.Y.) Times Union
Albany (N.Y.) Knickerbocker News
Columbus (Ohio) Citizens Journal
Madison (Wisc.) Capital Times
Wisconsin State Journal (Madison)
Urbana (Ill.) News Gazette
Arkansas Democrat (Little Rock)
Chattanooga (Tenn.) News Free Press
Chattanooga (Tenn.) Times

Knoxville (Tenn.) Journal
Birmingham (Ala.) News
Florence (Ala.) Times Tri-Cities Daily
Tuscaloosa (Ala.) News
Mobile (Ala.) Register
Albuquerque (N.M.) Journal
Arizona Republic (Phoenix)
Phoenix Gazette
San Diego Union
Manchester (N.H.) Union Leader
Portland (Maine) Press Herald
Worcester (Mass.) Telegram

INDEX

Jumping Frog of Calavaras County,
 110, 114
Der Junge Lord, 99
Junior League of Boston, 85–86

Kahlet, Neils, 44
Keith, Benjamin Franklin, 144
Kelley, Kevin, 36
Kelley, Norman, 85
Kelly, Emmett, Sr., 98
Kennedy, Joseph, 144
Kerner, Leighton, 180
King Priam, 105
Kipnis, Claude, 58
Kipnis, Dinah, 62
The Knot Garden, 105
Kolodin, Irving, 5, 57, 59
Komische Oper, 17, 41, 69, 103
Koussevitzky, Serge, 14, 131
Kraus, Alfredo, 132
Kresge Auditorium at MIT, 81, 82, 86
Kubelik, Raphael, 94
Kurka, Robert, 84–85

Lachner, Franz, 173–74
Lahat, Shlomo, 154
Lally, Francis T., Monsignor, 27, 28,
 31
Lamb, Joseph, 144
La Montaine, John, 130
Lane, Gloria, 77
Larson, Susan, 180
Leacock, Richard, 184–85
Lee, Ming Cho, 40, 41, 111, 118
Leigh, Adele, 56
Leinsdorf, Erich, 163
Leland, Sarah, 33
LeLoraine, Jacques, 101
Levin & Weintraub, 78
Levine, James, 128
Lewis, Richard, 57–58

Lewis, William, 111–12
Lexington Choral Society, 36
Libermann, Rolf, 157
Libman, Lillian, 78
Life Goes to a Party, 19
Life magazine, 26, 72, 106, 166
Lincoln Center Film Society, 185
Linyou, Wang, 154
Lloyd, David, 54, 86
Loew's State Theater, 24, 28
London, George, 43, 57
London Symphony Orchestra, 118
Louise, 2, 87–88
Luchetti, Veriano, 100
Lucia di Lammermoor, 82, 158
Lufthansa Airlines, 183
Lulu, 54, 68–72

McConathy, Osbourne, 39, 40, 43, 44,
 58, 61, 71, 73, 88, 103–4, 162–64
McCracken, James, 88, 149
McNally, Thomas, 166
Macbeth (Verdi), 44, 82
Macbeth (Shakespeare), 138
Madama Butterfly, 19, 39, 40–41, 110,
 111–49, 179
Magic Flute, 155, 179
Mahan, Christopher, 51
Makas, Maxinen, 57
Making Music Together Festival, 3, 4,
 147, 183
Makropulos Case, 158, 172
Malas, Spiro, 180
Manon, 34–36
Manuel, Michael, 63
Marcos, Ferdinand, 151, 154, 156
Marcos, Imelda, 151, 154, 156
Marcoux, Vanni, 165
Margrave, Wendell, 133
Marsee, Suzanne, 110
Marshall, Lois, 25, 67

ABOUT THE AUTHOR

Having not missed a Met season since 1954–1955, **Daniel Kessler** gladly confesses his passion for opera, one that has sustained a lifetime of attendance beyond his home base to performances as far-flung as Salzburg to Sydney, and Boston to Buenos Aires. His involvement as a real estate broker and vice president of several of New York's top real estate firms underwrote these peregrinations.

In the early 1990s, following the demise of the Opera Company of Boston, it became apparent to Mr. Kessler, having witnessed a fair number of performances of Sarah Caldwell's company, that something important and unique to the U.S. operatic scene had been lost. Even if Ms. Caldwell's story is a cautionary tale, it is important to examine her genius at play to better understand the events that brought her company to its final performances after thirty-two years on the boards. It is hoped that this biography will foster a greater appreciation of her unique gifts, vision, and love of the medium.

Mr. Kessler is a contributor to *Opera Quarterly* and has lectured for the San Francisco Opera. He lives in New York City.